Third Edition

PILOTS
IN COMMAND

Your Best Trip, Every Trip

KRISTOFER PIERSON

AVIATION SUPPLIES & ACADEMICS, INC.
NEWCASTLE, WASHINGTON

Pilots in Command: Your Best Trip, Every Trip
Third Edition
By Kristofer Pierson

Aviation Supplies & Academics, Inc.
7005 132nd Place SE
Newcastle, Washington 98059
asa@asa2fly.com | 425-235-1500 | asa2fly.com

Third edition published 2022 by Aviation Supplies & Academics, Inc. Second edition published 2017. First edition published 2014.

The 4R Model of Leadership discussed in Chapter 14 is used with permission from Dr. Mark McCloskey.

ASA-PIC3
ISBN 978-1-64425-065-5

Additional formats available:
eBook EPUB   ISBN 978-1-64425-066-2
eBook PDF   ISBN 978-1-64425-067-9

Printed in the United States of America
2026 2025 2024 2023 2022   9 8 7 6 5 4 3 2 1

Library of Congress Cataloging-in-Publication Data:
Names: Pierson, Kristofer, author.
Title: Pilots in command : your best trip, every trip / Kristofer Pierson.
Description: Third edition. | Newcastle, WA : Aviation Supplies & Academics, Inc., 2022.
Identifiers: LCCN 2022021612 (print) | LCCN 2022021613 (ebook) | ISBN 9781644250655
    (trade paperback) | ISBN 9781644250662 (epub) | ISBN 9781644250679 (pdf)
Subjects: LCSH: Air pilots—Training of. | Air pilots—Vocational guidance. | Airplanes—
    Piloting—Human factors. | Leadership—Study and teaching. | Flight training.
Classification: LCC TL712 .P54 2022 (print) | LCC TL712 (ebook) | DDC
    629.132/52071—dc23/eng/20220630
LC record available at https://lccn.loc.gov/2022021612
LC ebook record available at https://lccn.loc.gov/2022021613

CONTENTS

PART I: It All Begins Here

PART II: Getting on the Line

PART III: Professional Excellence

ACKNOWLEDGMENTS

When I set out to make a career as an airline pilot, I never imagined I would write a book about how to be a better airline pilot. There are many people who are responsible for inspiring, mentoring, and pushing me to succeed in ways I never dreamed.

Thanks to the loving support of my wife and best friend, Sarah, this project has taken the shape it has. I also thank my children, Evelyn and Oliver, who cheered me on. It is because of my parents, Dave and Julie, that I have my wings. The advice and mentorship of my dear friend Dave Burkum motivated me to take a series of blog posts and make it into this book.

This book is dedicated to friends and colleagues who challenged me to be my best at my job. Dr. Earl C. Benson, my high school band director, took me for my first flight in a small airplane. Above the band room chalkboard in giant yellow letters were the words, "RESULTS NOT ALIBIS!" My profound respect for SOP and standards has been in imitation of Capt. Paul Kolisch (ret.), who made the industry a safer place by pushing for the best in training and standards across the industry. My writing skills, diligence, and vision have been inspired by Ms. Jane Schraft. She has spent her career helping pilots fight for safety and professionalism from within their ranks, and to work with the airline managers who are just trying to keep things on time. There are countless captains and first officers I have flown with who never settled for anything less than the best on every trip, and they all have my gratitude.

Thanks also to Dr. Mark McCloskey, Kristine Tichich, Jackie Spanitz and ASA, and to my airline employers, past and present. Finally, this book is in honor of my father, Dave Pierson, who always was so excited about my flying. He was, and is—even in his passing—my primary mentor, hero, professional role model, and patron saint, inspiring me to make every trip my best trip.

ABOUT THE AUTHOR

Captain Kristofer Pierson is a Line Check Airman for a major U.S. airline. He holds an ATP with type ratings on the Boeing 787, 757, and 767, Airbus A320, Bombardier CRJ900/700/200 Series, and Saab SF430. Captain Pierson has over 12,000 hours of flight experience as both a Captain and a First Officer, flying for regional and major carriers, domestically and internationally. He has a B.S. degree in Airway Science–Aircraft Systems Management from Rocky Mountain College in Billings, Montana. For more information and resources from Captain Pierson, visit his website at krispierson.com.

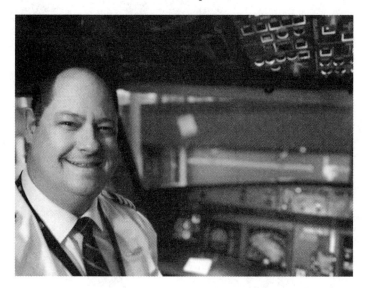

INTRODUCTION

Thanks for reading the latest edition of Pilots in Command: Your Best Trip, Every Trip. This is the third edition, and the biggest expansion of content, for this title. This book was, in its original form, targeted towards airline pilots who were ready to upgrade from First Officer to Captain, taking the role of Pilot in Command (PIC) firmly in grasp. Now, a decade after I started drafting the first chapters of this book, we are experiencing a new era of demand for professional pilots.

We need fresh resources to aid this new influx of professional aviators. Pilots who commit to achieving an airline career—whether coming from a military or a civilian background—will find themselves upon an ever-steepening learning curve. In days past, a pilot would work towards an airline career by attaining their Private Pilot Certificate, Instrument and Multiengine Ratings, followed by their Commercial Pilot Certificate and possibly their Flight Instructor Certificate, and then building flight time experience towards the hiring minimums posted by the carrier. When the FAA changed the standards for pilots at air transport carriers to require at least a "Restricted" Airline Transport Pilot Certificate (R-ATP), the landscape changed significantly.

Prior to those changes, air carriers were hiring pilots with anywhere from the minimum required time experience for a Commercial Pilot Certificate (250 hours) to 1,000 hours or more. Now a pilot will have a minimum of 700 hours (if transitioning from a military flight program), 1,000 hours if graduating from an accredited collegiate four-year degree program, 1,250 hours if graduating from an accredited collegiate two-year degree program, or 1,500 hours. Upon reaching the 1,500-hour mark, a pilot may attain a non-restricted Airline Transport Pilot Certificate (ATP). The gap from 250 hours to 1,500 hours is commonly being filled with flight experience from flight instruction to cargo and charter operations.

On paper, an aspiring pilot can go from zero experience to having an R-ATP—and ready to fly at an airline—in *two years*. Most pilots will end up working for a regional airline (also known as a "fee-for-departure" carrier) that operates smaller aircraft than the major airlines to gain more experience in order apply to a major. Others will apply to a carrier upon exit or retirement from the military. Some will transition from a general aviation or corporate background. But on any of these pathways there seldom are resources for pilots to learn what their worlds will look like as an airline pilot once they make it to the airlines—regardless if it is flying a regional jet (like the Embraer EMB175) or a widebody (like a Boeing B787). In all cases, they will need valuable information on how to navigate the airline world, particularly when it comes to training as a new hire, and more importantly when they become an airline captain for the first time.

This edition addresses many of the questions and I have fielded from new pilots and is based off of the common experiences and practices new pilots face when entering the airline industry. It keeps intact the knowledge I have shared in the previous editions and expands upon a few areas. Overall, this book will undoubtedly come in handy for a pilot embarking on an airline career and a pilot already onboard and seeking to improve as professional aviator.

Here is some background on how this book even came to be. I have maintained a personal blog and website for more than a decade—since before Facebook, Twitter, and others changed the shape of the World Wide Web into the vast and global Internet we now know. Though the frequency of my blog posts has been sporadic, I have always enjoyed having that outlet for writing and that connection with people who took the time to read what I had to say. My writings meandered between several personal interests—family, fishing, food, religion, politics, and of course, flying.

Early on in my blogging exploits, and only about four years into my airline career, I wrote a blog post about a tire blowout I experienced on landing. It occurred on a midwinter flight in the Dakotas on the Saab SF340, a 34-passenger turboprop and the workhorse of several regional airlines in the early 2000s. I was the First Officer on the flight, which, all things considered, was rather uneventful. We were used to the winter weather challenges posed to crews flying in the upper Midwest on turboprop airliners, hopping between small outstate airports and large city hubs. Snow and ice were a constant battle, especially when the cruise altitude rarely got above 17,000 feet MSL.

Early that morning we preflighted a cold-soaked plane that had been sitting out on the ramp overnight. An area of freezing rain had moved through, glazing the landscape with a thin layer of ice. The Saab had already been sprayed down with Type I deicing fluid—a heated mixture of glycol and water that removed any accumulations of ice, snow, and frost from the plane, and which was viscous enough to remain on the wing to help protect it from further accretions of frozen contaminants. The station agents did a thorough job, as during my preflight I was practically wading through the pink slime as I walked around the plane. There wasn't a trace of ice left anywhere on the aircraft. The skies were overcast, but no precipitation was falling at departure time. However, the band of freezing rain (FZRA) had set up just off to the north of the airport, and we encountered it during the climb out.

Our flight was quick, as we were heading only about 20 minutes north to our next stop to pick up the remainder of our passenger and cargo manifest before heading back to the hub. We picked up a bit of ice along the way, but the Saab's deicing boots handled it just fine. The Automated Surface Observing System (ASOS) indicated arrival weather of low overcast skies, light winds, five miles in mist, and a temperature of around freezing. We set up for the ILS approach to the main runway and headed in. The approach was completely normal. We ran the deicing boots all the way in with one last cycle just inside the final approach fix, and we had plenty of mixed ice piling up on the windshield wipers. I think we gave a PIREP to air traffic control of "moderate mixed" icing on climb and descent.

The Captain was flying this leg, and I was the pilot monitoring. We broke out of the overcast layer about 500 feet AGL, and the captain made a sweet, light-as-a-feather touch on landing. It was a true greaser (which really isn't hard in the mighty Saab with a snow and ice-packed runway). DING! The master caution sounded just as I was complementing his touchdown and calling out "80 knots my tops," taking control of the yoke as the captain transitioned to the nosewheel tiller. "Antiskid," I reported and canceled the master caution. Antiskid cautions were pretty normal occurrences on the SF340 during crosswind landings, with one main gear touching and spinning up before the main on the other side. The indication typically extinguished a few seconds later when the antiskid computer detected wheel speeds that made the logic report, "OK, this is normal."

But this time it didn't extinguish. The captain had already taken notice and said, "Well, the brakes seem to work OK." He was decelerating smoothly down the runway. The passengers were probably still sleeping! We made the turnoff, cleared the runway, and I called Center to report our arrival and cancel IFR. After getting off the radio, while I was doing my after landing flow and checklist, the captain became concerned.

"Something doesn't feel right in the tiller. It's like it wants to pull a bit to the left."

"Even when you are off the brakes?" I queried. (Sometimes pilots would ride the brakes to control taxi speed; in some planes that are light, this is needed due to the excess thrust at idle.)

"I'm not even on them, and I'm in beta on both engines, and she pulls. Then even when I bump up the power she pulls, even asymmetric power," the captain explained.

"Well, maybe the antiskid failed and a brake is dragging or something," I offered. After all, the antiskid caution light was still on, and we hadn't really addressed it yet.

"Nah—if the antiskid failed, its fail-safe is to release the brakes, not engage them, right?" he asked.

I really didn't remember exactly. It sounded right, but what if it was some other brake failure? True enough, part of the antiskid system was "touchdown protection," which ensured the brakes were not locked up on touchdown but then allowed the brakes to engage when a certain wheel speed was sensed. Spin-up of an airplane's wheels to that speed takes less than a second. After that, the system works to prevent lockups and resultant skids between the four main gear wheels on the SF340.

We were continuing down the taxiway to the terminal. Despite the captain's complaints, I really didn't feel any dragging or difference in the smoothness of the taxi compared to normal.

"Well, do you want to run the QRH or anything?" I asked.

"It seems like it's getting better, and the brakes are working fine," he said as he gave a couple demonstrative pumps to the binders. "Let's get parked, and we will run the QRH before we shut down. We've got time."

We did have the time. The flight was over-blocked (scheduled with a longer-than-average flight time) and we often sat at the gate with at least one engine running with the prop in feather just to keep the passengers warm while we killed the time. As it was, we would have about 45 minutes before we would need to head back out, and we were only boarding five more passengers. The QRH (Quick Reference Handbook) checklist for "ANTISKID" would hopefully resolve our issue, if one existed.

As we pulled into the ramp area we spotted one of our regular station agents headed out to the parking line with wands and chocks in hand. As we approached, he started to marshal us in. Then, very oddly, he got this look on his face as if he was seeing something unexpected and strange. His signaling motion slowed and he was staring at our left main gear. He guided us in to park, gave us the signal to stop, placed the chocks in around the nose gear, gave the chocks-in signal, and then very excitedly started pointing to the left main gear. "What the?! I'm shutting down the left side for now," said the captain as he feathered the props and shut down the number one engine.

As the left side spun down, he popped open the flight deck door and asked the flight attendant to open up the main cabin door. As soon as the main cabin door was opened and airstairs lowered, the agent bounded up them and stuck his head into the flight deck. "Guys, you have got to see this! You have a totally flat tire!!" I guarded the brakes as the captain went outside to see for himself. When he got back, I knew exactly what he was going to say even before he said it.

"We aren't going anywhere for a while."

We shut down the right engine, briefed and deplaned the passengers, and headed inside to call maintenance. Sure enough, the left main outboard tire was completely flat. Surprisingly, the inboard tire was intact, but under some stress from having to carry a bit more of the load. The captain was right: we were stuck for a while. The mechanic arrived with a new tire (three hours later) and changed it out. He called us out from the station office to take a look at what he found. The tire had a hole in it about 3 inches in diameter—a literal hole, not a crack or a slice, but an area where there simply was no more tire. It was a gaping hole from where the tire had been dragged all the way in from touchdown to the gate.

The wheel assembly itself had been locked frozen with ice. The same ice we PIREPed on the way in: moderate mixed ice. Typically, main gear can handle the ice because the impact of landing and wheel spinup breaks any ice accretion. This was not the case for our left main outboard wheel. It had never spun up, and we had been oblivious. We thought the antiskid had failed. Well, it had, but not on its own accord!

To make a long story short, we were on our way to Minneapolis after a four-hour delay. It truly could have been longer, but we worked hard to prevent that from happening. How? We simply took actions that kept the lines of communication open between our resources. The captain focused on coordination with dispatch and maintenance, and he delegated the task of keeping the local station, passengers, and crew scheduling in the loop. When the mechanic arrived, this meant I was also assisting him since he was the only one sent by the airline. I ensured he had what he needed to do his job, including borrowing a forced air heater from the local FBO to get the wheel assembly thawed out.

It was a good example of threat and error management, crew resource management, and overall pilot leadership skills being applied in a rather everyday type of outstation breakdown. It was what we were used to and how we operated at that carrier. I posted this story, or something very close to it, on my blog. I was extremely proud of our actions as a crew, and I thought it was a remarkable story, with the iced-up gear and all. I received great responses from people about it for the few days it was online. Then I was called into my chief pilot's office. The company's CEO evidently had read my post and asked that it be taken down. Back then, social media policy hadn't yet been invented (and, as I said, neither had Facebook or other social media sites). It was an ultimatum against which I didn't have a good argument, since my chief cited that (1) the employee handbook clearly stated that all public and media relations about flight events have to be approved by corporate communications, and (2) the request was coming straight from the top.

Alas, my blogging about flying days seemed numbered. But I always wanted to relate more than just cool stories like "There I was…cheating death again." I wanted to write about crews, captains, and people. I wanted to share experiences with passengers, ramp workers, and gate agents. And I especially wanted to write about the schoolhouse, and relate the good, the bad, and the ugly of airline pilot training. My tact would not be one of an exposé writer, pulling back the curtain to see behind the scenes. Rather, I wanted to share experiences that would help other pilots become better at their jobs. I wanted to take the valuable, non-dramatic, factual, and results-not-alibis type of conversations from the flight levels and the crew rooms and bring them forward.

So a couple of years ago on a long layover, I started drafting a blog post. It was going to be about pilot roles and the responsibility and authority of the PIC. Captain's authority is a subject that has a long legacy of debate—between pilots and management, between management and the FAA, and among scholars and laymen. But the rubber meets the road every day, on every flight, as PICs make decision after decision to ensure the safe operation of their flights. It came to my mind that captain's authority is not just something that can be defined and interpreted from the Federal Aviation Regulations (FARs) and company operating procedures. Instead, it is a vested capacity of pilots to work with their crews and resources to enable the flight operation to take place. The blog post got longer and longer as I drafted it. I started thinking about doing a series of posts. As I worked through my ideas, however, it dawned on me that I didn't have a collection of blog posts so much as I had a book. And, so, *Pilots in Command: Your Best Trip, Every Trip* was born.

I wrote this book with every pilot in mind: the college student working their way through an FAA-approved curriculum to be an airline pilot; a new hire at the regional/express carrier; a new hire at a major/national carrier; a captain upgrade candidate; and pilots who want some extra insight, tips, and tricks of the trade. I also wrote this from the viewpoint I think all pilots share: we all want to be better. We all seek improvement and we want to keep the blade sharp. As I worked through each topic covered in the book, I developed an approach of "best practices" for pilots. From briefings to handling non-normals, and from reviewing a dispatch release to getting a good night's sleep, I have written this book with a practical approach, filled with simple steps to take, mnemonics to remember, and checklists to complete in your everyday efforts to be the safest, most responsible leader you can be both in and out of the flight deck.

Thanks for reading. Fly safe!

PART I:
It All Begins Here

1

You Made It! Welcome to the Airlines

Perhaps, like me, you knew at a specific point in time that you wanted to be a professional airline pilot. I have met so many pilots who *just knew* they had to be at the controls, taking to the skies, and challenging the laws of nature. Flying, for many pilots, is the primary attraction. Simply breaking free from the ground, soaring among the clouds, climbing to vantage points known not even to most birds, and then gracefully navigating towards the landing strip, trading off energy for altitude and speed in order to return safely for a full stop.

Then the realization comes that there can be an intersection between the love of flight and a career. It might have been walking through the airport, watching the pilots go about their business. You noted the professionalism, the respect, and the purposefulness they exuded as they went about their duties. Maybe you saw the twinkle in their eyes as they greeted a wide-eyed child into the flight deck, and felt the tug at your heartstrings as another human gets bitten by the aviation bug.

So, you made a decision. You planned, you saved, and you invested. No matter what road you took, it was focused on the future career inspired by your dreams. And as you transition from student pilot to commercial pilot, building time and experience at the controls you knew the day would come where you would join the ranks of thousands to be a Pilot-in-Command at a commercial airline.

Your training, experience, and preparation have been waiting for a payoff. That time has come if you made it through the interview, got a class date, and are ready to step through the classroom door to begin your new-hire training at an airline. No matter the brand or designation of your carrier, the routes you will fly, or the type of airplane you will operate, your experience should be one that looks and feels like nothing else you have experienced in a professional training environment.

The job of an airline pilot is not one that merely works 9 to 5, confined to a cubicle with the exception of regular coffee and lunch breaks.

Your schedule is completely non-traditional, which has definite upsides and downsides. The view is second-to-none, and the office itself is pretty awe-inspiring in all of its technical glory. Your commute will undoubtedly require ground transportation to an airport, but could also mean the use of non-revenue flight privileges to reach your base. At the airport, your uniform, badge, and credentials as a professional pilot will grant you respect and trust unlike your average, everyday passenger—from the security lines to the gate podium, and even on board your flight, you have a job now that people hold in high regard. Although only through the lens of what pop culture has shown them, non-pilots understand it takes years of training and hard work to achieve the career of an airline pilot. Only you and you colleagues know the real truth of those matters, what the years leading up to this point have entailed, and that the years to follow will be so much more.

As a result, embarking on the training process as a new-hire, and becoming a part of the airline pilot world holds the distinction and advantage of being specialized for your job. It involves intense amounts of information, hours of independent and cooperative study with your colleagues, support from knowledgeable training personnel, and a results-driven curriculum that ensures you are fully qualified to take the helm of a transport category aircraft as pilot-in-command. All of this while imparting to you the importance of your position, the role you have in the success of the operation, and the opportunity you have to grow and become a leader from the flight deck.

AIRLINE CULTURE AND YOU

When you interview for an airline job, the panel of people evaluating you will not just be looking for someone who is going to fly the airplane. Their charge is to select individuals who are leaders; pilots who will not just do the basics of the job, but who will take the job to the next level. From working with fellow crewmembers to delivering friendly and genuine customer service, the candidate selection process will find people who are a good fit with the culture of the carrier.

Truly, each carrier's culture has much more to do with shared corporate values across all employee groups. There is a commonality among pilots, however, that our number one value is safety. An appropriate safety-based culture and mindset is anchored in place by pilot-leaders who set a strong example of how each and every flight is operated with safety and security at top priority.

So, no matter what culture your airline has developed and implemented globally, for flight operations personnel safety culture headlines the operation. During your first few weeks of new-hire training at the airline, the impact of safety culture on your career and how you operate will become clear.

Other aspects of culture indoctrination—customer service, cost control, efficiency, employee standards, and other guidelines and policies—will most definitely be presented and even trained to you. This part of your training gets overlooked by some, as it seems like fluff. However, knowing how varied culture aspects and values including safety work together to make your airline succeed is a vital part of being a respected employee. More importantly, by setting proper examples of your company's culture as you perform your duties as a pilot, you will advance your professionalism and leadership qualities to a higher level.

Over the years, the airlines have leveraged the ability of their employees to cooperate in a way that produces operational results. Becoming familiar with the values that motivate things like on-time performance, missed bag rates, fuel efficiency scores, and even stock price is something that is done almost subconsciously by individuals. For example, an employee might lean into the value of achieving personal bests when it comes to personal metrics. The baggage runner who is able to prevent bags they are responsible for from misconnecting, the gate agent who continuously gets the boarding door closed by a certain target time prior to departure, or the line technician who is able to perform routine maintenance checks under a specified limit fall into this category.

During your first few weeks of training, and certainly during your first few weeks on the actual flight line, you will find that pilots hold a unique position when it comes to meeting or exceeding operational metrics goals. When all other employee groups have done what they can do to get a plane to depart on time, it all comes down to if and when the pilots release the parking brake. The decision to do so includes an affirmation by the pilot-in-command—the captain—that the number one goal and cornerstone of airline culture, safety, has been assured. As it has been said by many before me, "The airplanes don't move without the pilots!"

YOUR JOB: BE A LEADER

Becoming an airline pilot has less to do with the technical aspects and operational skills of flying an airplane than it does with the soft skills of working cooperatively with others. Your training will undoubtedly spend a good chunk of time on this. Some carriers utilize exercises involving personality assessments, team building exercises, and other challenging scenarios to build up people's abilities to work well with one another.

At my first airline, a memorable part of both my new-hire and a few recurrent training sessions involved our Crew Resource Management (CRM) training module. The Human Factors Team at the regional carrier had cherry-picked some of the best course material from executive management training sessions, CRM programs from major airlines, and some leading-edge crisis management exercises for first responders. They were able to put it all together in a single-day session and they made it fun. It wasn't fluffy; it was by no means a charm school. Rather, it was a class that took the realities of interpersonal behaviors, cultural influences, and true-to-life stories and scenarios and applied them in an active, adult education format that taught us to be honest about our strengths and limitations.

Moreover, the course enabled people to tap into their own leadership skillsets. If your airline is doing it right (and under current standards they likely are) your training experience from Day 1 to the end of your new-hire training sequence will be geared in the same way. At every stage—not just in your crew resource management module—you will find opportunities to grow and evolve as a leader. If the feedback I have heard from countless pilots across the industry is accurate, nobody has considered it *work* as much as they have considered it *rewarding*. What's better than that?

Your job in training is not just to learn to fly the plane the way the carrier wants you to fly. Your job is to become the pilot leader they are counting on you to become. That is a big part of what this book, and all of your training throughout your career, will be about.

Let's get started!

2

Basic Indoctrination—Setting a Course for Success

Becoming qualified and maintaining proficiency for a commercial airline has evolved tremendously over the last thirty years. There are currently two sets of training and checking regulations for airlines on the books under 14 CFR Part 121. The traditional set of regulations (known colloquially as "Subparts N and O" for the applicable subparts of Part 121) have been kept in place as a backstop to the more current, scientifically backed, and widely utilized Advanced Qualification Program (AQP) regulations. To appreciate AQP and what it means for you as a pilot, I would like to offer some background.[1]

Between 1970 and the mid-1980s, airline flight crew training—both to qualify and remain current in transport category aircraft—was centered on each individual pilot proving that they could perform certain maneuvers to a standard of accuracy. Airmanship was tested mainly on stick and rudder skills and rote learning. Evaluations were conducted in strict pass-fail environments. Pilots can recall dreading the "pink slip" of a failed proficiency check. There was little room for do-overs.

The biggest drawback to the traditional airline pilot training and checking regulations is that they were written as individual training requirements and standards. Pilots subject to Subparts N and O *are not* checked as a crew. Alas, I remember when I took my first Captain upgrade checkride. I was PIC during my ride in an airplane that I had over 4,000 hours in as a Second in Command (SIC). My training partner was new to the airline industry, had zero turbine time, and was struggling. For about two-thirds of the checkride, I was allowed by the examiner to do some minor coaching—reminding my first officer about missed items here and there, calling out deviations, and helping share the mental model of a maneuver to help him through. After he lost control of the airplane on his second attempt at the V_1 cut maneuver, I attempted to intervene. The check airman froze the simulator, repositioned us to the end of the runway and laid a gentle hand on my shoulder. I turned around and he had his index finger to his lips, gesturing to me that I needed to stop helping. My partner repeated the same mistake (losing aircraft control on the V_1 cut for the third time) and the checkride was over. I had my new PIC type rating and was headed to back to the line. My new hire first officer had a pink slip and was luckily facing one last try at retraining rather than termination from the airline, thanks to a process agreed to with the pilot union.

Scenes such as this are commonplace during proficiency checks where pilots were checked as if they were operating single pilot. This is the environment under the *old rules*—and I think it's fair to call them this as they were authored in the 1970s and aside from updates related to technology, terminology, and changes in related regulations, they haven't really been overhauled.

Beginning in 1987, the Airline Transport Association and the FAA put together a joint task force to find solutions to the problems with airline flight crew training. They chiefly recognized that crews fly together as a crew—aiding, assisting, and dividing duties and tasks appropriately. This went hand-in-hand with the ongoing development of CRM, simulator technology, and a quality management systems approach to airline operations and safety programs. By 1990, a special regulation (SFAR 58) and accompanying Advisory Circular (AC 120-54) had been issued to create AQP. Notably, the FAA knew that there needed to be distinction between the old rules and this new program, and thus stated plainly in the AC, "Most accidents are attributed to crew error. Traditional training programs focus on individual training and evaluation. Under AQP, the focus is on crew and individual performance in both training and evaluation." This is the headline benefit of AQP.

Additionally, AQP integrated CRM skills in training and evaluation curriculum-wide, as opposed to CRM training being a separate a la carte curriculum for operators using the old rules. Accordingly, an AQP syllabus will utilize scenario-based lessons and evaluations. Rather than simply training and checking maneuvers (takeoffs, approaches, emergency procedures) in a routine, check-the-box Proficiency Check (PC), the scenario-based approach of a line-oriented evaluation integrates flight skills with a real-world approach. Suffice it to say that under these *new rules* for training and checking, the experience is to truly validate proficiency and competency through *training* and *knowledge enhancement*. Gone are the days of fear and loathing of the traditional Proficiency Check.

WHY CONTINUING QUALIFICATION IS IMPORTANT

If this is your first airline job after having built time in the civilian world, whether it was flight instruction, pipeline patrol, banner towing, or any other general aviation mode of flying, you are used to the Part 61 rules for keeping current and your pilot certificate active, namely the biennial flight review required by 14 CFR §61.56 and the landings requirements of §61.57. These regulations ensure that pilots holding Private Pilot Certificates are to some extent self-checking their proficiency, especially before flying the wife and kids to a pancake breakfast a few towns over. Pilots who make money while at the controls, holding a Commercial Pilot Certificate, fly more often than the weekend warriors but also have to comply with these same regulations.

The stakes are higher for pilots flying at the air carrier level, and thus the level of proficiency must also be elevated. Rather than only seeing an instructor or evaluator every 24 months, you will be headed to recurrent training even more often, and under some AQP curriculums will be exposed to some sort of training requirement or completion deadline every 90 to 120 days.

Some may think that sounds like too much. Others, having lived under the old rules of Subparts N and O, may think that the increased frequency of training means more exposure to "jeopardy" checking events. Both of these viewpoints require a better understanding of what *continuing qualification* training, specifically under AQP truly means.

First of all, the term *continuing qualification* is very much related to the term continuing education. Professionals from all sorts of backgrounds, disciplines, and careers, whether compelled by their employer, regulation, board, or personal interest, engage in continuing education throughout their careers. From time to time, these professionals take courses, attend seminars, or engage in training to enhance their skillsets and advance their levels of professionalism. It makes sense, therefore, for airline pilots—the experts of the craft, responsible for the carriage of life and property safely from departure to destination—to likewise undertake such efforts.

We pilots, however, are qualified as such under *federal law* and have been for close to a century. The first pilot certificate was issued by the U.S. government in 1927, and in 1928 formal regulations were issued on practical testing and recency of experience requirements. Under Subparts N and O, qualification was renewed via tests of skill of an individual pilot. Under AQP, qualification is continued via a curriculum that ensures that individual pilots have skills that are proficient through facilitated training and that crews are evaluated on the merits of their ability to operate safely in real-world operational scenarios.

While each carrier will infuse their own culture and operating fundamentals specific to their operation into their AQP curriculum, every carrier under AQP is putting into practice continuing-education values in concert with the regulatory requirements for pilot qualifications and standards. Whether your carrier employs distance learning and opts to forego formal classroom sessions for general subjects, aircraft systems, and other ground school topics, or chooses to still use a few checking standards from the old rules, or even has emergency equipment training conducted separate from days you are scheduled to be in the simulator, one thing will be consistent: you will continually be in some part of a training and qualification cycle throughout your career. The outcome, assuming your active and earnest participation, will be enhanced airmanship skills, mastery of CRM proficiencies, and higher levels of professionalism and crew leadership.

BECOMING THE PILOT YOUR CARRIER WANTS

In Part III of this book, we will look deeper at Continuing Qualification and what you can expect from your journey through a career of continual training and evaluation. For now, however, let's set our minds on what it will mean, look, and feel like to start a career as a pilot for an airline.

Your first couple of weeks of initial qualification training will be spent in what is known as Basic Indoctrination, or BI. This is where it will be made plain what your carrier expects out of you. The indoctrination aspects include understanding your job, what tasks are associated with your job, and how the carrier expects you to perform those tasks. As you may imagine, you will learn not only information specific to flight operations during BI, but also company-wide topics ranging from employee services and human resources to corporate divisions, values, and culture.

However, as an airline pilot, BI will lay a foundation for your training and performance as a pilot for your specific carrier. Major subjects covered in BI are general in nature, oftentimes apply across all fleets in the airline, and serve to unify and standardize the pilot group in how all flights are conducted. Some of these major subjects and topics may include, but certainly are not limited to:

- Use of manuals and documents
- Aircraft performance
- Emergency procedures
- Crew Resource Management/Threat and Error Management
- IT and computer systems
- Fatigue risk management
- Security and dangerous goods
- Dispatch and network operations
- Part 121 and Operations Specifications

Notably, some subjects in a BI syllabus that would seem to be aircraft specific, like performance and emergency procedures, are oftentimes common across all fleets for most airlines. Performance procedures are unified due to common dispatch procedures. Emergency procedures are generalized because carriers exercise them in a harmonized way across employee groups (i.e., flight attendants, ground and airport operations, etc.)

BI includes taking your skills as a pilot leader and advancing them to the level required for airline operations. This is where the proverbial rubber meets the runway, and where you land will determine your success moving forward throughout your initial qualification training.

The next four chapters, therefore, will serve you well in BI training as they discuss some fundamental subjects that airline pilots learn. Knowing how the airline world works in terms of command authority, roles and responsibilities, crew coordination, and resource management is crucial to your work and foundational to your professional development.

Chapter 2 Note

1. Training and qualification is still conducted by some carriers under FAR §121 Subparts N and O, and it stands for them as the regulatory method and standard. This book will focus on, and refer to, the Advance Qualification Program (AQP) which has not only been widely adopted in the U.S., but also replicated and adopted across the world in the form of similar programs.

3

Defining a Pilot-in-Command

In every modern transport-category aircraft flight deck, two or more individuals are employed in the task of flying the airplane. Nine out of ten of these flight deck crews are flying passenger-carrying equipment which requires additional professionals on board the aircraft to oversee the passenger cabin. A very small percentage of the crews who ferry passengers about do not have flight attendants—most likely due to aircraft size—and are responsible for the passengers themselves. Some other crews at the aircraft controls are the only souls on board their aircraft, for a myriad of reasons.

However, all of these flight deck crews share one very important characteristic: There is one—*and only one*—member of the crew who holds all responsibility for the flight alone: the pilot in command. The Federal Aviation Regulations (FARs) are explicit in their charge to this person.[1] 14 CFR §91.3 states:

Responsibility and authority of the pilot in command.
(a) The pilot in command of an aircraft is directly responsible for, and is the final authority as to, the operation of that aircraft.
(b) In an in-flight emergency requiring immediate action, the pilot in command may deviate from any rule of this part to the extent required to meet that emergency.
(c) Each pilot in command who deviates from a rule under paragraph (b) of this section shall, upon the request of the Administrator, send a written report of that deviation to the Administrator.

Three simple sentences exist in this concise regulation. Sentence (a) tells us what the pilot-in-command is responsible for. It is a one-line description of his or her ultimate role when flying an airplane. Sentence (b) describes the latitude the pilot-in-command has to "break the rules"— and it is a very small amount of latitude. Finally, sentence (c) places the requirement of reporting to the FAA, upon request, how much latitude a pilot-in-command exercised in accordance with sentence (b) in the case of an emergency.

When student pilots conduct their first solo flight, they are the sole operator of the aircraft. Nobody else is there to help. The only carriage is the pilot and their personal items, no other passengers or cargo. It is hard to find a professional pilot today that doesn't vividly recall their first solo flight, the primary right-of-passage for every pilot. How hard was that first solo? Preflight, taxi, takeoff, two touch-and-go landings and a full stop, park and shut down, postflight the airplane, and then it's time for pictures and celebration. For many of us it was a hard, stressful experience, as well as one of the biggest accomplishments of our lives, and really our flying careers.

This one moment in time for each and every pilot establishes them as a pilot-in-command—"PIC". As a matter of fact, it is the first logged time that goes in the "PIC" column of the logbook. Furthermore, it is the very first time 14 CFR §91.3 applies directly to the pilot. What makes a pilot a PIC during first solo is the fact that they are all alone. They are indeed *"directly responsible for, and the final authority as to, the operation of that aircraft."* No flight instructor is present to hand controls off to when the flare doesn't look right. And the solo pilot's flight instructor, sitting back at the flight school lounge sipping coffee in a supervisory fashion while their student goes it alone, is not logging any time for that flight either. Only the solo pilot is.

After the first solo, a pilot's experiences as PIC accumulate over time. Those experiences make them better PICs as their behaviors change and they learn more about how to operate and handle abnormal situations. Certificates and ratings are earned as milestones along the way. Then, at somewhere between 500–1,500 hours of logged PIC time, pilots who get hired to fly for a living—on equipment from crop dusters to cargo, and from business jets to Boeing 747s—take on much larger roles in operating an aircraft. They go from flying for themselves to flying for someone else, and with that the responsibilities increase ten-fold. Some pilots, like the crop dusters, will still be flying solo. Others will start flying as a crew. However, they all retain the primary instincts of their first solo flight—the instinct to be the pilot-in-command. As we will see later in this chapter and throughout the book, being a PIC is not merely about having to act on your own. Quite to the contrary, the most effective

PICs rely on their crew, their resources, and the factors surrounding the entire flight environment to fulfill their role under 14 CFR §91.3.

Yet many pilots find 14 CFR §91.3 to be the most complicated FAR to comply directly with, especially those who are responsible for a larger crew or larger aircraft. Roles and responsibilities not only get delegated, they also get shared. The higher workload levels of larger aircraft, while to some extent mitigated by adding more crew to the ship, complicate adherence to §91.3 even more, simply because there is so much more to keep track of. Finally, the very primary tenet of PIC, the title of §91.3 itself—the responsibility and authority of a PIC—is challenged not only by uncontrollable circumstances and conditions, but also by the very regulations, procedures, and practices pilots and operators employ in the name of safety.

This chapter examines these challenges to the PIC, and gives a primary look at how they can be eliminated.

FLIGHT DECK CREW ROLES

Modern airline transport flight decks have been developed, engineered, and automated to the maximum extent possible. A single pilot could more than likely fly a transport category airliner on their own, and in emergency situations, it may be necessary to do so. But that is not the intent of flight deck design. State-of-the-art technology and automation will never replace the function of a crew.

So, let us consider the flight deck crew of a modern airliner. The majority of these crews consist of two pilots: the pilot-in-command (PIC), and the second in command (SIC). More colloquially, these roles are named in company manuals and airline labor agreements as "captain" and "first officer," respectively. Some aircraft require other flight deck crew, perhaps a "second officer" (typically a flight engineer), or maybe an "international relief officer" or "relief pilot" (which is an additional SIC pilot or pilots who relieve the primary flight crew during extended flights for the purposes of rest). No matter what the combination of flight deck crewmembers is—captain and first officer, captain and two first officers, two captains and two first officers, three captains and one first officer—there is always one, *and only one*, pilot designated as pilot-in-command.

A challenge naturally presents itself between PICs and SICs, and it has to do with the "PIC instinct" I mentioned earlier in the chapter. All pilots are programmed with that instinct, and despite experience, certification, ratings, or any other auxiliary qualifications, many pilots see themselves as equals because we all know what it means to be PIC. The challenge therein lies in the ability for SICs to let go of their authority instinct a bit, and for PICs to fully assert their authority instinct.

Many airline pilots are familiar with the phrase "right-seat captain." It is not a flattering characterization of a pilot. If someone is characterized as a right-seat captain, it means that a personality conflict occurs between the crewmembers and that assertiveness is imbalanced. There is a healthy way to cure the imbalance, and it involves the clear distinction of roles and responsibilities between the PIC and SIC.

Much of this distinction is accomplished by the standard operating procedures outlined in company manuals. Even more is accomplished in specialized crew resource management (CRM) training courses given to airline crews. From both of these sources, we can find common determinations of which roles and responsibilities traditionally belong to each crewmember. Here is an example:

PIC:
- Reviews and approves preflight planning and dispatch release.
- Initiates and oversees the proper reporting of mechanical discrepancies.
- Gives appropriate briefings to other crewmembers.
- Makes appropriate go/no-go decisions using all available resources in the aeronautical decision making (ADM) process.

SIC:
- Reviews and gives input on preflight planning.
- Coordinates with the ground crew, cabin crew, maintenance, etc. to make sure that aircraft servicing needs are met.
- Becomes PIC when the PIC is not present in the flight deck, is on rest break, or is otherwise incapacitated.

Granted, standard operating procedures (SOPs) differ from carrier to carrier. But the PIC has the primary responsibility to ensure that SOP is followed in the conduct of a flight. It follows then that the PIC also must determine the roles and responsibilities of his or her crew. Simply put, a PIC must have the ability to *delegate*.

The Random House Dictionary's definition of the verb *delegate* is "to commit (powers, functions, etc.) to another as agent or deputy."[2] A captain's crew members are his agents—his deputies. Therefore, it is indeed one of the primary duties of the PIC to commit, assign, and empower his crew with roles and responsibilities that are not necessarily already defined by company manuals, FARs, SOPs, etc.

Most importantly, PIC and SIC designations are *not necessarily* synonymous with "pilot" and "co-pilot." In fact, those terms are perhaps the most antiquated, yet still the most commonly utilized by the general (non-aviation savvy) public. In the aeronautical sense, a pilot is a person duly qualified to operate an aircraft in flight. The word pilot originates from the Greek word *pedotes*, which means "helmsman." Clearly the origin and the definition leads one to understand that a pilot has the primary task of operating the aircraft. But being a pilot, and thus having the skills to operate and steer the ship, does not make one a PIC.

How about co-pilots? Are they any more or less of a pilot than a pilot? It's weird to think about this question, isn't it? Co-pilots do, however, have the distinction of being subordinate—despite the prefix of "co" which typically means "with", "in partnership", or "cooperation." A co-pilot is definitively subordinate to a pilot. Many modern dictionaries define co-pilot as a pilot who is second-in-command of an aircraft.

It almost leads us to wonder, in the end, who is really flying the airplane? Or at least it begs the question, who is *supposed* to fly it? This is where the PIC and SIC barriers are erased, or at least blurred, as most operators and crews operate with a joint-control format. One pilot is controlling some aspects of flight, while the other pilot is assisting or is controlling other aspects of flight. Many carriers have now adopted the delineation of "pilot flying" and "pilot monitoring."[3] These roles can be assigned to either the SIC or the PIC. It is traditional among many carriers for the roles to switch between the two pilots with each leg.

The "pilot flying" (PF) is typically responsible for the following:

- Manipulation of primary flight controls during all phases of flight
- Navigation
- Aircraft systems management

The "pilot monitoring" (PM) is typically responsible for the following:

- Manipulation of secondary flight controls upon command by PF
- Monitoring flight control and navigation of PF
- Air-to-ground communications

The above lists are based on the age-old order of aeronautical priorities for a pilot in flight: Aviate, Navigate, Communicate. Both the PF and PM follow that priority in carrying out their duties. Here is a typical sequence of actions and duties performed by a crew during an approach to landing, listed as the flight proceeds inbound from the final approach fix:

PF	PM
Initiates final descent to runway	Monitors descent rate
Calls for final flap and gear configuration	Selects and confirms configuration
Navigates vertically and horizontally down the approach course to touchdown	Monitors navigation, calls out deviations
Promptly corrects any deviations	Communicates with ATC

So what is the big deal, anyway? Why do we need these roles, names and ranks all clearly defined? There must be a driving force—a clear, underlying reason for the ranks, the order and division of duties, the authority, and the boundaries of that authority. Why must we have captains and first officers, pilots and co-pilots, pilots flying and pilots monitoring?

Because pilots are human. And, as Alexander Pope said, "To err is human..."

INTRODUCING THREAT AND ERROR MANAGEMENT

Alexander Pope's quote, from *An Essay on Criticism* (1709), in its entirety is, "To err is Humane; to Forgive, Divine." Pope was writing to, and about, critics of his own work (he was a poet) and admonishing them on how to critique fine art. The essence of Pope's comment is that there needs to be recognition of the natural occurrence of error in anything we do as humans. By divine grace, messing up every once in a while is forgivable. The relationship between human error and divine forgiveness is dramatically demonstrated by the act of human flight.

My first flight instructor once made the sage observation, "If God intended man to fly, Adam would have been born with wings." I am sure he had heard this said somewhere else, but as a teenager, it sounded original to me. Professional aviators realize that to have "slipped the surly bonds of Earth" is to have done something we were not intended to do naturally.[4] Thus, a great amount of respect must be given to the science of flight. It is an imperfect science in many respects, but perhaps none more so than in the respect of human factors.

Human factors have been studied extensively since World War II when aircraft manufacturers, psychologists, physiologists, and engineers collaborated to refine aircraft controls and designs to improve safety. Oftentimes, the term "ergonomics" has been linked, almost like a synonym, to human factors. The International Ergonomics Association defines ergonomics as "the scientific discipline concerned with the understanding of interactions among humans and other elements of a system…in order to optimize human well-being and overall system performance."[5] The organization breaks down the discipline into three distinct domains: physical, cognitive, and organizational. In the air transport application, the organizational domain of ergonomic study is home to both *Crew Resource Management* (CRM) and *Threat and Error Management* (TEM).

CRM started when NASA released a study implicating human error as the chief cause of aviation accidents. Early CRM theory and training models focused on the utilization of all available resources to the aviator during operations. The use of knowledge and skills from other crew and team members, the recognition of differences in attitudes, barriers to communications, situational awareness, problem solving, decision making, and teamwork have traditionally been core focuses of CRM. The field expanded extensively in the 1990s, with several airlines running CRM in accord with FAA mandates.

In 1994, the University of Texas and Delta Airlines partnered to begin a new way to evaluate whether CRM concepts were being applied on the actual flight line. The method of evaluation, called *Line Operations*

Safety Audits (LOSA), used observations made from the flight deck jump seat on actual flights. While the initial observations focused on evaluating CRM behaviors, error management observations were included soon after. Observers noted when errors occurred, including who made the error, who responded to the error, and the outcome.[6]

Researchers yearned for more context on the errors being observed, however, and full-fledged threat and error management concepts were woven into the program. Aircrews at Continental Airlines were first exposed to the marriage of CRM and TEM. LOSA observations using the CRM/TEM model started there in 1996, and soon expanded through the industry and worldwide. In 2006, the FAA issued the final advisory circular (AC 120-90) on LOSA and TEM.[7]

TEM model developers at University of Texas's Human Research Project introduce TEM using the following simple definitions:

Threats are defined as events or errors that:

- occur outside the influence of the flight crew (i.e., not caused by the crew);
- increase the operational complexity of a flight; and
- require crew attention and management if safety margins are to be maintained.

Errors are defined as flight crew actions or inactions that:

- lead to a deviation from crew or organizational intentions or expectations;
- reduce safety margins; and
- increase the probability of adverse operational events on the ground or during flight.

If errors are not managed, the result could be an *undesired aircraft state*, defined as a position, speed, attitude, or configuration of an aircraft that:

- results from flight crew error, actions, or inaction; and
- clearly reduces safety margins

CRM/TEM training models therefore emphasize the mantra, "Managing THREATS is managing the future, managing ERRORS is managing the past."

The (now "classic") Swiss Cheese Model

In 1990, psychologist James Reason published *Human Error*, in which he introduced the "Accident Causation Model."[8] Commonly referred to as the "Swiss Cheese Model," Reason paints a very simple picture of how an accident happens through the impact of several causes, actions, and latent threats. This model has now been adopted across many procedurally-driven vocational fields and industries.

Conceptually, each layer of an operation can be visualized as a slice of Swiss cheese. If you have sliced Swiss cheese, you know that the block of cheese itself does not have holes that run all the way through. Instead, air bubbles that are trapped in the cheese are scattered randomly throughout the block, and when the cheese is sliced, these bubbles become holes in the slice. If you stack up varying slices of Swiss cheese, there is a chance that the coincidental alignment of holes in each slice could make a hole that passes through the entire stack. But odds favor that the slices and their holes will not line up in such a way.

So we can imagine each slice as representing a part of an aircraft operation in which threats to the safety of the operation occur. If a threat to safety is not detected and trapped, it can turn into an error. An error can be visualized by a hole in the cheese. If there is an error in the first layer, it becomes incumbent on the second layer to detect that error and resolve it, or suffer the same fate—allowing a hole in the cheese to enable the error to pass on. If each layer fails, an accident or incident can occur.

Many different organizations have presented the Reason's Model with different roles for each layer. Reason himself approached his theory relative to the operations at a nuclear power plant. The top layer is typically characterized by some sort of organizational influence. This could be training, culture, or management. The next layers may represent different types of "latent threats," which are barriers to unsafe operations that may or may not be detectable by the flight crew. If they remain undetected, errors develop. The final layer is the "last chance" layer which represents either an action or inaction to stop the developed chain of errors from causing an incident or accident.

Any number of examples could be used to demonstrate Reason's model in action. One of the chief accidents that gave rise to a fostering of a TEM model at Continental Airlines was Flight 1713, a DC-9 that crashed on takeoff at Denver's Stapleton International Airport in November of 1987. The NTSB report summary reads as follows:

The National Transportation Safety Board determines that the probable cause of this accident was the captain's failure to have the airplane deiced a second time after a delay before takeoff that led to upper wing surface contamination and a loss of control during rapid takeoff rotation by the first officer. Contributing to the accident were the absence of regulatory or management controls governing operations by newly qualified flight crew members and the confusion that existed between the flightcrew members and air traffic controllers that led to the delay in departure.[9]

Although the NTSB primarily cited the captain's failure to have the aircraft deiced a second time and the first officer's improper aircraft handling in their findings, the other "contributing factors" tell us that there was more going on here than meets the eye. These are the "slices" of the Swiss cheese that TEM models seek to tackle. The weather was a threat. The experience levels of both pilots were a threat. The poor ATC clearances and traffic management in and out of the deicing pad were threats.

Threat: Crew Inexperience	**Error:** Inexperienced captain allows first officer to perform takeoff.
Threat: ATC/ground traffic issues	**Error:** Non-compliance and errors in taxi clearances further delay the departure, increasing the threat level of aircraft contamination.
Threat: Aircraft icing	**Error:** Captain fails to have aircraft deiced a second time.

In terms of errors, we can see the chain begin to get put together. Each threat—or slice of cheese—that goes undetected, or worse, unmanaged, can lead to the undesired aircraft state (UAS). Here is how, in a simple fashion, the unmanaged threats developed into errors that led to the crash:

We can furthermore take each of these errors and show how they formed an "error chain" that produced the undesired aircraft state (the crash):

    Error: Longer delay leading to further aircraft
       contamination
+ Error: Captain fails to have aircraft deiced a second time
→ UAS: Degraded aircraft performance
    Error: Inexperienced captain allows first officer to per-
       form takeoff
→ UAS: First officer over-rotates aircraft on takeoff causing
       engine compressor stalls/surges

    Error: Captain fails to arrest rotation
→ UAS: Degraded aircraft performance

The "final errors" of the crew of Continental 1713 were compounding errors. The NTSB doesn't say this, but the TEM model and definitions we have described above puts it all together for us. The errors led to a deviation from crew or organizational intentions or expectations, reduced safety margins, and increased the probability of adverse operational events on the ground or during flight. They hit all three defined characteristics of an "error." What's more, the error of the over-rotation was compounded by the error of the captain (not arresting it). Both errors would have been prevented if the crew had identified the threat of inexperience.

Each layer of the causation model, each layer of the Swiss cheese, had an error hole that lined up with the next, but only because threats were not detected, or were ignored. The crash of Continental Flight 1713, which resulted in 28 fatalities, was preventable.

Pilots-in-command need to remain cognizant of the classic Swiss cheese model, watching for each slice and the holes that may exist.

Putting TEM/CRM To Work

(The following is a fictional account of the beginning of a threat-intensive trip.)

    The alarm jolted Captain Elroy D. Jones from his slumber. Rolling over towards the clock, he realized that it was not the 0500 wakeup he was expecting as the cyan "3:12 AM" display blared back into his eyes. He listened more carefully, and allowing another pulse of drowsiness to wash away, he sat straight up in bed. It was the car alarm.

    Parked outside on the curb because Jones had been trying to finish the cabinets in the garage last night before he had to pack for the trip, the Jones's Jetta was beeping at the entire block. Capt. Jones's wife murmured something to the effect of "Turn it off before the kids wake up," but he was already at his bureau fumbling for the keychain remote. With a quick click of the button, he silenced the vehicle's protest…only to hear another. His daughter, three-year old Lucy, was now crying and he knew that it would only be moments before his son, five-year old Jack, would be up too.

"I'll get the kids, you go check the Jetta," Jones's wife said. As he headed downstairs he began to fume. He knew the whole family would have trouble getting back to sleep. And he was leaving for a four-day trip at 6:30. "Great," he thought.

The Jetta was fine. The sound of a whimpered screech as he approached and the muddy footprints on the hood indicated it was a raccoon. "Nice work parking it next to the garbage, idiot," Jones criticized to himself. He reflected on the events leading up to the nocturnal disruption: started the cabinets late, stopped when he realized he needed to pack, left Jetta out on street, packed and went to bed hoping to quickly fall asleep, reminded by wife that tomorrow was garbage day, got out of bed to do garbage, left garbage totes next to Jetta instead of either moving the car or putting garbage on other side of the driveway.

Back in the house, the kids were being cooed back to sleep by Mrs. Jones. Capt. Jones slipped back into bed and closed his eyes, praying that he could get back to sleep. It seemed like only 30 seconds later when the next alarm went off. This time it was the alarm clock.

An hour later, Capt. Jones was on his way to the airport to start a four-day trip. Sipping his coffee to get warm and increase his wakefulness, he began to think about the day ahead, and tried desperately to forget about the sleepless night. He was headed into JFK by way of PIT. He would spend a couple hours sitting in JFK before the last leg of the day to ORD. The car radio, tuned to the local sports talk station, had the local weather guy giving his admonitions about travel across the Great Lakes today. The first winter storm of the season had raced up from Kansas overnight and Chicago, Milwaukee, Detroit, and Cleveland were all in the crosshairs for later today. "Great."

After clearing security, Jones headed to the crew room for check-in. As he rounded the corner, he ran into Ryan Essex, his first officer for the trip.

"Hey, D.J., good morning! Nice four-day ahead of us—snow-storm and all!"

"Hmpf. Yeah, sounds like it might get interesting. Par for course, though. It is November, ya know."

"Right, right. Well, I am going to grab some coffee, you want something?"

"Yeah, sure. I'll get ya back tonight in Chicago. How about a blackeye?"

"You got it boss, see you at the gate, I think we are at 22."

Jones had been with the airline now for 18 years, and several of the more senior F/Os he flew with knew him pretty well. To them, he was "D.J." or "Deej." Same with some of his closer friends, and of course, his wife. He was glad he had Essex on for this trip. It could turn out OK, but given the night before, the weather situation, and the general propensity for problems of the unexpected to arise, he would need a good F/O.

After checking mail and logging in to the scheduling system to check in for the trip, he headed to the gate. As he approached the podium there was Essex, coffee in hand, with a smug "You're never gonna believe this" look on his face. Next to him was a mechanic and a perturbed-looking gate agent on the phone.

"What's up?" Jones queried.

"They can't get a code to clear on the leak detect system, so they are grounding the plane," Essex replied.

"OK. How long?"

"Don't know, Captain," replied the mechanic. "Could be something we could have done in 15 minutes, could be something that could take all day. We tried 'control-alt-delete' a bunch of times, so don't ask."

Computers ran the systems on the plane more than pilots in Jones's airliner. It was a running joke that all you had to do was "re-boot" to clear a mechanical discrepancy. The unfunny part of the joke was that sometimes it worked, but only until the computer realized the plane was still broken...which could prove to be too late if proper procedures were not used.

"Well, I assume you are holding boarding if you are up here at the podium," Jones asked the mechanic.

"Yeah, well I can't do that, technically, but she is talking to OPS to see what the plan should be."

Essex rolled his eyes, and handed D.J. his coffee. "Right. OPS. I am sure they have this all figured out."

D.J. knew what Essex was saying. OPS (short for "Operations") was responsible for gate assignments and servicing requests. But they also coordinated gate services, and thus, the gate agents always thought they had some control over whether or not a flight operated. In the realm of Gate 22 (and every other gate on the C concourse), "OPS was in control of everything." Essex's sarcasm cued D.J. for his next move.

"OK, I am going to step over here and call dispatch and find out what they know," he said calmly and with a smile. He gestured to Essex to come away from the podium. "Let's take a walk."

Over the years, D.J. learned that delays of any kind—whether they are mechanical, weather-related, or otherwise—take time. They don't get resolved quickly. If they did, they wouldn't be called delays. And once a flight got delayed, it got de-prioritized as resources were shifted off of it to work another flight. Hanging around the gate and waiting for the gate agent and mechanic to find answers was going to be a lost cause.

D.J.'s cell phone buzzed. "Right on cue," he said dryly to Essex.

"Yeah, Jones here," he answered. He knew who it was.

"Hey, Captain Jones, this is Anna in Crew Scheduling. We are notifying you that your first flight is delayed this morning."

"Really? Until when?"

"Umm, I think they are posting an 8:45 departure now."

D.J. looked at the flight information screen that he and Essex were passing in the concourse, and confirmed that his departure time now showed 8:45.

"OK. Thanks for the call, anything else I should know?"

"Not right now, but we will call you if anything else happens with the flight."

"Great…hey, do me a favor, would you, and patch me over to the dispatch supervisor?"

"Sure thing, please hold."

Another thing D.J. learned over the years is that pilots were the last to hear from dispatch and maintenance about details of any plans, but the first persons asked out on the front lines. The phone clicked and rang a couple times as his call transferred over. Thankfully, a familiar voice answered.

"Dispatch, this is Flo."

"Flo, there are people trying to get to the Steelers game," Jones teased.

"D.J., what the heck did you do to that airplane now!"

Florence Bena had been at the airline for 30 some years. She started out as a gate agent, then became a flight attendant, and now was a duty manager in the airline's System Operational Control center or "SOC." She had known D.J. from his first day on the job.

"You know, it's just not my day, Flo. I didn't even touch the damn thing!" D.J. laughed.

"Mmmm, hmmm! I bet you looked at it cross-eyed, though! When are you gonna learn, son." Flo was about the same age as D.J., but due to her motherly instinct, she found it necessary to call him and other pilots "son" out of fondness.

"Hey, what is the real scoop on that thing? You know the gate is going to ask me after OPS admits to them they don't know anything."

"Well, sit tight. I posted the 8:45 because we might swap you to another ship, and they might get it fixed. We gave maintenance another hour to try and get her patched up, and if they don't you will get swapped."

"OK, sounds good. Hey, if you and Jimmy are free the weekend after Thanksgiving, let me know if you want to come on over for a couple drinks. The kids would love to see you guys."

"We just might be. So long as your wife makes an extra pecan pie for Jimmy. He raves about it every year!"

D.J. said goodbye and looked at Essex.

"Well?" Essex asked.

"Well what? We are delayed to 8:45. Sounds like they are close to fixing it. If not, we swap planes."

Even before he steps into the flight deck for the first leg, the threats have already piled up on Captain Jones:

- Fatigue
- Snowstorm
- Distraction (still worrying about things back at home)
- Broken plane
- Delayed flight

Many pilots tend to look at threats naturally as obstacles to "a good day." However, whether you have a good day or a bad day at work is irrelevant. These issues are legitimate threats to the operation occurring normally, and could result in degradation to safety of flight. Suffice it to say, whenever a pilot has something affecting them that causes them to say, "Ugh, this isn't going to be a good day," the alarm bell is ringing—a threat has presented itself.

Some threats, as Reasons pointed out, we just don't know about. These are called "latent threats." A great example of a latent threat is fatigue. In fact, it is perhaps the most dangerous of latent threats due to its tendency to be unrecognizable until it is too late. Take Capt. Jones, for example. He very well may have arrived to the airport feeling awake (due to caffeine and perhaps the brisk walk through the terminal) but the fact of the matter is that he slept poorly the night before. As he begins his flight duties, he may be completely unaware of the onset of fatigue because he feels completely alert.

Threats may already have manifested themselves into errors. An example is if an aircraft is dispatched into known icing conditions with an anti-icing system deferred. Obviously, such an action is unintended, but for some reason the threats (broken anti-ice system and forecast icing) were not trapped by the dispatcher. They combine to cause an error which must be *trapped and mitigated* by the flight crew. If the flight crew fails to do so, the airplane could encounter icing conditions in which sustained flight is impossible. What would happen if that encounter caused an unsafe condition, up to and including an aircraft accident? This would be eerily reminiscent of Continental Flight 1713, but nonetheless is a sequence of events we know we have seen before. The only difference is whether or not the sequence—the error chain—is broken.

It is extremely important for flight crews—and especially the PIC—to be cognizant of threats and errors. The PIC, having ultimate responsibility for the safety of flight, needs to be wise and resourceful in trapping/stopping threats and resolving/mitigating errors. Proper crew briefings will enhance the success of TEM. Another great help will be the PIC's ability to manage his or her workload.

WORKLOAD MANAGEMENT

Many airline operators have specific task roles all set in place for flight crew members, for different phases of the flight operation. For example, during preflight, the first officer may be responsible for conducting the external preflight and the captain may be charged with flight deck set-up. During cruise, the pilot monitoring may be responsible for recording and transmitting position checks while the pilot flying may be required to check engine parameters. Whatever the case may be, duties are oftentimes shared so that each member of the flight crew is carrying a shared burden.

This isn't to say, however, that workload management is conquered by such a prescription. What happens when several threats or errors suddenly present themselves? The workload goes up exponentially for both crew members, but particularly for the PIC due to the level of responsibility. It is at these times that a PIC will need to tweak their workloads, and the workloads of the other crewmember(s).

	Normal Operations	**Engine Failure**
Pilot Flying	• Flies the airplane	• Flies the airplane • Radios • Coordinates with cabin
Pilot Monitoring	• Radios • Checklists • Coordinates with cabin • Performance data lookup	• Checklists/Non-Normal

Taking a somewhat "elementary" example of engine failure in flight (only because it is practiced in recurrent training all the time by professional operators), we can examine the workload shifts that *could* occur.

During an engine failure, everyone's stress level skyrockets. The pilot flying (PF) must concentrate directly on his role. The pilot monitoring (PM) has to amplify his workload a bit, which was already the "busiest" to begin with. Now the PM has to run additional non-normal procedures and checklists. In an effort to free up the PM for these tasks (which are crucial to managing the emergency—securing the engine and preparing for a safe emergency landing) the PF, once he has assured he has control of the airplane and needs no additional assistance in flying, can offload the PM. In the example, the PF takes on the duties of radio communications as well as coordinating with the cabin. This leaves the PM free to work on the checklists, both normal and non-normal.

It is common that the PIC will want more of a communicative role in an emergency situation, meaning that the PIC will want to be the one to coordinate with ATC and company, briefing the cabin, etc. More properly, the PIC should want to be in a position where he can best *supervise and manage* the situation. The same model of workload management in the engine failure scenario can be used in this case:

Normal Operations	
Pilot Flying	• Flies the airplane
Pilot Monitoring	• Radios • Checklists • Coordinates with cabin • Performance data lookup

Engine Failure	
SIC	• Flies the airplane • Radios* • Coordinate with ATC*
PIC	• Checklists/non-normal procedures • Coordinates with company* • Coordinates with cabin

Notice that the roles during the engine failure scenario have been determined by PIC/SIC designation, rather than by PF/PM. The asterisk (*) denotes radio communications. Because the SIC is already handling primary radio communications with ATC, he may as well coordinate any emergency requests with them. The PIC can utilize the second radio (two or more VHF communications radios are typically onboard modern aircraft) to coordinate with company, operations, etc. In this model, from a task perspective, the two pilots are balanced, and the PIC can have a much more supervisory role with hands-off of the flight controls.

Coordinating these roles in emergency situations is the duty of the PIC. They can be established either in a preflight briefing, or at the point in time when the emergency occurs, but getting this figured out in advance is preferable. An emergency will be enough of a surprise, and having disagreements over who should handle what is an added surprise that should be avoided.

When coordinating this in the preflight briefing, the PIC has to ensure that the SIC understands *exactly* what the roles being assigned entail. This may seem odd, since it would make perfect sense that if a captain says, "If we have an inflight emergency, I want you to operate the radios and fly while I handle the non-normals," the first officer would know exactly what is meant. But a better way to brief it is for the PIC to say, "I want to be able to manage the situation." This is an all-encompassing way to describe the role. The PIC will not only handle the non-normal checklist, but will also coordinate with ATC, dispatch, maintenance, cabin crew, and others. Managing the situation involves being able to take focus off of flight controls and instruments in an effort to gain perspective.

Another important point that needs emphasis in this briefing: the PIC needs backup. The SIC is going to focus on the basics of aviate/navigate/communicate, but also needs to keep an ear open to what the PIC is saying to dispatch. The PIC needs to aid this by keeping the SIC in the loop on all plans and decisions being contemplated. They must work together as a crew in concert, not as a crew completely compartmentalized.

RESPONSIBILITY AND AUTHORITY

This chapter opened up with a quick review of 14 CFR §91.3, which (as a reminder) is titled "Responsibility and authority of the pilot in command." The first clause in the regulation gives us the FAA's number-one rule when it comes to PICs:

> (a) *The pilot in command of an aircraft is directly responsible for, and is the final authority as to, the operation of that aircraft.*

How can we interpret this rule more clearly than how it is plainly written? In a way, this entire book is an answer to the question in that it explores many aspects of being a PIC and covers many things that a PIC is responsible for. It starts with understanding all of the elements that are brought together to conduct an aircraft operation: airplane, flight deck crew, cabin crew, dispatch, maintenance, customers, cargo, refuelers, loaders, servicers, caterers—they all have a part in making the aircraft operation happen. And the PIC is responsible for *every last one of them*.

Many of you may be incredulous when reading that last paragraph. "How could I possibly be responsible for the guy who dumps the lavatories on the airplane?" you may ask. In response, I would ask, "Does he touch your airplane?" Since the answer is yes, I can tell you that the PIC is 100 percent responsible for that servicer's actions.

Not only is the PIC responsible for that person, he also retains *full authority* over that person. Again, the reason is that the lavatory servicer is in contact with the airplane under the PIC's authority. If a valve gets left open or a panel gets latched improperly, and one of these causes an incident or (perish the thought) an accident, who will have to file the report and be *responsible* for how the aircraft was operated at the end of the day? The PIC.

A PIC is very much like the CEO of a large company. The CEO has direct authority over, and responsibility for, everything that affects the operation of the company. And while the CEO may have many management layers below him, he is still responsible for every move made by every employee of that company, right on down to the part-time payroll clerk.

We discussed threat and error management earlier in the chapter, and it is this concept of the PIC's overall authority that makes TEM so vital in safe aircraft operations. If there is an opportunity for any of the personnel who have a hand in operating the aircraft to detect, trap and eliminate a threat, or correct an error, it should be exercised. If the PIC detects a threat or finds an error caused by others, it is incumbent upon the PIC to take action.

To revisit the lavatory dump operation: If the PIC conducts a post-flight inspection and finds that the lavatory servicer didn't latch the panel correctly, what should happen? The PIC should of course call the servicer back to correct the problem. And should the lavatory servicer follow the PIC's instructions and carry out his request? Absolutely. The PIC, in this circumstance, is not "crossing any lines" of authority.

Some would argue that the PIC is not the lavatory servicer's "direct report," and this author strongly disagrees. The lavatory servicer may indeed report to a lead, supervisor, or manager, but a PIC is the "CEO of the Airplane." The PIC is in charge of every aspect of the airplane's operation. The lavatory servicer's supervisor can be in charge of that employee's time card and performance review, but when it comes to the interaction he has with an airplane, he reports (like everyone does) to the PIC.

When we define a pilot-in-command, we are not only identifying a role. We are also identifying a leader. Responsibility and authority are invested in the PIC because even among a team, there is still a leader that is in charge. The remainder of this book points to the PIC as having the identity of the one and only person on a flight that everyone will look towards for direction, for command, and for resolution of conflict.

Chapter 3 Notes

1. All Federal Aviation Regulations cited are part of Title 14 of the United States Code of Federal Regulations, most easily retrieved online from faa.gov/regulations_policies/faa_regulations

2. Retrieved from dictionary.reference.com

3. "Pilot Monitoring" took the place of the extremely passive term "Pilot Not Flying" as CRM/TEM concepts developed in the twenty-first century.

4. I am clearly echoing the immortal words of John Gillespie Magee, Jr., and his sonnet *High Flight*, which was his reflection on the joy of flight and the inherent divine relationship to flight. He closes the poem, "And, while with silent lifting mind I've trod the high untrespassed sanctity of space, Put out my hand, and touched the face of God."

5. From "What Is Ergonomics?" on the International Association of Ergonomics website: iea.cc

6. I strongly encourage you to read, "Defensive Flying for Pilots: An Introduction to Threat and Error Management" by groundbreaking researchers at the University of Texas. A copy of this paper is archived by the Flight Safety Foundation at skybrary.aero/sites/default/files/bookshelf/1982.pdf

7. All advisory circulars are searchable and downloadable at faa.gov.

8. Reason, J., *Human Error*. (Cambridge, England. Cambridge University Press, 1990).

9. NTSB Number AAR-88/09.

4

Crew Briefings

If you work for an airline that encourages and facilitates crew briefings, and requires that it be done at certain places and certain times, you are ahead of the game. Hopefully this section provides a review for you and perhaps some tips you hadn't thought of. If you don't work for the airlines, or have never come across this kind of advice before, keep an open mind, and as you read think of situations where appropriate briefings could enhance each and every flight operation you conduct. If you are in the passenger airline industry, you probably know that "What's the flight time?" is perhaps the most commonly uttered question between flight crews. Coming in a close second, or perhaps even a dead heat, is "When do we arrive?" Some crews may have the experience of overhearing or participating in a crew briefing that consists of nothing more than one or both of these questions. That's just plain wrong.

What if on every flight you prepared for, all you knew was the flight time? As a pilot, it would be like walking into the flight deck with nothing but a boarding pass. No flight plan, no weather briefing, no load manifest—nothing else. Armed with only the flight time, you would only be as knowledgeable as your passengers.

And your flight attendants? Truth be known, many flight attendants don't get much more information from their crew briefings. Lots of pilots get on the plane and say, "Hi, it will be 2:30 to Houston," and then they disappear into the flight deck. How fair is that?

Is the flight time really, honestly, the most important aspect of any flight? Of course it's not. How many other factors affecting the flight need to be communicated to the entire crew? What about factors affecting the whole trip (which might encompass several flights across several days)? If you sit down and make a list, it could look similar to this:

1. Time
2. Safety
3. Weather

4. Security

5. Maintenance issues

6. Gate services

7. Special passenger needs

8. Sterile flight deck procedures

9. International procedures

10. Deicing

11. Personal issues (rest, food, etc.)

12. Schedule issues (legality, breaks, etc.)

13. Special boarding or deplaning issues

14. Crew meals

15. Entry to flight deck

16. Emergency procedures

17. Special considerations

Truly, the list could go on and on. But in reality, do crews brief all these things? Are they all necessary? When and how could such briefings be conducted? Effective PICs and SICs ensure the entire crew (flight deck and cabin) is properly briefed, and briefed as often as possible and necessary.

THE SEA-ICE METHOD OF CREW BRIEFINGS

To be effective in your crew briefings, you need to know what information your crewmembers have, and what information they need to know. While each operator will differ in specifics, there are four basic categories of information that are common between all operations that crewmembers will need to have in order to effectively perform their duties. These categories are listed in the following table.

SEA-ICE Categories for Crew Briefings
1. **Safety** and **Security** issues and considerations
2. **Equipment** issues (inoperative equipment, etc.)
3. **Abnormal** procedures
4. In Case of Emergency (**ICE**)

And, naturally in the world of aviation, we have a nifty mnemonic made from the abbreviations for these categories: SEA-ICE.[1]

In the following sections, you can easily employ SEA-ICE to your briefing techniques, starting with the first briefing you give and ending with the last post-brief.

THE FFOT (FIRST FLIGHT OF TRIP) BRIEFING

Let's begin by talking about the very first briefing you give at the beginning of the trip. The "First Flight of Trip" or FFOT briefing is the absolute, number one, most important briefing you can conduct because it sets the tone and establishes the lines of communication between the crew. The elements of a good FFOT brief will be covered a bit later in this chapter. First, let's talk about first impressions.

First Greetings and Introductions

It should be natural for a crew to start out every trip with basic greetings, introductions, and small talk of the day. For the majority of crews this occurs when everyone arrives at the gate or the plane. For some crews it could happen in the crew room or a facility where "check in" is conducted. In any case, this first point of contact is *crucial* to the success of the entire trip. As the saying goes, "You never get a second chance to make a first impression."

The following advice should be taken as a strong recommendation, and not be taken lightly. No matter where you are, how you feel, who you are greeting, or how you feel about them, remember that the PIC sets the tone. Captains are 100 percent responsible for making *the best* first impressions. When you greet a crewmember, you should smile, provide a firm (but not knuckle cracking) handshake, look in their eyes, and say "Good Morning!" (or "Good Afternoon," "Good Evening," or whatever is appropriate) and "my name is _____."[2] Even if you don't feel enthusiastic, *sound enthusiastic*. If you want to know how you should look, sound, and act during this greeting, simply recall the best job interview you ever had: Remember how you greeted the interviewer and how excited you honestly felt to greet them (because you wanted the job so bad). THAT is how this, and every greeting, should go. Why? *Because every first officer and flight attendant you meet for the first time is interviewing you.* They will size you up in a matter of moments, so the way you handle this introduction is really vital.

The next step is your call, but at the very least you need to tell this person when they can expect to hear more about the flight (i.e., when you will brief them). The natural thing to do is to launch into some small talk. Maybe you know this person from a previous trip? Perhaps you wanted to ask them how they are doing. Whatever the small talk is, finish up with either the briefing itself or details about when they can expect a briefing. This is crucial in order to demonstrate that you are PIC, that you are confident, and that you have a plan to brief them. They want to hear from you, so ensure them that they will!

When and Where

If you are going to tell a crewmember when or where you will conduct the crew brief, you should have it planned out in advance, if at all possible. The best time to conduct any pre-flight briefing is as early as possible before the start of passenger boarding. The best place to brief is completely up to you, but the location should at the very least be comfortable and free of distractions. If you have access to a briefing room, use it! If you are in the gate area, find a place away from the bulk of passengers (if possible). If you are on board the aircraft, move to a location in the cabin that is away from the boarding door(s) and free from noise and distraction.

Airline crews are all too familiar with the gate agent who comes down to say, "Ready to board?" with the passengers already at her heels. So another strong recommendation is that if you have not completed your briefing, tell the gate agent to wait. Asking for more time doesn't always help, though; in an industry run on "countdown to on-time departure" procedures, they may start getting passengers down the jetway anyway just to avoid the risk of any delays on their part. If you find yourself mid-briefing when a passenger shows up at the door, *ask them to wait*, and when you are finished with the briefing, make sure to *thank the passenger* for their patience while you finished your "safety and security briefing for the crew."

Let me repeat this point with an example:

[Scene: Passenger arrives at the boarding door while the captain is mid-briefing with the crew a few rows back in First Class.]

Passenger: *[stepping onto airplane.]* "Um, hello?"

Captain: *[Approaching passenger.]* "Hi there! Say, we will have you onboard in about 90 seconds. Could I ask you to wait back in the jetway for just a bit while we finish up some preflight duties?"

Passenger: *[Stepping back into jetway, somewhat perturbed.]* "Oh, um… I guess so. Sure."

[Captain thanks the passenger and heads back in to finish up his briefing, in a non-rushed, confident manner. He then heads back to the passenger and ushers him back onboard.]

Captain: "Hey, thanks for waiting while I finished up the safety and security briefing for the crew. I appreciate it!"

Passenger: "Um. Yeah, right, no problem. Glad to help!"

Did you notice the word choice of the captain in the example above? He told the passenger he was finishing the "safety and security briefing." In a nutshell, a preflight briefing is exactly that, but that isn't what is important about his choice of words. What is important is that the captain told the passenger exactly what was happening. Here are the benefits from the way the captain handled the situation:

- The passenger feels very confident that the captain is an in-charge type of person, and has safety and security as the top priority.
- The crew feels taken care of, and can tell this captain means business when he prioritizes the briefing ahead of the passengers.
- The crew and the passenger feel good about the level of confidence exuded by the captain, and therefore grant him trustworthy status.

The FFOT Briefing Itself

You can put SEA-ICE to good use when addressing details about the FFOT brief. That big list a few pages back comes into play when fleshing out SEA-ICE. But beyond the typical considerations you must make for every flight, this briefing sets the tone, and is intended to help everyone make an overall assessment of how the trip will function on a crew-coordination basis.

For this reason, you need to bring in some of the more "touchy-feely" aspects of briefings. This is the hardest part of crew briefings for many pilots. It is not easy to ask seemingly intrusive and personal questions to people you may have just met. But when it comes down to brass tacks, pilots-in-command are really *required* to know whether or not their crew is up-to-task. It is part of their overall responsibility for the operation of the aircraft.

To point, prior to covering the items you will discuss based on SEA-ICE, you should consider two additional mnemonic reminders:

IMSAFE

NEEDS

The "IMSAFE" mnemonic is at the top of the list, and as you will see in a later chapter, the classic abbreviation (representing Illness, Medication, Stress, Alcohol, Fatigue, Emotion) is vital in assessing your (or your fellow crewmember's) fitness for flight duty. When I brief my crew, I don't start out by asking, "Okay, folks! Has everyone done a self-evaluation with 'IMSAFE' today?" Nor do I query them on each of the different points: "Are you sick? Are you on meds? Are you stressed? Have you been drinking?" (Seriously, could you imagine doing this?)

I make one exception, however, in relationship to fatigue. Crew rest is at a premium these days, and until better rules and practices actually manifest themselves—and even when the day comes when they have—I will tend to ask crew if they feel rested.

For assessing the remainder of IMSAFE, rather than approaching it as an interrogation, all I do is size them up just like I would do when greeting any friend or family member. You can tell in an instant if something "isn't right" with a person. If you aren't exactly sure what I am writing about here, or need more details, see Chapter 5.

"NEEDS" reminds me to let the crew know that they should feel free to ask for whatever they need—and I don't mean just what they need to conduct their duties. I tell them if they need to take care of something personal, or need extra time, food, or anything else, that they can ask me and I will make sure they get what they need.

So, what does IMSAFE and NEEDS look and sound like all put together at the beginning of the FFOT? Well, here's an example:

*"Hey everyone, let's take a few moments to do a briefing. [Everyone gathers around] OK, well, we have a nice little three-day trip ahead of us. I know it is an early morning; did everyone get some good rest last night? [Hopefully everyone responds affirmatively] Awesome. Well, I want every one of you to know right away that if you **need** anything—whether it is a bite to eat, some extra time during a turnaround to take care of something personal, or*

something that pertains to getting your job done right, let me know. Even if it will take some additional time, I want to make sure that you get everything you need. [Everyone will be nodding along in agreement now]. Does anyone have any questions about the schedule or the trip, or anything so far?"

After completing the IMSAFE and NEEDS segment of the FFOT, roll into the SEA-ICE briefing for your first flight. By the way, every time a pilot-in-command has a crew change—including a *cabin crew* change—it is imperative to do the IMSAFE and NEEDS portions of the FFOT briefing with the new crewmembers.

SEA-ICE in the FFOT

Remember, we are going to employ SEA-ICE in all of our briefings. Again, the four categories are shown below.

SEA-ICE Categories for Crew Briefings
1. **Safety** and **Security** issues and considerations
2. **Equipment** issues (inoperative equipment, etc.)
3. **Abnormal** procedures
4. In Case of Emergency (**ICE**)

These four categories can be readily broken down into specifics. (Not all specifics are included below, but these are for example).

- Safety issues and considerations
  - Weather/turbulence
  - Special boarding or loading
- Security issues and considerations
  - Flight deck security
  - Law enforcement officers/federal air marshals
  - Secured passengers
  - Customs procedures
- Equipment issues (inoperative equipment, etc.)
  - Deferred equipment
  - Alternative procedures due to inoperative equipment

- Abnormal Procedures
  —Enplane/deplane non-standard (i.e., airstairs, no jetbridge, etc.)
- In Case of Emergency (ICE)
  —Flight deck expectations/responses
  —Cabin expectations/responses

If there are no considerations to be made for one of the categories above (for example, if there are no equipment issues), that is fine—but it still needs to be briefed.

Here is an example briefing for the cabin crew using this five-category approach:

"Whatever you do back here in the cabin, please think of safety first. Ensure passenger safety and your own safety in every move you make. If there is ever a doubt, stop whatever it is you are doing, and make sure it is safe to continue. If there is anything we pilots can do to help you in this, let us know. Our flight today will have pretty good weather en route, but expect a few bumps about an hour in. If we get any reports of turbulence that we feel may jeopardize safety, we will give you a call to suspend service until we are sure we can remain in smoother air. Please ensure to use proper procedures when we need to go in and out of the flight deck, making sure passengers are seated and the aisle is blocked. The gate agent has not informed us of any special security concerns, and no LEOs or FAMs have been made known to the crew. If any do board, however, please let the flight deck crew know where they are seated. We should have a normal boarding process today, with one aisle chair passenger that will be loaded first. Seat 12A is deferred, and the aft potable water is inop, so we have requested that moist towelettes are stocked in the aft lavatory since the sink water is unavailable. There are no other abnormalities expected. In flight, if the flight deck becomes aware of an emergency, we will contact you as soon as we are able and let you know at a minimum the nature of the emergency, if it will cause us to make an emergency landing, how much time we have remaining until landing, and whether or not it will be a braced landing, evacuation, etc. If you become aware of an emergency situation, please contact the flight deck with discretion and advise us. The captain will determine the course of action to take. The flight time is 2:30. Please let us know if you need anything, including if you need any extra time—including for any personal issues. Any questions?"

Note that the flight time is given, but at the end of the brief. Also, for the emergency situations, the "T.E.S.T." method (Type, Evacuation, Special Instructions, Time) method was generally covered. However, company policy may dictate more specific briefing points. Some carriers use terms like "Red Emergency or Yellow Emergency" to denote the nature of the emergency and whether or not an evacuation is likely. Also, some operators utilize the "emergency chime", "alert", or "multichime" to clearly indicate that an emergency situation is present; others use more discrete methods to communicate emergency information between the flight deck and the cabin.[3] In the end, all five categories were covered in the example brief. In addition, every good brief should end with an indication that you are open to the needs of the crewmembers. Always close with "Any questions?"

In review and summary of this section dealing with the FFOT, remember:

1. IMSAFE
2. NEEDS
3. SEA-ICE

THE STANDARD PREFLIGHT BRIEFING

When I was a newbie airline pilot, part of my airline Basic Indoctrination was to memorize what was known as "The Standard Brief." Before learning anything about the airplane, and while absorbing tons of information from 14 CFR Part 121, operations specifications, company polices, and general subjects, all of the new hires had to memorize a paragraph describing what happened if an engine failure occurred after we were committed to takeoff (at V_1 speed). It was similar to the following (you will note the term "autocoarsen," which is particular to the Saab SF340):

"If we have an engine fire or failure at or after V_1, we will set max power and continue the takeoff. With a positive rate, we will select gear up, establish V_2, and verify autocoarsen. If negative autocoarsen, we will confirm the appropriate condition lever and select it to fuel off. At 1,000 feet we will retract the flaps and complete the memory items..."

While this little paragraph was nice in describing some of the considerations and procedures we would use if we had an engine failure at or after V_1, it was not a complete takeoff briefing. *Not even close.* But for some reason, we took this rote-learned recitation and treated it like that was all there was to a takeoff brief. It got ingrained in us *that all we needed to think about was engine failure after V₁*—so ingrained, in fact, that when some crews got to the "crew brief" item in the checklist, they would just state "standard" as the response.

After some time, a sea change took place in our airline's training department. During proficiency checks, pilots were taken completely by surprise when additional threats and errors went undetected because all they were focused on was the "V_1 cut". Check airmen and instructors started implementing some sweeping changes to get the fleet back to reality when it came to the preflight briefing. And the changes meant that when the crew had to conduct their briefings, a simple response of "standard" would no longer suffice.

Because what does "standard" mean anyway? In primary aviation training, the term "standard" is applied in terms of the conditions used to describe an airplane's performance. Pilots learn that a "standard day" means that the atmosphere has the properties of a parcel of air at sea level with a pressure of 29.92 in. Hg and a temperature of 15°C. We also tend to add in some lore-based qualities like, "If Chuck Yeager was testing our airplane..." After all, Yeager was the epitome of "standard," right?

So pilots assessing any briefing as "standard" are really lying to themselves. Every single flight a pilot performs is in actuality quite *non-standard*. The weather and atmosphere have a 99.9 percent chance of being non-standard. The airplane likely is not factory new, and even if it was, many airplanes that have just been delivered have yet to be "standardized" per customer order. It is more likely the airplane has some mechanical discrepancies. And again, as for Yeager, can we really call any test pilot one who operates within standards?

The "Standard Preflight Briefing" I am addressing and promoting here goes by so many different names and flavors across the industry. But the concept is the same and it focuses on one unilateral truth about every flight: nothing is standard. Every time you do a preflight briefing, you have to focus on this; otherwise you will miss so much.

The challenge lies in how to do this. Let's face it: many pilots fly in and out of the same airports day after day. They have the airport layouts, frequencies, SIDs, STARs, waypoints, approaches, and more ingrained into their memories. It is so easy to slip into talking about the things that are "the same way they are every time I do this flight." And pilots do so by not saying very much at all. Honestly, just eliminate the word "standard" from your briefings and focus on what might be different about the particular flight, at that particular moment.

This is where SEA-ICE helps out a bunch. You can certainly acknowledge the fact that you can expect the "normal route," or "typical departure," or the like. But you especially need to focus on what isn't routine, or what just happens to be plain different.

Again using the four categories, below is an example brief from one pilot to another. This could be the captain briefing the first officer, or even the pilot flying briefing the pilot monitoring. Each carrier or operator will have a specific routine to follow regarding who briefs what and when. My recommendation, however, is that no matter what prescribed briefing procedure you have to follow, the pilot-in-command still should ensure that information in each category of SEA-ICE is covered. Again, the PIC can say something for every category, even if it seems obvious. And please note that the word "standard" is gone from the vernacular.

> "Let's keep an eye on safety. If we see something that could potentially be unsafe, let's call it out, stop what we are doing, and correct what needs to be corrected. We have good VFR weather here and MVFR weather at the destination requiring an alternate. Our chosen alternate's weather is legal, and we have confirmed the fuel load on board for departure that includes the alternate fuel requirements. We have no special security concerns, and the cabin crew has been briefed to advise us if that changes. The aft potable water is deferred, and we have a slat access plate missing that will cause us to take a performance hit, but there are no other MEL/CDL procedures that need to be complied with. We have to deal with the hard-stand parking spot at our destination, so we will make sure to include a word about using the airstairs when we talk to the passengers. In case of any other abnormal or emergency situations, we will follow checklist guidance."

Some readers may think the above brief is a bit short or lacking some crucial information. But I would submit that it covers everything the pilots need to be on the same page for:

- *Safety/Security*—The brief starts out with a general "eye towards safety" statement. The brief covers the weather expectations, as this flight doesn't seem to be operating in "severe clear" conditions. Security-wise, the brief acknowledges that there is nothing special to consider, and that the cabin will advise if something affecting security arises.

- *Equipment*—The brief covers the deferred equipment, and points out the performance and procedure considerations.
- *Abnormals*—The brief points out the use of the airstairs being a consideration.
- *ICE*—The brief simply states that the crew will follow checklist guidance. Does the crew need to review emergency checklists and procedures? No. In fact, as a requirement of their training, certification, and recurrent qualifications they should know exactly what those checklists say and how to perform them.

Does the briefing need to include finite details about how the take-off will be performed? Or how about how the takeoff will be aborted? Maybe, if your aircraft operation is so complex that you need to brief those aspects on every flight (or, even more to point, if your company procedures require it). But consider this: do we brief how to recover from a stall every time we prepare for departure? Not likely. That being said, here is an example of a SEA-ICE takeoff briefing that focuses on actual aircraft operation:

Safety: "We will plan to take off from runway 22R from intersection Whiskey. Safety-wise, let's make sure we verify runway properly with signage, markings, and aircraft heading."

Equipment: "For this departure, we will arm LNAV, and acceleration height of 800 feet set up with no speed restrictions set into the FMC. Any speed control we need on the departure will be done with speed intervention on the MCP."

Abnormal: "Looks like on the pre-departure clearance they have given us the Newark One except to maintain 2,500 feet, so in that case I will ask for Flight Level Change rather than VNAV when we reach our acceleration height. I may keep the speed at 210 until we get cleared above 3,000 feet."

ICE: "If we have a power loss or engine fire after V_1, we will continue the takeoff, and with a positive rate retract the gear and climb out at V_2. We will let ATC know and declare emergency and ask for runway heading. At 800 feet I will call 'Vertical Speed plus 100, set clean maneuvering speed' and we will patiently accelerate and retract the flaps on schedule. Once cleaned up, I will call, 'Flight Level Change, Set Clean Maneuvering Speed, Set Max Continuous Thrust,' and start heading towards the engine failure checklist."

Customize your briefings to include what you need to for operational reasons and in accord with your standard operating procedures. But keep your preflight briefings pertinent to things that may not be normal or standard, especially within the framework of "SEA-ICE."

I have one last word on briefing and preflight readiness. Sage pilots are always wary of anomalies that may impact the safety of flight. However, what makes a sage pilot a *safe* pilot is whether or not they are verbalized in the flight deck. I have flown with several captains, and as a captain also performed this final check with the other pilot when we approached the end of the taxiway prior to takeoff:

"[Insert Pilot Name Here], is there any reason it would be unsafe for us to take off?"

Boom! That's it. It would be a rare day indeed if I was given a reason. But it gets asked anyway.

SEA-ICE ON ARRIVAL

Using the SEA-ICE briefing method for arrival briefings is helpful for focusing on what might get missed. There are plenty of other mnemonics, methods, and procedures for how to set up for an arrival and approach brief, but some elements are always common between them:

- Current and expected weather conditions must be considered.
- Flight instruments, FMCs, navigation and communication radios, and other avionics must be programmed and set up.
- A verbal approach briefing must be exchanged between the pilots.

SEA-ICE can help improve your briefings to hit some other points, too. Let's take a look.

First, set up the equipment for the arrival or approach. Program the FMC/FMS, tune the appropriate frequencies for nav and comm radios, set or select airspeed reference bugs, etc. Ask your flying partner to do the same before you commence the brief. If you are lucky, your partner has already set everything up for you!

Safety: The briefing (ideally done well prior to top-of-descent) should start out with the safety considerations. First points of information on safety come from current weather and NOTAM reports. Pull them up, read them off, and talk about any impacts. Secondary safety points typically involve procedures—either the instrument approach procedure itself or the airplane procedures for the particular approach. Brief them as thoroughly as you can, making sure to read or recite special notes or procedures as required.

Equipment: Review the equipment set up that you did prior to the beginning of the brief, confirming verbally the frequencies and courses. Discuss when autopilot/automation modes will be called for and executed.

Abnormals: Talk about what may be expected or anticipated on this arrival or approach that may not be "as briefed": ATC clearance changes? Runway changes? What about if the weather changes dramatically? Windshear? Crosswinds? Discuss both procedure and technique. This is also a good time to brief what a missed-approach or go-around will look like, even to the extent of running through the standard callouts for your aircraft. (Let's face it—they are not all that common. A little refresher never hurts!)

ICE: What kind of emergencies can happen on an approach? Basically, the book is as wide open as it is for any other in-flight emergency. Fires, equipment failures, passenger issues, security issues, you name it. You can't (and you don't need to) anticipate every possibility in the brief. But you should have a plan of attack for three different stages of the approach:

1. *When in the arrival environment, but not yet on the final approach segment.* Brief whether you will continue toward final approach, or ask for a delay/hold while the situation gets worked out.

2. *When on final approach, but not below 1,000 feet AGL/short final.* Discuss what type of emergencies will cause you to conduct a missed approach/go-around, and what types of emergencies you will continue for landing. Any fire situation should commit you to land immediately, and any situation which would cause the aircraft to possibly become unstable or uncontrollable on final approach or landing would trigger a go-around. Most everything else you will likely be able to continue the approach to a landing.

3. *1,000 feet AGL/short final.* You are seconds away from landing. If and only IF the aircraft will become dangerously unstable or uncontrollable upon landing, execute a go-around. All else, commit to landing.

THE POST-FLIGHT BRIEFING

Post-flight briefings seem to have been deemed useful only in the training environment. Flight instructors and check airmen utilize the post-flight brief to cover what happened in the lesson or check ride—the good, the bad, and the ugly. Why don't we see post-flight briefings used in the real-world, live action, operational environment? Perhaps it is because of the stigma the post-flight brief carries with it—that of critique. "Leave the critique for the schoolhouse!" is a protest I've heard.

What are we afraid of? As pilots-in-command, don't we have a responsibility to review the flight and learn from anything that may have happened out of the ordinary? *Are we so bold to think that every flight is so close to ordinary that we cannot point out what anomalies did occur?*

The fact of the matter is that post-flight briefs may be a missing link in the quest to create a safe culture within an air carrier operation. And guess what? It doesn't have to be critical at all. Again, if you utilize the SEA-ICE framework, post-flight briefs become easy to run as well as beneficial to the operation you are responsible for.

Safety/Security: Discuss/debrief what happened during the flight that resulted in threats to the flight's safety and/or security, and what threats remain that need to be addressed.

Equipment: Discuss any equipment malfunctions or abnormalities and what, if any, action needs to be taken to remedy them.

Abnormals: Debrief any abnormal situations that presented (or which have presented themselves) and how they were handled, or how to handle them in the future. (The future could be the very next flight.)

ICE: Was there an inflight emergency? Debrief and discuss what the next steps are (typically taking time to review, make notes, and coordinate reporting requirements).

Don't worry about making the post-flight briefing too formal. In fact, I would be willing to bet that we all cover parts of the SEA-ICE framework in natural post-flight chatter. For an illuminating example, read the following:

[The crew has just completed the shutdown checklist and are waiting for the jetbridge to get put into place.]

Captain (CA): "Well, I think we handled that misunderstanding with ATC well. They clearly had their hands full and it was the right thing to do to set the brake and wait until we could get a clear exchange of information over the radio. Otherwise, we could have had a problem going head-to-head with that A380!"

First Officer (F/O): "Yeah. I am glad we did that. I was totally confused, and I could tell ATC wasn't paying attention."

CA: "Now that we saw the slat fault posting again in EICAS, I will check if it has been reset before, and if not we can do the reset procedure. If we can't reset it, we will just have maintenance handle it."

F/O: "OK, yeah, I don't think I saw it in the logbook. But while you look, I will get out the MEL and start looking it up."

CA: "Cool, thanks. Also, it seems that they don't have ground power here yet. If we can't get it, we will have to coordinate getting everything powered back up and cooled down before we get back to it two hours from now. I'm not burning the APU the whole time we sit here."

Now, in the above exchanges, the SEA-ICE framework was followed, and the post-flight brief occurred disguised as a normal conversation. There was no "ICE" portion, but thank goodness! Note that the captain took the opportunity to touch on the issues during some idle time. Also note that there was no, "OK, Billy. Let's debrief!" It simply isn't necessary. Just use SEA-ICE as a personal mnemonic reminder, and strike up some simple, casual conversation.

The example also did not contain any critique. PICs need to use careful, "honest discernment" when considering whether or not to give critique in a post-flight debrief.[4] If a critique is requested (e.g., *"Hey, how could I have handled that transition into the flare differently given that quartering tailwind?"*), take it to heart that your flying partner is asking because they (a) genuinely want to improve, or (b) they see you as having expertise and advice to lend, or (c) they need to confirm they did something right or wrong. Be honest, use some mentoring skills, and let them know your critique.

If no critique is requested but you think one is due, again use some discernment. Do not offer critique unless you are fully prepared to also provide advice. It doesn't do any good to say, *"Hey, Billy, that landing was a little bit of a clunker. You really need to get that worked out."* and then simply let poor Billy hang, wondering how he went wrong. If you don't have any good advice, save the critique, and instead seek out someone you can ask for the advice you would have liked to have given out yourself.

Chapter 4 Notes

1. SEA-ICE is just the first mnemonic in this book. And it is simply the one I have found most useful. If you come up with your own briefing system, or a different way to remember how you brief, that's fine!

2. The blank here is for you to insert your name. Whether you give your first name or your professional name ("Captain Pierson") will depend on your airline's culture and your personal preference. By the way, it's OK to call yourself "Captain_____." After all, you are the captain and proclaiming your title exudes confidence. If you are familiar with Captain Jack Sparrow of the "Pirates of the Caribbean" movie franchise, you know how much he dislikes it when people don't refer to him as "Captain," even when he is without a ship to be in charge of. After you introduce yourself with title, feel free to say, "You can call me [your name]."

3. Each carrier is different, but what seems to be pretty consistent is that pilots brief how emergencies, and specifically aborted takeoffs, are to be handled. Part of this emphasis comes from the scrutiny that high-speed aborted takeoffs have received from the FAA and NTSB following the PSA Airlines Flight 2495 accident in January 2010.

4. "Honest discernment" is one of the virtues of a transformational leader, as described in Chapter 13.

5

In Charge Behind the Flight Deck Door

In Chapter 3, we examined in depth the nature and primary responsibilities of being PIC. But as we pointed out, the crew is not simply comprised of pilots. Cabin crewmembers are an integral part of the whole "team" that ensures that a flight carrying passengers is conducted safely. In this chapter, we will look at the role of the modern flight attendant, including a quick peek into history to discover how flight attendants came to be. Thereafter, we delve into communications issues and how to keep the crew cohesive and anchored in trust.

LIFEGUARDS OF THE SKIES

As the commercial aviation industry transitioned from its infancy and started carrying people (rather than air mail and cargo) aboard airplanes in the 1910s and 1920s, it competed directly with the railroads. For decades, railroads (and ship lines) employed stewards to ensure passenger comfort and accommodation was well tended to.

The general public has a skewed perception of the role of the flight attendant today. I can say this because I witness it daily. United States domestic airline passengers, as a result of the low-cost-airline era of air travel in the twenty-first century, have developed a diminished level of respect for the flight attendant. One of the challenges of being an effective leader as pilot-in-command is to empathize with your crew, and this is so important with cabin crew. Let's face it: As pilots we close the flight deck door and work in our cozy little front office, enjoying the view and the company of one or two other people. Meanwhile, our flight attendants are conducting their duties in a very different environment.

A very good flight attendant whom I have had the pleasure of working with several times wrote the following description of her job on her blog:

> "Flight attendant" is the label that I prefer, as it is the title of the job that I applied for and work under. Yes, I was trained to fight fires,

evacuate the aircraft, assist in medical emergencies of many varieties, and serve drinks, but I'm not a firefighter or an EMT. Nor am I just a bartender, which I've also been called. I am not just another skirt running for your entertainment. My job has purpose. It's an honest job and it's satisfying, especially since most people don't recognize that my number one priority is to protect the safety of my passengers and the integrity of the aircraft...I see an average of 304 people a day, traveling coast to coast, from all over the world. I have seen more skin tones than I thought were possible, heard many languages that I can't define, understand, or speak, and I have smelled the smell of a thousand different cultures through food, incense, body odor, and perfume. As someone who keeps an eye out for able-body passengers and people who might be up to trouble, I find that first impressions can never be underrated and labels cannot be used to define first impressions. An open mind is imperative in witnessing human interaction between strangers. Judging is impossible, because there will always be a surprise.

I think her assessment in this post speaks volumes about her job—particularly the aspects we don't always think about. Especially in the tight-quartered environment of regional jets, most of which run at 80-percent capacity or better, the amount of interpersonal interaction is intensified for the flight attendant. And, problematically, a good number of the passengers don't realize the *real* reason the flight attendants are there.

I once carried a jump-seating pilot who had just finished a charter flight on a 737 full of deportees. The passenger load he was in charge of taking care of on a flight between the United States and a destination in South America was mainly foreign, illegal immigrants who had been rounded up by the ICE/INS and escorted to the charter. According to the pilot, many of the deportees were nabbed from workplaces, as some still donned janitorial, fast food restaurant, and other blue collar uniforms. Accompanying the deportees were ICE/INS agents and a full complement of flight attendants.

But the flight attendants were not there to serve peanuts and soda. Instead, as required by the FARs, they were there in case of an emergency requiring evacuation. Water was served, and the deportees were allowed to use the lavatories. However, the flight was as no-frills as one could be.

This anecdote really puts the true role of a flight attendant into perspective. The general public knows that the cabin crew will demo the seat belts and oxygen masks, point to the exits, and show them the safety briefing cards before departure. But after the flight gets airborne, how many passengers truly look upon the role of the flight attendant as *lifeguard*?

The FARs do not list "customer service" or similar skills as requirements for flight attendant training curriculum. As a matter of fact, 14 CFR §121.421 says only the following subjects are required:

General subjects:

- The authority of the pilot-in-command.[1]
- Passenger handling, including the procedures to be followed in the case of deranged persons or other persons whose conduct might jeopardize safety.
- Approved crew resource management initial training.

And, for each airplane type:

- A general description of the airplane emphasizing physical characteristics that may have a bearing on ditching, evacuation, and inflight emergency procedures and on other related duties.
- The use of both the public address system and the means of communicating with other flight crewmembers, including emergency means in the case of attempted hijacking or other unusual situations.
- Proper use of electrical galley equipment and the controls for cabin heat and ventilation.

In these six subject areas, there is nothing having to do with customer service. (The requirement for "proper use of electrical galley equipment" is for safety of operation, and not a requirement to learn how to prepare food.)

Here is the upshot: each flight attendant needs to be trained and remain competent in their abilities to keep passengers safe. The remainder of this chapter will examine some ways that pilots can assist flight attendants in carrying out this charge.

Starting out, the best way pilots-in-command can ensure their flight attendant crew is focused on safety and playing their very important part in the operation of the flight is to establish positive two-way communications. Starting with enabling communications pathways through positive rapport, enhancing the communications through meaningful briefings, and following through with in-flight contact will encourage, support, and empower your cabin crew to be effective in their role.

COMMUNICATIONS NEED A CLEAR PATH

Developing two-way communications has its beginnings in establishing a positive rapport with people you are communicating with. This is so true among flight crews: if you have negative relationships between crewmembers, they don't communicate. (And keep in mind that communication is not simply verbal.) Developing that positive rapport will establish a *clear path* for communications. In the previous chapter, briefings were covered at length, and to return to one tidbit from that discussion, it cannot be stressed enough how important setting the tone in your crew briefings is to opening up two-way communications.

To provide some framework, let's discuss when you as PIC want to hear from your crewmembers. When do you want them to speak up? Obviously we know that training, procedures, and plain instinct will cause a flight attendant to contact the pilots in the case of an emergency or some other urgent situation (security threat, equipment malfunction of a critical nature, disruptive passenger, etc.). But what about at other times?

I think we can agree that the sterile flight deck concept should be adhered to unless there is an urgent message that needs to get up front. Beyond that, however, wouldn't you agree that you would rather hear from the cabin crew about their concerns and observations *whenever* they arise...*whatever* they may be?

Many people might shy away from agreeing with this idea because they fear that they might get an earful of stuff they don't need to or *want to* hear. For example, many pilots will identify with the experience of flying with someone who wants to dump all their life's troubles on their co-workers. You know, that flight attendant who wants to tell you all about how her kids don't respect her, and her house is falling apart, and her husband won't do anything about it...on, and on, and on? Too much information!

It can be tough having to listen to all of that. We have our own problems so why should we listen to others' troubles? Welcome to Leadership 101. You have to listen to at least some of it, and you have to remain *positive* or all other lines of communication come crashing down. The moment that a captain blows off a flight attendant, acts indifferent to their gripes, or diminishes their concerns, that flight attendant will decide the captain is unapproachable on any topic, including job-related ones.

I have worked with several flight attendants who work under some sort of "speak only when spoken to" edict. These attendants *need to be asked* if there is anything they have to tell me or ask me about. This begs the question: Who put them in a situation where they felt they had to keep their mouths shut? Many of them are *not* the types that complain, whine, or gush with too much information about their personal issues. More often than not, they are the types who you would like to hear more from and maybe even get to know better. But for some reason, one day someone shut them down.

So instead of shutting someone down when they go "TMI" (too much information) on you, let them know you heard what they said, but turn the conversation back to something work related. For example, when someone says, *"Ugh, I just can't stand my cats anymore. But I love them! Do you love cats? I have other pets, too. But my boyfriend hates them! Do you have any fish or pets?"* simply say, *"No I don't, but that reminds me there is a good fish special at the hotel we layover at tonight. Remind me to tell you about it later, I have to get back to preflight duties."* Or make up some other duty-related escape mechanism. Be kind. Don't roll your eyes. And if the fish special comes up in later conversation, be prepared!

By giving your crewmembers the sense of a positive rapport—even when they annoy you with meaningless talk—you can open up the lines of communication, rather than closing them down. There is an alternative to avoidance. Simply avoiding or ignoring someone's banter is not good, as you need that person to communicate with you at times when it is important. By ensuring that you don't cut the lines of communication, you can set a positive tone that will carry through the trip.

BRIEFINGS

In the previous chapter, the SEA-ICE mnemonic was introduced as an aid in creating crew briefings. This table provides a quick review:

SEA-ICE Categories for Crew Briefings
1. **Safety** and **Security** issues and considerations
2. **Equipment** issues (inoperative equipment, etc.)
3. **Abnormal** procedures
4. In Case of Emergency (**ICE**)

Every briefing you do will be different, depending on the situation. The challenge, however, is not so much remembering what to brief, but making the briefing *meaningful*. This is especially true for cabin crew briefings, and the reason is that when pilots brief each other during pre-flight, it is likely based on SOPs. For most operators and most aircraft, a designated outline, flow, or checklist is provided for the pilots to follow when conducting briefs. Some operators may also provide such procedures for flight attendant briefings, but many do not. So because there is not an operational briefing for flight attendants, in order to make your briefings meaningful, you need to approach the SEA-ICE method with an eye to the number-one priority job of flight attendants: safety.

Passenger safety cannot be taken for granted. My experience with flight attendants has been that they are keen on keeping everyone safe, even when people continue to ignore crewmember instructions. On the day I wrote this chapter, I had flown a trip. Towards the end of the de-planing process, one of the passengers said to my lead flight attendant, "Thanks. I wasn't one of the seven, you know," as he smiled and walked off the airplane. The flight attendant explained to me that she had made an announcement as we approached the gate (but had not yet parked) when she noticed people were already unfastening their seat belts. She had said something like, "I know there are about seven of you who have already unfastened your seat belts..."

She was totally in the right to make the announcement, as I have seen passengers stand up in the aisle to reach something in the overhead bin during taxi only to be thrown forward when the aircraft makes a sudden stop. Effective pilots-in-command will empower their flight attendants to perform their duties in such a way that focuses on safety as the top priority.

To return to the briefing itself: Since SEA-ICE begins with safety and security, why not launch your flight attendant briefing with something similar to the following (which might look familiar from Chapter 4):

"Whatever you do back here in the cabin, please think of safety first. Ensure passenger safety and your own safety in every move you make. If there is ever a doubt, stop whatever it is you are doing, and make it safe to continue. If there is anything we pilots can do to help you in this, let us know."

These three simple sentences establish a tone and a mode of operation that will dictate eveything, which is important. It empowers the flight attendant team with the mindset that their job is safety first. Nothing else matters, really, if safety is in jeopardy.

After opening up with this statement, SEA-ICE is very straightforward. Outline any other known safety and security considerations, point out any equipment issues, address any known abnormal procedures or situations, and talk briefly about what will happen if there is an emergency. All of this, of course, can be done in line with established company procedures and policies. (Refer to the multiple examples I provided in Chapter 4.) Just as a review here, how about this very *brief* cabin crew briefing. Consider this example to be a brief given mid-trip (not FFOT) perhaps during a quick turn at an outstation:

"Alright, just a reminder, keep it safe back here. If anything is out of line safety-wise and you need our help, let us know. Weather is good en route, so turbulence shouldn't be a concern. Security-wise we have one LEO, back in 19B, and we also will have a jump-seater. Same airplane, so we know about the deferral of the aft lav. Nothing abnormal to deal with, and same considerations in case an emergency arises that we talked about before. Flight time should be around 1:45. Any questions?"

I can't think of one flight attendant who didn't appreciate a crew briefing that was meaningful, and that addressed real issues for the flight beyond just how long the flight would be. If you conduct crew briefings with useful content and in a consistent manner, you earn the respect of your crew and create an environment which fosters safety and efficiency.

IN-FLIGHT COMMUNICATIONS

Gone are the days when we could open up the flight deck door at will, invite the cabin crew up to chat or see the sights, or have casual discussions with them while en route. Since the tragic events of September 11, 2001, security measures have made flight deck security the highest priority when it comes to preventing another terrorist attack that uses an airplane as a weapon.

Each operator will have additional tweaks to their policies, but two common themes exist across every policy and procedure governing in-flight communications between the flight deck and the cabin, and the relationship this has to flight deck security.

First, a sterile flight deck begins upon the securing of the flight deck door pre-departure (and in some operating procedures even sooner during pre-flight briefings) and does not end until indicated by the flight crew. This includes (per 14 CFR §121.542) times of high workload, taxi, takeoff, operations below 10,000 feel MSL, and landing—and really any other time as determined by the PIC. All *non-essential* communications are prohibited during sterile flight deck operations.

Second, in-flight communications between the flight deck and cabin when the flight deck is *not sterile* are to be limited as much as feasible to the operation of the flight. In addition, any communications must be conducted by interphone when the flight deck has been secured. Additionally, primary and secondary barriers are employed to defend the flight deck and prevent unauthorized entry. Flight deck security is serious business, and any attempt to breach the flight deck will be met with force.

These two themes set a standard that raises the bar of safety and security to a high level. Sterile flight deck, while not by any means a "new" concept post-9/11, has been re-emphasized due to the secure nature of the flight deck. Once the flight deck door is closed and locked, the only way it is opened in flight is if a pilot needs to attend to physiological needs (receive food, beverage, or use the lavatory). And in such a case, a strict challenge-and-response procedure is typically prescribed before the door is opened. If a pilot needs to leave the flight deck to use the lavatory, another crew member must enter the flight deck to re-secure the door and watch/guard the flight deck.

Overlay the typical restriction of communications via interphone to the flight deck to an operational-only nature, and the environment can seem extremely muted from a communications standpoint. Even more poignantly, these rules serve to isolate the flight deck from the distraction of the cabin. Flight attendants can feel isolated from the pilots, and rightly so—it is by design. So how can an effective pilot-in-command ensure that the rapport, tone, mood, esprit de corps, or positive vibe set from the briefings and preflight interactions doesn't die away?

Just as I mentioned earlier in the chapter, the lines of communications must remain open and clear. PICs *want* to hear from flight attendants, but they know and respect the procedures outlined above. On practically every flight I operate, the last words before we are closed into the flight deck by the flight attendant are, "Talk to you in [name of destination city]" Sometimes that is several hours away! Pilots must endeavor to make the first move when it comes to in-flight communications. And I don't just mean when it's necessary (for example, when calling the cabin to confirm service requests for the arrival). Pilots need to reach out to their crew to ensure that they are not cut off by the strict procedures. Here is how to do it.

Call them.[2]

How simple is that? Just call them. But be reasonable and considerate towards their duties when you do. For example, most operators have the cabin crew commence meal and beverage services upon receiving the 10,000-foot/non-sterile flight deck indication. Take into consideration the amount of time it will take for them to accomplish their tasks, and then make a quick call to them with the following points of conversation (as a recommendation):

- Is the cabin comfortable?
- Are there any passenger issues?
- How are they doing?
- Flight time remaining, weather ahead, service requests, etc.

I can't tell you how many times I have learned about something that would require either my attention or advice (both as a PIC and SIC!) when I made this call to a flight attendant. And I can't tell you how many times I have been thanked and complimented by flight attendants *for actually thinking about them!*

The argument that calling the cabin outside of the times prescribed under an operator's SOP is in violation of SOP is baseless, and frankly, nonsensical. If our charge as pilots-in-command is to have responsibility and authority over the entire flight operation, shouldn't we make such calls to our flight attendants? Emphatically, YES!

None of the four bullet point items I listed above can be characterized as non-operational. Not even, "How are you doing?" because it is essential to the safety of the operation to ensure that your crew is capable of performing their duties.

Just call them.

POSTFLIGHT AND DEBRIEFS

When the aircraft parks at the gate and the flight deck door is opened again, it is an interesting environment. Sometimes the stress level is going down, much like the air slowly being let out of a balloon, as the passengers empty out the plane. Other times, an issue presents itself during the deplaning process and the stress level amps up a notch. In any case, the deplaning and postflight process remains a vital time to ensure that communications between you and the cabin crew continue, and that your support and enablement of the flight attendants' number-one job (passenger safety) is never in question.

The first way pilots can do this is to be present near the boarding door during deplaning. Sometimes carriers require it, but oftentimes our duties prevent it. Many pilots argue that "it's not my job" to greet and say goodbye to passengers. This is nonsense. Without getting on a customer service tangent (an entire chapter is devoted to it later), let me just touch on this one point briefly. *Passengers like to see the pilots.* Why? The pilots are the bosses of the plane. They run the show. If it was good or bad or so-so, the passengers would love to put a face to the experience. (Hopefully it was a good show.) I am not making this point to downplay the flight attendants; certainly not, as this chapter is devoted to the support of flight attendants. But I make the point to drive home the fact of the matter: the flight attendants are not responsible for the operation of the flight. The pilot-in-command is!

So, I implore you to stand next to your flight attendants. Say "goodbye and thank you" to the passengers. *Smile.* Look like you were happy to get them safely to their destination. (You should be.) This gives your flight attendants support in the customer service role, you are present as an authority figure for them to rely upon if an issue arises, and again, passengers like to see the pilots—and to thank them.

The second way pilots can support the flight attendants in the post-flight environment is to ask them how things went. This is a sneaky way to enter into what can truly be considered a postflight debrief with your cabin crew. Try on this possible conversation:

Captain (CA): "How'd it go?"

Flight attendant (FA): [Sigh] "Oh, fine I guess."

CA: "Any problems?"

FA: "Not really…Well, it's not a big deal but we had to warn this guy in 12C to keep his seat belt on a billion times and then he got all pissy with us. I think he was a little lit up, too. He calmed down a bit after the guy next to him told him to shut up, I think."

CA: "So, he chilled out though and deplaned without any issue."

FA: "Yeah, but he was a super-deluxe-elite-miles club guy and he kept saying he was going to write a letter of complaint about it."

CA: "I wouldn't be concerned. You were doing your job, nothing less."

FA: "Thanks. Oh, by the way, could you call for a new set of blankets to be brought on, we had to throw some in a bag due to a spill."

CA: "Sure I can!"

FA: "Also, we have a reading light out in 20A and a gasper vent stuck at 5C."

CA: "Great, thanks for letting me know. I will make sure to call those in."

Again, the opening is simple. "How'd it go?" The flight attendant could have simply said, "Great! No worries!" and that would have been sufficient. But more often than not, there is some issue—perhaps small, but an issue nonetheless—that needs attention. The example above included service and maintenance issues, but also another issue needing attention—perhaps more attention than any others.

The flight attendant was in need of some reassurance and support for the way she handled a difficult passenger. I don't consider anything more important than listening, supporting, reassuring, and encouraging my cabin crew. There have been so many times that I have encountered situations such as this as a PIC, and even more times when I was a first officer. Sometimes it just meant being a sounding board. At other times the situation required my direct intervention. In any case, pilots are looked to as resources by flight attendants when they have to handle difficult situations. They look to pilots for advice, reassurance, and support.

MAKING THE CREW

Communications, briefings, and the feel-good theory of working together well with your entire crew are worthless unless you actually take action. This chapter has primarily focused on the role of the flight attendants, but to round out the chapter it's necessary to briefly discuss how pilots-in-command can "make the crew." There are three primary ways to bring the crew together with ease: teaching and exemplifying trust, being an honest resource, and fostering inclusivity and accountability.

First, on teaching and exemplifying trust: Don't worry—my take on this is not a call for pilots to start admonishing crewmembers about trust. It has much more to do with the example-setting side of the equation, which begets the teaching side. Setting an example in any action is an everyday exercise of teaching skill. So, this is more like a call for pilots to be trustworthy in order to set the example.

What does trustworthy really mean? For me, it is best defined by the Boy Scouts of America, who claim "Trustworthy" as the first point of twelve which comprise the Boy Scout Law:

A Scout is Trustworthy. A Scout tells the truth. He is honest, and he keeps his promises. People can depend on him.

Consider the role of pilot-in-command once again. Due to the nature and definition of the role, *everyone is depending on the PIC*. Pilots can teach trust by *depending on others*. Demonstrate to your fellow first officers, flight attendants, ramp agents, gate agents, refuelers, dispatchers, mechanics, and operations personnel that you depend on them. This is how trust is taught: through the demonstration of dependency.

This definition of "trustworthy" also serves as a nice segue into the rest of the formula for "making the crew." At the core of trust is the characteristic of integrity. Truth and honesty are described in the Scout Law as the manifestations of a trustworthy scout. As a pilot, one of the best ways you can "make the crew" is to be an honest, truthful resource to your crewmembers. This means remaining factual, reliable, and straightforward in everything you say to them, and in every action you take with them.

Don't sugarcoat the truth, and don't embellish or mislead from the truth. Weather, mechanical problems, operational situations, even your take on the current economics of the airline industry—why hide what you know and understand as true, undeniable facts from people you are depending on to help you run a safe, efficient, and reliable flight operation?

Finally, foster inclusivity and accountability among your crew. Even if personalities occasionally conflict on some points and levels, you cannot exclude or otherwise ostracize a crewmember. You actually have to bring such people in closer, so to speak. Ensure that everyone gets briefed (ideally, together). Ensure that everyone's concerns are well vetted and addressed. Ensure that even the distant, distracted, and disliked are being included.

Moreover, ensure that everyone understands the concept of accountability. It truly goes hand-in-hand with trustworthiness. Simple displays of humility will get you a long way in this regard. So do statements such as, "Hey, I am not perfect by any means, so let me know if I get something wrong. Feel free to speak up!" The more your crewmembers see you as trustworthy and humble, the more they react to your example and emulate it, repeating your actions that demonstrate inclusivity and accountability. This unifies everyone in a way that makes people feel free to be themselves, to stretch professionally, and to excel in their duties. Make the crew!

Chapter 5 Notes

1. I find that the requirement of flight attendants to understand the authority of the pilot-in-command speaks volumes about both the job of the PIC as well as the job of the FA. The FARs serve to clearly delineate the authority chain here. Regardless of the fact that large airline crews depend on pursers/lead flight attendants/service managers to act in a supervisory role over the cabin crew, the PIC is still responsible for all.

2. Quite frankly, they may call you first if you don't. If they do, embrace the communication.

6

Rediscovering the "Lost Art" of CRM

The first airline CRM program was actually called "Command/ Leadership/Resource/Management" (or "C/L/R") and was developed by United Airlines in order to respond to a need for increased safety culture on the property as well as to comply with new FAA regulations requiring training in human factors. C/L/R attempted to dovetail the "old school" ways of captain's authority with the new "touchy-feely" inclusiveness approach in human factors applications. Former United Airlines Captain Al Haynes, PIC of the infamous crash of United Airlines Flight 232 in Sioux City, Iowa, in 1989—and regarded by many as the most prolific spokesperson for CRM—said in a presentation to NASA in 1991 that "Up until 1980, we kind of worked on the concept that the captain was THE authority on the aircraft. What he said, goes. And we lost a few airplanes because of that. Sometimes the captain isn't as smart as we thought he was. And we would listen to him, and do what he said, and we wouldn't know what he's talking about... SO if I hadn't used C/L/R, if we had not let everybody put their input in, it's a cinch we wouldn't have made it."[1]

Haynes's success in saving lives at Sioux City, and his major promotion of C/L/R (which evolved to CRM under guidance from NASA and researchers at the University of Texas), made every operator worldwide take notice. Moreover, many types of industries immediately latched onto CRM; nuclear power plants, maritime crews, and fire departments are a few examples of the wide-reaching appeal of CRM. But one unique element eludes many of these professions: a federal regulation vesting all power, authority, and responsibility into a single person.

Chapter 3 touched on CRM as it explored the essence of the pilot-in-command role. As the predecessor of threat and error management (TEM), CRM really has deep roots and has been studied extensively for decades. Because the FAA mandates CRM training, the industry has come up with all kinds of variations on the original CRM model. Think of CRM like ice cream: long ago ice cream was invented in a very basic form, sometimes sweetened with just a little fruit or juice. Now thanks to Baskin-Robbins, Ben & Jerry's and others, we have countless flavors of ice cream, but all are based on the same original model. Airlines create their own flavor, and hopefully develop new flavors over time. Unfortunately, some operators have had only one flavor for years now, and it is frost covered and freezer burned.

It takes culinary artistry to come up with new flavors while respecting the original recipe. So, in some operating cultures, CRM has become a "lost art." In an effort to revive some of the freshness of CRM, I want to dig more directly into CRM's essence. This chapter is not so much a CRM primer or history; instead, it will focus directly on a "New CRM." Through techniques that pilots can employ in the flight deck to get the most out of the more common CRM cornerstones, and the awareness of some core truths about what makes CRM work, we can gain a new appreciation for the lost art of CRM and create some new flavors.

THE NEW CRM

Particularly in the United States, consolidation has moved the major airlines into new categories of size and structure. In 2016, United, American, and Delta all boasted pilot groups that have in excess of 12,000 members. All three have multiple pilot bases, each serving multiple fleets and varying types of flying. It is common to hear pilots describe their carriers as feeling like "airlines within airlines" because of the sheer size of the fleets and bases.

The immense amount of attrition of older pilots and the demand for growth that is happening globally are spurring a fresh hiring spree. New faces are appearing not only in new-hire classes, but also in the flight decks. The biggest challenge for flight departments has become crew cohesiveness as a result of the massive turnover in the ranks. Generational differences, a variety of flying backgrounds, and the exposure to new, twenty-first-century technology presents challenges to how crews operate together. The "New CRM" aims to level the playing field, cutting through these challenges and focusing on one simple fact: we are all just pilots.

The core truths of the New CRM are shown in the following table.

The New CRM
1. A crew will not work together if they misunderstand the variation of personalities among them.
2. A crew will not work together if they allow personalities to become negative in the face of challenges.
3. A crew will not work together if a member is not well from a physiological or psychological standpoint.
4. A crew will not work together if a member does not comply with standard operating procedures.

Note how each of these core statements are worded. "A crew *will not* work together..." It isn't "*may not*" or "*might not*." These truths are based on an "all-or-nothing" approach to renewing the way we approach CRM. The New CRM is rooted deep within the human-factors side of the original CRM model, and demands that we approach our crew relationships with an eye towards perfection. It is hard to accomplish because we are not perfect—but the quest, the push, the effort to conduct our duties as a crew as close to perfection as we possibly can makes us that much safer, that much more efficient, that much more proficient, and certainly that much better in interpersonal efficacy.

Who is This Guy Next to Me?

Good, safe pilots have an incredible sense of awareness of the personalities they deal with on the job, and they adapt. First officers, not having the "distinction" of being PIC, have to adapt somewhat more than captains. In some respects they are like chameleons, adapting to the PIC in order to make sure everything goes smoothly. This can be good and bad, but in the end, every pilot makes an assessment of their partner. Every pilot, whether in the right seat or left seat, naturally asks themselves, "Who is this guy next to me?"

Recognizing that every one of us has a unique personality, inclusive of how a person acts in a crew environment, is the underpinning, and first, core truth of the "New CRM":

> *A crew will not work together if they misunderstand the variation of personalities among them.*

Capitalizing on the instinct as a pilot to size-up your flying partner, you can and should think critically about who that person is, and how it will affect your crew coordination for the trip. Clearly, nobody needs to do a full-scale psychoanalysis of their co-worker. What we are talking about here is simply a cursory assessment of the overall demeanor, behavior, and personality of your flying partner. Here are some considerations:

- Is he/she distracted?
- Does he/she seem open to conversation?
- Is he/she worried about something flight related when it's unwarranted?
- Has this person reached out to me about something personal?
- Is this person "all business"?

In no way am I suggesting that this should be some sort of verbal "interview." All of these questions should be performed in your "inner monologue." Also, don't be too concerned with emotions unless they are extreme—for example, if your first officer starts crying, or if your captain starts losing his temper by throwing things across the flight deck. If extreme emotional displays are occurring, clearly a huge problem underlies the emotion, and the safety of the flight is likely in jeopardy.

Your general analysis, however, should give you a good idea of:

- What level of professionalism to expect.
- What personal boundaries are in place.
- The amount of preparation the person has done for the flight.

These three characteristics of your flying partner will be paramount to effective CRM. And your response to these characteristics will determine the effectiveness of your crew coordination.

This kind of assessment and response needs to extend beyond the flight deck door, as well. Focusing again on core truth number one of the New CRM, you need to establish an understanding of the personality of each and every crewmember on the airplane. Realistically, the variations between personalities will be many. But you can certainly appreciate each using the rubric outlined above: level of professionalism, personal boundaries, and amount of preparation.

Returning again to the core truth, "A crew will not work together if *they* misunderstand the variation of personalities among them." The word *they* implies a very important point. Each member of the crew needs to be understanding of the different personalities they are surrounded by in the work environment. This is not something simply for the captain to figure out for everyone. Encourage your crewmembers toward understanding each other. And remember this is not an all-call to run a popularity contest. *You will fly with people you absolutely dislike.* But it is the understanding of that person's personality that will make you effective as a fellow crewmember.

When Personalities Fail, You Can't!

Everyone has bad days. But sometimes certain people make bad days into even worse days by projecting their misfortune on others. When you encounter someone who wants to "bring you down" with them into their realm of misery, your defenses need to be ready. You also need to do everything you can to stop the person from continuing to rain on the parade. This upholds core truth number two of the New CRM:

A crew will not work together if they allow personalities to become negative in the face of challenges.

Let's say you have the following encounter with your flying partner while settling into the flight deck:

You: "Good morning! How are you?"

Him: "Ugh. I really am sick and tired of flying out to JFK. We are always out there. Now we are starting another 4-day of nothing but JFK flying. I hate my life!"

How do you respond? Clearly this guy is unhappy about this trip, and it has barely started. There is a really easy, three-step process to respond to a negative statement like this.

Step 1: Acknowledge the problem. This does not mean you have to agree with the problem or any aspect of their negative statements. All you need to do is make a counterstatement letting this person know that you heard their complaint, and that you understand it. For this example, you could respond with, "Well, I know JFK has its problems."

Step 2: Offer an alternative view of the problem. Again, this does not mean you need to affirm or deny this person's problem. All you are doing is looking at the same problem from a different point of view. It is well known among aviators that every airport has its share of things to complain about. So an alternative view in this example would be to point out that other airports also have problems: "Well, I know JFK has its problems, but so do MSP and DTW."

Step 3: Provide an alternative response to the problem. This is where you can do your best work to get things on a more positive course. Clearly the person in this example is not looking forward to JFK, and perhaps you can suggest a way to *enjoy* JFK. Maybe it works, maybe it doesn't. But what will count is your effort.

> You: "Well, I know JFK has its problems, but so do MSP and DTW. Let's make the best of it. Hey, we have a three-hour sit in JFK, and I hear there is a good new restaurant in Terminal 6. Want to check it out with me rather than just sitting in the crew room?"

Honestly, making this effort can be hard, especially if you yourself are not having an especially good day. But making the effort will pay off in huge goodwill dividends with your crew.

Good pilots, and especially good captains, set a tone of positivity—all the time. Even in the darkest of situations, the tone should remain positive. Try on this quick snippet of a captain's briefing to the cabin crew:

> *"We have a very full flight, and one of the air conditioning packs is deferred. It is going to get very hot and sticky—even more than it is now. Once we depart it is going to be bumpy as we deviate around some weather en route. We will still do normal cabin signals, but please remain seated and don't get up to do service until we call you. That call may not come due to the rough air. Once we get in, we will have to deplane onto the ramp since there is not a jetbridge available. And it will be pouring rain. It is going to be a doozy of a flight, but once we are done, we are going to laugh. I want to hear about every funny thing you see in the cabin when we get in."*

The captain is laying out the truth of the situation: the flight is going to be uncomfortable, and there are some definite obstacles (and threats) ahead of the crew. But when they are all done, he wants the crew to laugh about it. The simple request to hear some comic anecdotes from the cabin post-flight sets a positive tone despite the negative setup.

Every day you fly, you will encounter personalities that will challenge you. Make every effort to remain positive, use humor when appropriate, and enforce the fact that there is still a job that needs to be done. When personalities fail, you can't.

I'M SAFE, Are You?

Our own physiology deeply affects personality on a moment-to-moment basis. How we feel in terms of our health will undoubtedly affect our personality, attitude, disposition, and eventually job performance. In the New CRM, being aware and proactive about bodily health is a core truth:

> *A crew will not work together if a member is not well from a physiological or pyschological standpoint.*

Chapter 4 discussed IMSAFE as an element of crew briefings that cannot be overlooked. However, it didn't cover the full details of IMSAFE as it applies to briefings. Instead, I discussed doing a cursory check—a passing assessment, if you will—of the health and fitness of your crew to fly. Now we can go into deeper detail about what exactly to look for when doing such assessments.

Let's walk through the "telltale signs" of fitness to flight using "IMSAFE" as a guide.

Illness. Sick people are easy to spot: drooped eyes, pallid complexion, coughing, or sneezing, or strained voice. You can just tell when someone is sick. Another manifestation of illness is a latent and dangerous one: the inability to act or perform duty. Whether illness consumes someone because it is all they can think of, or whether illness consumes a person by shutting down basic body functions, working while sick is asking for trouble. Another consideration is the effect on co-workers. Airline crews work in close quarters, and it's hard to avoid sharing germs and viruses. If one person boards an airplane with influenza, there is a high likelihood that all other persons that get on that plane will contract the illness. Flying sick simply gets everyone else sick, too.

Medication applies to the medications that make someone act in a way that may have an adverse impact on their duties. Keep in mind that this could be the result of a person *not* taking a prescribed medication. There are people who simply cannot function normally without their medication. Extreme lethargy or overt anxiousness, unusual comments, or an overall withdrawn demeanor may be indications of something else, but very often they are due to a medication issue—use of or lack thereof! Even simple allergy medications (Benadryl®, Claritin®) can have a sedative effect on people. But also keep a sharp eye out for over-the-counter pain medications. If one of your crewmembers is downing ibuprofen (Advil®), acetaminophen (Tylenol®), or naproxen (Aleve®), check up on them! If something as simple as a headache or joint pain is enough for them to be self-medicating, it is worth your time to make sure they will remain fit to fly while on the medication. Remind them that if at *any* time they feel their pain getting worse, or feel ill in some other way, they should let you know immediately. This is for their own sake, as well as the sake of the crew and passengers.

Stress. We all know that there is an inherent amount of stress involved in any job, but in the vocation of being an airline pilot, the stress level is above-average from time to time. Professional airline pilots learn to cope with the stress of the job by practicing good CRM and TEM, verbalizing and engaging with crewmembers about things that are causing them stress, and seeking resolution to stressful situations. If your flying partner shows signs of stress but does not verbalize it or ask for help to diffuse it, you need to step in. Some signs of stress very common with pilots include profuse sweating (when not caused by heat), rapid stammering or mumbling speech, nervous habits (fidgeting, foot tapping), and perhaps the most dangerous—complete checkout or withdrawal. If you see somebody sit down at the controls with symptoms of stress, you need to engage them and see if you can help. Offer to offload them. "Hey, take your time getting settled in. I will grab the preflight and set up the FMC for you. Can I get you some water?" Let them know you recognize their stress level and are offering some reprieve. Offering the choice of flying roles to them is also a good idea; some pilots de-stress when they are pilot flying, some find pilot monitoring better. Allow them to choose what is right for them, and keep an eye on the stress level they exhibit in that role.

Alcohol is another one that is easy to spot. If you smell alcohol, or notice intoxicated behavior, it's time to ask the hard question. But what may be harder to spot are signs of alcohol abuse. In today's social environment, the consumption of alcohol is a big player. The pressure to drink is tremendous. And while some people have figured out how to control their consumption levels, others have zero control. In the IMSAFE rubric of evaluation, all too often we focus on the hard-and-fast rules: 14 CFR §91.17 specifies that no crewmember may *attempt* to act as a crewmember within 8 hours of alcohol consumption (though company regulations may be more restrictive) and blood alcohol concentration cannot exceed 0.04. Remember that this limit is even lower in foreign countries. But the overt abuse of alcohol has associated effects and behaviors that can be just as problematic as a person operating while intoxicated. Fatigue due to lack of restful sleep while alcohol levels are heightened is a big one, followed by mood swings, lethargy, and lack of concentration and focus. What is troubling is that sometimes it is hard to determine if someone abuses alcohol. If you have a crewmember that talks about booze a lot, seems to be making frequent comments like, "Boy, I can't wait to hit the hotel bar tonight," or relates stories about being drunk in a way that makes it seem they want you to think that behavior is acceptable, be alert.

Fatigue is perhaps the most prevalent IMSAFE condition contributing to aviation accidents and incidents—so much so that Congress recently passed new laws to create amended, more restrictive FARs governing fatigue for crews. A part of that legislation underscored the requirement for each and every airman to take serious responsibility for their own personal fatigue management.[2] It may be somewhat elusive to see signs of fatigue. Fatigue is a very internal, often mental, manifestation of a lack of sleep. If I spot a yawn or even a comment of, "Man I got to bed late last night," I become curious. But crewmembers have a tendency to mask fatigue; they want to complete the mission, and let's face it, schedules can often be pretty hard on people's sleep schedules. Many times I will simply ask, "Everyone feel rested today?" If a negative response is given, my next question is, "Do you feel rested enough to work today?" I can say that in over a decade, I have only had one person say "no" to that question, and we arranged to have him removed from duty in accordance with our company fatigue policy.

Finally, *emotional* signs can also remain elusive, but the main concern should be any outward displays of emotion. I have seen *several* emotional outbursts in my tenure as an airline pilot, from pilots and flight attendants alike. Let's face it: airline work is done in a high-stress, high-workload, and high-danger risk environment. It doesn't compare to the Alaskan crab fishermen followed by the popular reality TV show *Deadliest Catch*, but in my opinion it can come pretty close. Remember to approach an emotional crewmember with a caring, leadership-based attitude. Find a way to respectfully and tactfully understand the reason for the emotional display. Your genuine concern will hopefully serve to diffuse the emotional stress affecting the crewmember.

Utilizing the IMSAFE method is an easy way to ensure beforehand that you *and* your crewmembers are not already handicapped from working effectively with each other. Simply put, if you feel like crap, you can't do your job.

Adherence to SOP—Why We Can't Afford Not To

The final core truth of the New CRM is:

> *A crew will not work together if a member does not comply with Standard Operating Procedures.*

If you have been in the industry for some time, you know well the stories from recurrent trainings, CRM classes and the like— all pointing to pilot error as the cause of an accident or incident, and in particular the inability of the crew to adhere to standard operating procedure leading to eventual disaster. Driving the point home even further is the avoidance and mitigation of developing incidents (events which are rapidly progressing down the error chain, passing through several holes in the Swiss cheese) when proper use of SOP is applied to the situation.

The conclusion on SOP discipline is clear: *apply SOP or risk everything.* So why do pilots need constant reminders, consistent reinforcement in training, and never-ending admonitions by authors, rule makers, evaluators, and the government on this point?

Perhaps we need to look a bit harder at our own human nature, and in particular the nature of a pilot. By and large, pilots are "Type A" personalities: naturally controlling and self-sufficient. They have a proclivity to do things their own way, with a great sense of initiative. For better, this disposition makes them good at their job. Flying airplanes demands strong personalities that can handle the exaggerated variety of elements, conditions, and challenges that are naturally a part of aviation. For worse, it also causes some pilots to become too cavalier, macho, and careless when facing anomalies to the expected "normal" modes of the operation at hand.

Chapter 9 goes into further detail on the handling of "non-normals" and the benefits of following checklists, procedures, etc. rather than just fixing the problem using (what the pilot assumes) is infallible systems knowledge and that "by the seat of your pants" instinct engrained in pilot culture. But this chapter is about CRM. So how do we put SOP adherence into that context, and moreover, how to we put it into the core of the New CRM I have discussed here?

Straightforwardly, following SOP is a *choice*. A crewmember, regardless of the orders of the SOP themselves to follow SOP, has to respect that order and *choose* to follow SOP. Even though the evidence is profoundly in favor of following SOP, human nature sometimes interferes and makes the choice confusingly difficult. Let me share a simple example of non-adherence to SOP that happens every day on hundreds of flights: sterile flight deck.

For those who may not be familiar, "sterile flight deck" refers to the rule under 14 CFR §§121.542 and 135.100 which prohibit nonessential conversation and distracting activities during critical phases of flight, including taxi, takeoff and landing, and all other flight operations conducted below 10,000 feet, except cruise flight.

This isn't just SOP, it is the *law*. And hundreds of pilots break it every day, mainly through non-essential conversation. Why? It's *human nature*. When on approach to New York-LaGuardia runway 4, pilots get a beautiful view of Manhattan. Invariably, undoubtedly, crews have remarked to one another on the sights of the skyline. Who wouldn't? I have been there, and the view of New York from such a vantage point is spectacular. It's seemingly innocent, but can we honestly say that all it would take is one tiny distraction, one interruption, to trigger a deviation? Yes. Could we guess that it has happened? Yes. Let's even pretend that one time, a crew was gawking at the Big Apple, talking about layover plans slated for Times Square, and missed a configuration call, causing them to abort the approach and go around. The critical phase of flight in a New York minute goes hyper-critical for that flight, that crew, ATC, other aircraft in the area; the threats multiply and extend well beyond the flight deck.

Hopefully my point is clear, and rather than using more space on a hotly debated subject that is really just common sense, it's important to make clear the link to CRM. It is this exposition of SOP adherence as a lifesaving *choice* that brings into focus the utmost importance of the three preceding core truths of the New CRM.

Earlier I focused on crew dynamics, rooting a positive crew dynamic in being aware of personality differences, dealing appropriately with those differences, promoting positivity in the face of challenge, and ensuring that physiological wellness is in check. SOP adherence is a *choice* that is most effectively *made*, and *supported*, in an environment where crew dynamics are positive, and everyone feels good—when we are all "on our game." The first three core truths of the New CRM, in essence, are the underpinnings of the fourth. SOP deviations are more likely when:

- We fly sick or fatigued.
- We don't like the person we are flying with.
- We don't appropriately respect or acclimate to the personalities of other crewmembers.
- We fail to recognize the difficulties our crewmembers may be facing themselves.
- We allow a negative attitude to permeate and affect the entire crew.

Recognizing the core truths of the New CRM and applying them practically leads us to perform our jobs in accordance to SOP. From this point we can then bring in other traditional CRM model components and merge them with the New CRM.

The New CRM—Realization of the Lost Art

Go to any CRM program, class, course, seminar, book, article, etc. and you will likely find the original CRM model elements are still firmly in place:

- SOP
- Communications
- Behavior
- Fatigue and Stress
- Situational Awareness
- Leadership/Professionalism

Already, one can see that the New CRM taps on the original model quite well. In fact, we can make the following categorical links pretty easily:

New CRM "Core Truths"	Original CRM Model "Elements"
A crew will not work together if they misunderstand the variation of personalities among them.	Behavior
A crew will not work together if they allow personalities to become negative in the face of challenges.	Communications/Behavior
A crew will not work together if a member is not well from a physiological or psychological standpoint.	Fatigue/Stress
A crew will not work together if a member does not comply with standard operating procedures.	SOP

But as you can see in the above table, not all of the original model elements find a categorical home that we can link up with a core truth of the New CRM. We are left to deal with situational awareness and leadership/professionalism.

Applying Situational Awareness to the New CRM

Situational awareness (SA) has been an immense focus for CRM facilitators over the years. Some of this has been driven by the accelerated advent of new automation in the flight deck that marries quite well with our information-driven society. Ironically, the "electronic flight bag" and several flight deck enhancements (flight management systems that come with all sorts of real-time data functions, including live weather, chart access, automated ATC information systems, etc.) were all developed with an eye towards increasing SA, not exasperating it. Unless these resources are used appropriately, with a cognizant effort to remain "ahead" of the automation, SA degrades and the automation and information systems become a threat.

A basic CRM course developed by Transport Canada, Western Region, offers a list of several "clues" to a loss of SA:[3]

Low Stress Level: When the amount of information being processed is significantly low, the level of situational awareness is low. Low stress level is common on long flights when pilots become bored or when they are fatigued. This lack of alertness will result in a loss of recognition of warning signals and reduce their ability to react quickly and correctly in an emergency.

High Stress Level: When the amount of information being processed is significantly above an individual's capacity. If a person's stress level is very high, that person will operate at low levels of situational awareness. This is commonly referred to as information overload.

Ambiguity: When information can be understood in more than one way, there can be a fifty-percent chance of an accident occurring. A classic example is the captain calling "take-off power" and the first officer reduces the power to idle.

Confusion or Unresolved Discrepancies: When information is unclear, or two or more pieces of information do not agree, we must search for information until the discrepancies are resolved. A simple example with catastrophic consequences is the acceptance of a clearance to descend below published minimum safe altitudes.

Fixation or Preoccupation: The ability to detect other important stimuli is lost when an individual is fixated, preoccupied or distracted. This situation can easily result in no one flying or looking outside the aircraft unless there is proper assignment of responsibilities essential to safe flight. The entire crew's preoccupation with a malfunctioning nose gear indication light resulted in an L-1011 crashing into the Florida Everglades. No one was monitoring the flight instruments; no one was flying the aircraft.

Departures from SOPs/Regulations: Violating minimums or using improper procedures puts pilots into a gray area without being able to predict safe outcomes with certainty. Consistent and blatant violations of rules often reveal other systemic problems within an organization.

Failure to Meet Planned Targets: In flight, pilots are constantly setting planned targets such as airspeeds, altitudes, checkpoints, times, etc. When planned targets are not met (e.g., being high and fast on an approach) pilots must question why and recognize the consequences of not meeting set targets.

Gut Feeling: This is often the most detectable and reliable clue to the loss of situational awareness. Our bodies are able to detect stimuli long before we have consciously put the big picture together. Learn to recognize your own signs, such as stomach butterflies, muscle tension, mood swings, etc. Trust your feelings; policemen sometimes trust their lives to gut feelings.

So how can we properly correlate SA into the New CRM? When you boil down the loss of SA situations, they come in two flavors: *loss of SA due to complacency, and loss of SA due to overload.* For each of the clues to SA loss listed above, we can list out the associated type or flavor of SA loss for each clue:

Loss of SA Clues	Type
Low Stress	Complacency
High Stress	Overload
Ambiguity	Complacency
Confusion/Unresolved Discrepancies	Complacency/Overload (could be both)
Fixation	Overload
Departure from SOP	Complacency
Failure to Meet Planned Targets	Complacency
Gut Feeling	Complacency/Overload (could be both)

Notably, complacency rings the bell in the majority of SA loss events. It is this strong link between complacency and loss of SA that we can work into the core truths framework of the New CRM. The following table cites some causations of complacency when the core truths are not rectified.

New CRM "Core Truths"	Causation of Complacency
A crew will not work together if they misunderstand the variation of personalities among them.	Crew acts independently from each other rather than finding common ground. Distractions from arising conflict cause complacency.
A crew will not work together if they allow personalities to become negative in the face of challenges.	Negative attitudes overrun and destroy morale; crewmembers divide into groups or individuals.
A crew will not work together if a member is not well from a physiological or psychological standpoint.	Illness, medication, stress, alcohol, fatigue, or emotion distract crewmembers, or worse, incapacitate them.
A crew will not work together if a member does not comply with standard operating procedures.	Not following SOP is blatant complacency.

Putting all of this in play, we can come up with a simple statement that places SA into the New CRM framework:

Situational awareness is only intact when crewmembers understand the variations of each personality, rectify negative personalities, ensure that everyone is fit to fly, and operate in adherence to SOP.

Applying Leadership and Professionalism to the New CRM

There are plenty of definitions of the words "professional" and "leadership," and the two words are certainly intertwined. In most definitions, they act symbiotically: leadership involves professionalism, and professionals employ leadership.

I think that going on at length here on what specific definitions of professional and leadership fit best with the New CRM is unnecessary. But I do want to highlight two very important leadership elements: integrity and duty.[4]

Leaders must demonstrate a high level of integrity. When you take a look at what integrity is—what it involves—you find that it comes down to consistency in values. The root of the word integrity is the same as the word integer, which means something is whole. Intact. Consistent. Safe, effective pilots-in-command do not allow their integrity to be compromised. They are consistent and honest in carrying out their responsibilities.

Leaders must also heed the call of duty. Duty involves keeping commitments and doing what you are supposed to do, when you are required to. The true meaning of duty, however, is to have debt. Those who have a true sense of duty can be said to have a sense that they owe a *debt*. Leaders in the flight deck who recognize the meaning of duty can apply it very practically every day: we owe it to our passengers and crew to be safe and proficient at our job. We have to understand and commit that duty we have to them.

At the end of Chapter 3, I expanded on the "responsibility and authority" aspect of 14 CFR §91.3: *(a) The pilot in command of an aircraft is directly* **responsible** *for, and is the final* **authority** *as to, the operation of that aircraft.* The context of that discussion was having responsibility and authority over the jobs of other people affecting the flight operation. Since the core truths of the New CRM go to personalities, attitude, fitness to fly, and SOP adherence, we have to look upon the PIC to have some level of responsibility and authority to promote the behaviors and actions that will yield good CRM among the crew.

Leadership is the active word in this discussion. It will take leadership to promote, exemplify, and have authority to ensure that personalities, attitudes, wellness, and SOP adherence among your crew produces a flight environment that operates under the New CRM model. When you lead your crew in the New CRM, through your own *professionalism*, morale will build and the job will get done right. Due to the professionalism of your crew, things will work well even when the weather goes down the tubes, the airplane breaks, and other elements of the operation create threats and obstacles. The product of the application of leadership and professionalism to the New CRM, quite simply, is *teamwork*.

The word "team" originated to describe a group of animals that was harnessed together to pull something, like a team of horses. Now the word describes any group of persons or animals which has come together to collaborate on a work project. Through their loyalty to one another, team members bond in order to do their best work together rather than separately. Airline crews, in order to operate safely, effectively, and efficiently, must engage in loyal teamwork. Effective pilots-in-command will step up to foster and develop the teamwork, leading their crew to accomplishment.

Hanging in my home is a framed advertisement for United Air Lines from a 1948 issue of *Newsweek* Magazine. The ad features a headshot of Captain R.T. Freng that fills the page. The caption reads "What Makes a Mainliner Tick?" The ad copy is a written as a testimonial from Capt. Freng on the contributions of mechanics, engineers, dispatchers, meteorologists, radio operators, and ground personnel to United's operations (see the box below for the full text). He closes with, *"It's the whole team that makes a Mainliner tick. They're experts, every one..."*

What Makes a Mainliner Tick?

"Add together all the flying United Pilots have done and you have hundreds of millions of miles of experience over the nation's first airline. But we pilots are not the only ones who make a Mainliner tick.

"You should see the hundreds of mechanics who keep our Mainliners in top flight condition. United always goes one step farther in extra care in maintaining its airplanes—spends millions in aircraft refinements.

"You should meet the engineers, who put the best equipment that can be had in United Mainliners. You should talk to the dispatchers, meteorologists, the radio operators who keep in touch with us while we're aloft. You should know the rest of the experienced ground personnel who contribute so much to operating your Mainliner from each airport.

"It's the whole team that makes a Mainliner tick. They're experts, every one...the best in the business. We know. United won't have anything less than the best—on the ground or in the air."

—Captain R.T. Freng

(Excerpted from United Air Lines advertisement, 1948 issue of *Newsweek*.)

History speaks volumes about it; all aspects of flying are teamwork based. It is inherent to the craft. Imagine Orville without Wilbur, or Lindbergh without Hall (Lindbergh's aircraft engineer). It is a part of our nature as aviators to rely upon others. Think of the frustration you sometimes feel when you can't get through to dispatch or OPS. Pilots depend on their team members. Good aviators seek to bring together their resources as teams. Previously illustrated at the beginning of this chapter was the example set by Capt. Al Haynes of United Flight 232. Haynes recruited a commuting DC-10 instructor from the cabin to assist the flight deck crew in controlling the disabled aircraft. Captains, admit to yourself that you have a team...not a team that you belong to, but one that you lead!

Once we get the teamwork part down, the rest of CRM is easy, right? No way! Getting CRM right every day, every flight is hard work. That is why our industry continues to study, redevelop, repackage, and represent CRM in some new fashion every year. Some of my colleagues would argue that true CRM is a "lost art." Many aviators have become disenfranchised by the seemingly oversimplified approach to understanding CRM—the "learn to get along, work, and play well with others" approach. But the core of CRM is even simpler than that.

Many pilots, dispatchers, mechanics, and flight attendants attend recurrent CRM training every year to hear some of the same concepts and stories over and over again. The New CRM serves as a simple way to refocus on the practical application of CRM which sometimes eludes crew members. Keep in mind the core truths, which all start with the words, "A crew will not work together..." and endeavor to lead your crew to actually work together. Add in the practical focus on situational awareness and leadership/professionalism in the context of these core truths and you will have rediscovered the lost art.

Chapter 6 Notes

1. Retrieved from yarchive.net/air/airliners/dc10_sioux_city.html
2. Read more on this in Chapter 17.
3. This resource has been archived on CRM developer Neil Krey's website: crm-devel.org/resources/misc/transcan/transcan7.htm
4. For an at-length discussion of leadership, see Chapter 14.

PART II:
Getting on the Line

7

Initial Qualification—More Than Just Learning a New Airplane

As pilots train and accomplish requirements to gain their Private Pilot and Commercial Pilot Certificates, Instrument and Multiengine Ratings, and even check-out on a new type of airplane that doesn't require a type rating, they are very much in single pilot mode. Part I of this book was written to aid your transition into the crew environment. You will no longer be in single pilot mode. Every aspect of every flight operation will involve working with others cooperatively to ensure a safe flight.

Starting with your first day in BI, all of your training will be done in a crew environment as well, and that certainly includes aircraft training. I introduced you to the basics of AQP in Part I of this book. Here we will look closer at the nuts-and-bolts of how training and evaluation under AQP works, and how you can do your very best to get the most out of the program your carrier has put together.

Let's start by looking at the basic components of an Initial Qualification course under AQP. You will see that each phase of your qualification course will involve different modes of training. This includes classroom lecture, coursework (using either computer-based training, workbooks, or handouts), Flight Training Devices (FTD), and Full Flight Simulators (FFS).[1]

AQP QUALIFICATION SYLLABUS OVERVIEW

This course overview is common among most air carriers utilizing an AQP for aircraft qualification. You will note the lack of the words "checkride," "stage check," or any sort of "check." This is clue number one that you are doing your aircraft qualification under AQP rather than a Subparts N and O syllabus. Rather than being checked along the way, the pilot is being validated or evaluated. In fact, the Line Oriented Evaluation (LOE)—the final assessment of a pilot's ability to safely operate the airplane—is geared to evaluate how the *crew* operated the flight *together*, rather than being a pass/fail of each pilot's airmanship and flying skills. More on this later.

Phase of Training	Mode of Training
Aircraft Systems Training	Coursework, classroom, FTD
Systems Validation (SV)	Written/computerized knowledge test
Flight Deck Procedures Training	Classroom, FTD
Procedures Validation (PV)	Briefing, FTD
Maneuvers Training	FFS
Maneuvers Validation (MV)	Briefing, FFS
Line Oriented Flight Training (LOFT)	FFS
Line Oriented Evaluation (LOE)	Briefing, FFS
Operating Experience	Live flight operations

An AQP training syllabus is designed to allow for the subjective nature of evaluation of aircraft knowledge, airmanship skills, and most importantly crew coordination and proper use of CRM. Grading and performance standards are applied during each flight training device, simulator, and line flying evaluation (where applicable). For data collection and tracking purposes (essential and required under AQP) as well as to grade performance during evaluations, crews and individuals are graded on a numerical scale. More on this later in this chapter.

Each carrier will employ a different mix of training modes and methods for each phase of the qualification course; therefore, I can't get into too much actual detail on how each phase is carried out. Instead, I can give you a general idea of how a qualification course typically runs.

Aircraft Systems Training

When the qualification course kicks off, there are some prerequisites of sorts that carriers typically employ, but they do not necessarily prevent the commencement of the course. Such requirements may include the completion of the BI course, some sort of line familiarization requirements,[2] and perhaps even a flight time or experience requirement. Beyond that, most pilots in the industry will enter a qualification course when newly hired by their carrier, or when transitioning to a new fleet.

Since it is the twenty-first century, it is very common for airlines to utilize computer-based training or distance learning rather than classroom time for much of the coursework required for training programs. The Aircraft Systems Training phase commonly leans on a large portion of the training being done by the pilot on their own via online courses. The benefit of this, primarily, is the reduced cost for the airline to conduct in-person ground schools. But the benefits of a flexible learning schedule and the ability to review on a pilot's own time cannot be overstated.

There are certain things, however, that a computer-based course cannot convey or teach. Therefore, it is especially common in this phase for pilots to attend a handful of lecture sessions that cover more detail on aircraft systems and allow for interaction with instructors that have high levels of technical knowledge.

The Systems Validation (SV) is used in AQP to validate the pilot's knowledge of aircraft systems. Depending upon the design of the course, and the fleet being trained, the SV may be performed upon completion of the online and classroom training. However, many operators have found that reinforcing systems knowledge with sessions in the FTD provides the best mode and method to meet proficiency standards in this phase. FTD lessons at this early stage of the course are driven very much in the direction of familiarization. The use of FTDs that provide functional feedback (being able to push a button or flip a switch and see an actual change in aircraft system state) are required for carriers that have FTD lessons in the systems phase.

I personally enjoy these lessons, both as an instructor and as a student. It's fun to turn on the APU, start an engine, and even see what lights up on the panel when something goes wrong *before* even knowing what the plane feels like to actually fly. As an instructor, I have found students actually saying out loud "Ahhhh," when they see a system run and cause an indication that they didn't understand completely from the book or computer lesson. The reinforcement is real!

The SV is given by a qualified instructor, and, in this technological age, is typically conducted on a computer testing platform. Like other knowledge tests you have done to achieve certification, a score of 80 percent is typically required. Also like previous knowledge (or "written") tests, scoring less than 80 percent does not mean you have failed the course overall. It does, however, incur more training. Rather than calling it retraining, which implies that the systems phase of the course has to be repeated, a pilot only is required to remediate the questions or subject areas missed to *proficiency*. Some airlines require a full re-take of the SV, and others require only a retest of the subject areas missed; again, it depends on the design of the course.

Flight Deck Procedures Training

After students have completed the SV, more work in the FTD is completed through a set of lessons designed to teach flight deck flows, procedures, checklist usage, and certain flight profiles all while reinforcing the systems knowledge previously learned. At this stage of training, actual time in the FTD is bookended with briefings. Your time in FTDs and FFSs will always start with a briefing that will not only give an overview of the lesson, but also serve to prepare the crew for the elements that will be completed. At the end of the lesson, the instructor will review the lesson, give feedback on what went well, what could be better, what to work on, and what comes next. Briefings are integral to the qualification course, allowing for feedback and providing opportunities to take deeper dives into the topics and elements of the lesson.

During procedures training, every flow and checklist done in a normal flight operation is covered. Aircraft acceptance, flight deck setup, programming and setting of flight management systems, radios, and navigational aids; preflight checklists, engine starts, pre-taxi and takeoff checklists, after takeoff, climb, cruise, descent, approach, and landing checklists; after landing flows and checklists, parking and shutdown procedures, and even some special operational checklists will be covered.

Also in this phase, it is common for airline training departments to reinforce, or perhaps reintroduce, common callouts, flow and checklist standard operating procedures, and other common procedures that are implemented company-wide, regardless of fleet. An example is altitude callouts: most carriers have a standard way for crews to verify and verbally confirm assigned altitudes on climb or descent. "NINE FOR TEN THOUSAND" could perhaps be called out when passing 9,000 feet MSL while climbing to 10,000 feet MSL. Also common is the standardization of how flight deck flows and checklists are completed, including who completes a flow, who reads a checklist, and who responds to the checklist.

If the FTD used in this phase is capable of simulating phases of flight—especially takeoffs, climbs, cruises, descents, and approaches to landing—learning and practicing callouts will be done real-time in simulation. This also allows for training of flight profiles, which are often built on a sequence of cues or triggers for a certain callout, maneuver, or activation of a system to occur. One example is the point during the takeoff profile that the landing gear is retracted: Commonly, the PF or PM will call out "POSITIVE RATE" upon recognition of an increasing trend of altitude and rate of climb, which triggers the response from the PF of "GEAR UP" which commands the PM to raise the landing gear lever.

For pilots who aren't used to flying in a crew environment, this phase of training is perhaps the most crucial. Single pilot flying drives aviators to become self-sufficient, managing their flight to their own personal choice of procedures and techniques. When flying as a crew, there is no choice for procedures other than the ones that have been standardized. Training occurs to ensure that all flows, checklists, callouts, and flight profiles are conducted in the same way by every pilot. To use musical metaphors, everyone reads from the same sheet of music and coordinates their actions in concert. The captain is the conductor, with all crewmembers following their cues. Understanding your role as PM or PF, captain or first officer, and how these roles have specific procedural responsibilities is crucial for flying in the crew environment. Learning the rhythms of each phase of flight and how the flight deck procedures produce those rhythms is crucial to the rest of the qualification curriculum, not to mention every safe flight operation you will be involved with moving ahead.

After completion of the penultimate lesson in this phase, the final lesson serves as the Procedures Validation (PV). Conducted in the FTD, the PV is completed when the crew shows they can meet safe, proficient standards when it comes to all normal operations SOP. Some carriers may also use the PV to conduct review of systems questions, or other topics that will underpin and serve as transition material as the crew moves into the Maneuvers and Line Oriented Flight Training (LOFT) phases.

Maneuvers Training

Traditionally known as "sim sessions," the maneuvers phase launches the crew into full flight simulation, in devices that are designed to operate exactly like the real-life airplane does. These simulators have state-of-the-art computers and components that produce motion, lifelike visuals, and all flight deck indications and responses. All flight controls operate identical to the real airplane, including feel and tactile feedback. The motion of the simulator, combined with the wrap-around visuals triggers a pilot's senses. It is more than a big video game—the FFS provides an invaluable training platform to demonstrate, replicate, teach, and evaluate a crew's ability to operate the aircraft safely in all kinds of conditions.

Maneuvers training begins with normal operating maneuvers. Taxi, takeoff, area departure, basic flight maneuvers, arrival and approaches are all focused on up front. Because each pilot does need to demonstrate proficiency as both PF and PM, the sequence of maneuvers is repeated for each pilot. Precision and non-precision approaches with all engines operating and the SOP for each kind of approach is tackled before non-normal procedures are introduced.

The most critical non-normal procedures aviators have to learn involve the loss of an engine or major aircraft system. Again, dependent on course design, crews can expect training on engine failures that occur during the takeoff roll, both prior to takeoff safety speed (V_1) and after, during initial climb, at cruise, and on approach. Engine inoperative approach, landing, and go-around procedures are also trained.

Along with the non-normal flight maneuver profiles and actions by the crew, a crucial element to the non-normal SOP is the conduct of non-normal checklists and associated procedures. Task management during a non-normal situation is trained per company policy (i.e., who flies, who takes the radios, who runs the checklists, etc.). CRM and TEM skills are developed, honed, and demonstrated at high levels during these scenarios.

The Maneuvers Validation (MV) is conducted as the final lesson of the maneuvers phase. After the briefing outlines the sequence of maneuvers the crew will demonstrate, however, it becomes clear very often that this is just another lesson—just with a more evaluative focus. Here is a common sequence of events in the MV:

- Taxi
- Takeoff
- Non-Precision Approach to a Missed Approach
- Missed Approach
- Landing
- Rejected Takeoff
- Takeoff with engine failure at V_1
- Single Engine ILS Approach to a Missed Approach
- Single Engine Missed Approach
- Single Engine Landing
- Low Visibility Taxi Out
- Low Minimums (CAT II or CAT III) Approaches and Certification

The simulator environment is set up to facilitate the MV and allow the crew to demonstrate their proficiency in the maneuvers themselves. Therefore, expect the instructor or evaluator to reposition the simulator, slew the location of the virtual airplane to different locations, and expedite vectors. Similarly, the instructor may freeze the simulator in order to allow a crew more time to complete a task (so long as it is completed safely and timely). The crew typically operates as if there are no passengers or flight attendants to worry about. Coordination with ground resources during emergency procedures are a given. The MV is all about showing you can fly safely, even when the airplane malfunctions.

Line Oriented Flight Training

The last phase of the qualification syllabus brings the crew through a series of FFS sessions that are scripted to simulate operations as they happen on an everyday basis. The emphasis switches from the maneuvers phase—where the crew demonstrated proficiency in PF and PM skills—to the LOFT phase where the simulator is flown and all decisions are made as if the pilots are operating a line flight.

To that end, every lesson in the LOFT phase starts out like any other normal real-world flight—with the crew pre-flight briefing the flight plan, weather, NOTAMs, and all pertinent information available to them for the flight. They get in the simulator, set up the flight deck, and conduct briefings in real time. The instructor plays the roles of gate agent, flight attendant, ATC, dispatch, ground personnel, and more to increase realism. Headsets and shoulder harnesses are used just like on the real flight line, all communications made via appropriate methods, and the entire flight is operated real-time—no repositioning or freezing of the simulator on these LOFT flights!

LOFT sessions allow a crew to truly consolidate their knowledge prior to the final evaluation session, the LOE, which also serves as a qualification session for issuance of the aircraft type rating, if applicable. At this phase, system knowledge is tapped several times as more non-normal procedures are explored, mainly in situations where an aircraft system fails. Advanced maneuvers that explore the operating envelope of the airplane are often lined up in LOFT scenarios—loss of control (upset recovery), terrain avoidance, turbulence escapes, emergency/rapid descents, ditching, and more find their way onto the syllabus in this phase.

All the while, the crew should be improving their CRM and TEM skills, learning how to best manage non-normal situations. Each flight scenario begins with normal operations and then devolves into the challenge of a non-normal. But some LOFT sessions are also designed to replicate a real-world event that the carrier wishes to use in a lessons-learned approach. Supplementary procedures, like adverse weather operations, alternate ground handling procedures, and maintenance procedures are also trained.

Line Oriented Evaluation

All the phases of the initial qualification course lead up to the LOE. If there is any singular point during the course where the crew would be embarking on a checkride, this is it. But, unlike checkrides for previous certifications and ratings, and certainly different from the proficiency check conducted under Subpart N and O, the LOE doesn't involve a comprehensive final exam–style evaluation of all of the maneuvers and procedures you learned during the course. Instead, the LOE is just another LOFT scenario. The crew is checked together as they operate within the margins of safety, completing the flight and handling any and all issues that may arise with appropriate CRM and TEM skills.

Prior to the FFS portion of the LOE, during the pre-briefing the evaluator may conduct what is termed an Operational Knowledge Review (OKR). Although very much akin to an oral examination, because pilots are being *evaluated* rather than checked under AQP, there is no jeopardy in the OKR. Typically, OKRs allow evaluators to ensure pilots are proficient on what must be recalled from memory (limitations, immediate action items, etc.), and can incorporate questions regarding general, non-aircraft specific, flight operations policies (dispatch legalities, security procedures, etc.). Again, because the pilots are evaluated as a crew, OKRs take on more of an open dialogue format than a quiz show format.

It has been my experience that LOEs are "busy," just like many real-world operations can get busy; and certainly not just because of a major system failure like losing an engine on the takeoff roll. If that was it, the LOE would be over in no time. Rather, how about a tow bar breakaway during pushback? What actions are required for a last-minute runway change during taxi-out? During climb on the RNAV SID, you get vectored off and then back on to meet certain altitude constraints, and during all the readback clarification you get a TCAS RA. Up at cruise, the flight attendant calls and says you have a passenger complaining of chest pain and feeling weak; a physician passenger assists and recommends getting the ailing passenger to a hospital as soon as possible. While declaring the medical emergency and beginning to divert to a new destination the first officer's radio control panel stops working. During the approach you can't get to the final flap setting on final due to a malfunction. After landing you get a cargo smoke indication on the taxi in.

All of those issues can arise during a single LOE. How the crew reacts, uses CRM, employs task and workload management skills, and *completes the flight safely* determines whether or not the LOE is completed successfully. Busy? Yes. Stressful? Undoubtedly. Realistic? Yes—albeit a very, very bad day for that flight! In fact, I have had all of those issues arise in the real world several times, some of them combined on the same flight. But please note, the LOE doesn't have to have an engine failure, hydraulic failure, rapid decompression, or some dramatic issue to be useful in evaluating the crew. It just needs to provide enough realistic challenge to the crew that compels them to show they have the knowledge, skill level, and overall capability to overcome the challenge and *operate safely*.

MAKING THE SYLLABUS WORK FOR YOU

Course Prep and Study

Any initial qualification course is daunting and can certainly be exhausting. Remember, the initial qualification syllabus isn't just for new hires. Whenever you transition or upgrade from one equipment type to another you will be subject to this sequence of training events. The question is how will you prepare and remain ready for every lesson and evaluation ahead?

Number one, the best thing you can do, if able, is to connect with your training partner. Solid programs pair crewmembers together for the entire course or as much of it as possible. Once you find out who that person is, and if you are able to reach out through company channels to make initial contact, do so. A simple message saying "Hi, we are paired up for initial qual. Just wanted to say hello and share my contact info with you. Looking forward to the course!" will work, along with your contact info.

After you reach out to your training partner, start gathering materials for your training. If you are able to get hands on manuals, syllabus, lesson plans, study guides, flight deck diagrams, flight deck posters, and other training *software*, do it sooner than later.[3]

Pilot Training Materials

While this list certainly isn't exhaustive, it includes the most common course materials used for initial qualification courses:

- Airplane Operating/Flight Manual
- Flight Operations Manual (and other relevant company manuals)
- Course Syllabus and Lesson Plans
- Flight deck posters and guides
- Aircraft systems guides and handouts
- Copies of normal checklists
- Copies of non-normal checklists (QRH, QRC, EmerCard, etc.)
- Handouts on flows, callouts, amplified procedures
- Systems guide
- Supplementary Procedures

A common question is "what do I need to study before I arrive at training?" The answer depends completely on your learning style, and how you are able to balance out other commitments before you arrive at the training facility on day one. Oftentimes, airline pilot students opt to not study prior to arriving at the schoolhouse. The reasons vary for this, and you too may choose to keep out of the books. But keep in mind that the course syllabus will be busy and efficient. Time for study during the course will limited. If you can get a head start on things by at least looking through the airplane manuals and browsing some of the syllabus, you certainly should.

Many carriers have implemented computer-based training as a part of the qualification syllabus. This is another area of study that you should consider completing in advance of day one. Once classroom or FTD lessons begin, you will be pressed for extra time to get caught up on the computer lessons prior to the SV.

Conquering the Paper Tiger

You may be familiar with the expression *paper tiger,* meaning someone or something that appears fierce, commanding, or even dangerous, but in actuality is weak and lacks substance. Amongst pilots, paper tiger refers to a flight deck mockup made of photographs or posters. They have been practically indispensable to pilots learning a new transport category airplane for years. At my first airline gig, we didn't have FTDs for the Saab SF-340 turboprop. Instead, we had flight deck panel posters glued onto plywood, erected in the basic shape and form of the flight deck. A classroom chair was positioned on either side of the mock center control pedestal. My training partner and I sat and practiced flows, button and switch positions, light logic, and even some imaginary flights. It reminded me of my kids making spaceships out of old cardboard boxes and playing in them, calling out orders and firing off imaginary rocket boosters. Not unlike my kids, in the paper tiger our imaginations were engaged in a way that would help solidify knowledge we needed to progress through our initial training course.

Why, in the twenty-first century, are we still practicing our amplified flight deck procedures in plywood and paper mockups? *Because it works!* No different than flash cards, flip books, handouts, even self-produced study guides and "gouge" on the evaluations. Training aids that pilots have been using for years still stand up against, and in spite of, technological advances.

When you turn to the pages of your flight manual that lists out the steps in a flow or checklist, you will see an ordered list of steps. Better manuals have diagrams accompanying those steps with arrows and numbers overlaid on a photo of the flight deck or panels involved in the procedure. But simply reading those pages and staring at those diagrams will not create the muscle memory needed to perform the procedure.

Use the paper tiger to your advantage to work out the bugs in your flows. Work with a partner to master cadence, speed, and proper sequence. All you are doing is pretending to throw a switch, click a button, or turn a knob—and for certain the paper tiger lacks the tactile feedback of such actions. But simply moving an arm, pointing or pinching a couple fingers, and saying out loud the action you are simulating will do amazing things to your brain in terms of memory and mastery of the procedure.

Operations Familiarization Flights

Pilots at Part 121 carriers are now required to observe two flights from the flight deck jumpseat get acquainted with the flight line operation at the carrier. 14 CFR §121.435 states that all pilots newly hired after April 27, 2022, fall under this requirement.

It is a ride-along of sorts, and rather than joining the passengers back in economy, you get a front seat!

Listing and check-in procedures to gain access to the jumpseat vary by airport and airline. Allow sufficient time to check in at either the ticket counter, gate, or in some cases both. After gaining access and checking in at the gate, introduce yourself to the Captain. It is at their discretion to allow you to occupy the jumpseat, a policy that applies to normal non-revenue jumpseat riding.

Once onboard, the crew will give you a quick orientation of safety equipment and brief you on your role and responsibility as a jumpseater. Believe it or not, when occupying the flight deck jumpseat—whether qualified in the airplane or not—you are an additional member of the crew! You are an additional set of eyes and ears available to augment the situational awareness of the pilots at the controls. You will assist in an emergency if one occurs, particularly during an evacuation, and you will be briefed on how the Captain expects you to assist in such an event.

Keep the following things in mind when occupying the jumpseat:

- Dress code is uniform, business, or business casual. Jumpseating is a privilege requiring professional conduct at all times.

- If you are able, wear a headset. Follow sterile flight deck rules,[4] but speak up when necessary.

- Remember to turn off your cell phone as soon as you enter the flight deck and cease text messaging.

- As you will be seated closest to the flight deck door, you be responsible for its security. This includes opening and closing the door when appropriate—always check with the Captain or First Officer when it is okay to open the door, including at the end of the flight.

- Always express your gratitude to the crew when deplaning!

Hopefully your observation flights will be uneventful. Your job during an orientation flight is to simply take it all in. If you are brand new to the airline operation, the first thing you will notice is the cadence and pace. At times, it will be busy. You will catch some things that you expect to see and hear during the flight and you will miss much more. But the whole experience will immerse and inoculate you and temper your expectations for how the flight operation runs in real time.

Keep some simple notes as you observe the crew perform their duties. Ask questions at appropriate times, and take into consideration that everything you watch will (hopefully) be done in accordance with SOP, but also with varied technique being applied.

Lesson Prep and Syllabus Engagement

Your carrier should issue you a copy of the training syllabus including lesson outlines and plans. The syllabus will have all you will need to know about requirements, evaluations, completion standards, materials, and lessons used in the course. Beyond getting to know your flight manuals well, reviewing your syllabus will serve as great preparation for the course.[5]

Prior to each lesson (or each day), make it a part of your study routine to read through the lesson plan. The lesson plans will likely be akin to the ones you got used to seeing as a student or instructor while you were earning your first certificates and ratings. They will have an objective or overview section, lesson content or subjects covered, and often an outline of the briefing to be covered before the lesson. Many lesson plans also have a sequence or profile of the tasks and maneuvers to be performed. Read through the plan while referencing other aids, like the flight manual, flight deck posters, profile handouts, or whatever you need and have access to, so that you can visualize and pregame the lesson.

Progress and Contingencies

Once you get started in the course, things should move along swiftly and smoothly, and carriers have all the incentive in the world to keep your training progressing and on schedule. Your training is a huge investment in cost and resources for the airline, so they are motivated to ensure your success.

As mentioned at the beginning of the chapter, performance during evaluations is graded on a numerical scale, typically 1 to 5. The general completion standard for any evaluation, including the performance of a maneuver or flight task by an individual pilot, typically looks like this:

- The flight flew within legal limits or there was appropriate use of emergency authority.
- The flight remained within SOPs or deviations were justified.
- Errors were identified and appropriate corrective action was taken in a timely manner.
- The successful outcome of a maneuver or procedure was never in doubt.

It is possible to score unsatisfactorily, meaning in essence that the crew did not perform with an adequate margin of safety, or that proficiency fell below training standards. In theory, an unsatisfactory grade should be pretty hard to come by if the training leading up to the validation event adequately prepared the crew for the next phase of training. In this way, the design of an AQP course should advance the proficiency of the crew as they complete it. Just like any good training syllabus, each lesson reinforces knowledge and skills learned in preceding lessons. Pilots learn to become more proficient at skills as they progress. For example, flight deck flows, checklist responses, and procedures are trained during the Flight Deck Procedures Training phase and evaluated at a primary level during the PV. By the time the crew does their MV, those procedures are proficient enough to meet all standards, and during the LOE the crew performs at a level that proves them worthy of qualification.

Just like in any other learning environment, there could be times where a student struggles with a lesson or doesn't complete a validation. If you find yourself at such a juncture during training, don't fret. The airline, oftentimes in consult and agreement with the pilot's union or training committee that represents pilots' best interests in training, has a plan in place for pilots who are struggling or who don't progress in training. Such a plan typically follows a prescription for re-training and further evaluation, all with efforts made towards eventual course completion.

If a pilot receives an unsatisfactory performance rating at any point during the course, they are then slated for what is oftentimes termed *short cycle*. Rather than returning to recurrent training for continued qualification at the normal interval, the pilot returns sooner. Upon successful completion of the recurrent training on short cycle, the pilot is returned to the normal interval of continuing qualification events.

TRANSITIONING TO THE LINE

Upon successful completion of your LOE, a training syllabus may include additional training for ancillary subjects that are specific to the fleet that were not necessary to be trained prior to the LOE. Otherwise, with your aircraft qualification complete, and Temporary Airman Certificate in hand with the fresh aircraft type rating, you will be headed back to the real world of airline operations. Say goodbye to the schoolhouse and the simulators with a feeling of accomplishment, and take time to celebrate, as you certainly have earned it!

If it hasn't occurred already, the airline's crew scheduling department will be arranging for your initial schedule on the flight line. Your first real, live trips will be flown as a part of your initial qualification training, and is commonly referred to as Initial Operating Experience (IOE). This is where all your prior training meets up with the live operation of the airline; where you actually put on the uniform, head to work, and climb into the flight deck of the actual airplane. It will be your first time at the controls of the real thing with real passengers and real cargo on board. In fact, there will be so much happening, IOE deserves a chapter all by itself!

Chapter 7 Notes

1. The difference between a FTD and a FFS is quite simple: FFS is a full motion simulator while a FTD is a fixed-base, non-motion simulator. A FTD can be as basic as a photorealistic mockup of the panels in the flight deck, or as advanced as an actual flight deck, so long that it doesn't actually move. Some operators will even utilize a full motion simulator as a FTD by simply taking the simulator off motion and disabling the visuals. The idea is that an FTD helps a pilot establish "muscle memory" for locations of controls along with flight deck flows without the distraction or interaction of aircraft movement and outside reference.

2. Such as visiting their pilot base or doing observation flights from the flight deck jumpseat.

3. *Software* in the educational aid sense, which could be books, flash cards, articles, as well as actual computer software. Many carriers are employing FMS/FMGC emulator programs that students can download or use online. I even used Microsoft Flight Simulator to start getting used to flight deck layout for the B757 when I was getting ready to qualify in that fleet!

4. During all operations below 10,000 feet MSL (and in some cases, higher if the Captain deems it necessary), all non-essential conversation must cease to allow the crew to focus. See 14 CFR §121.542.

5. Knowing how to find information in your manuals is perhaps more important than memorizing the information in them. You will certainly be required to memorize certain information like system limitations, but there is so much additional information contained in both the airplane flight manual and the air carrier's flight operations manual that unless you have a perfect eidetic memory, complete memorization of these manuals is impossible.

8

Initial Operating Experience—On-The-Job Training Like You Never Expected

Initial Operating Experience. Some think it is an antiquated misnomer, especially when applied to a pilot who may already have years of experience and thousands of hours under their belts. Some operators have even dropped the word "Initial" from the term, indicating that "OE" denotes enough connotation to describe what happens during this training phase.

Indeed, when I was hired on at the majors, I had spent 13 *(yes, thirteen)* years at the regionals during a time when hiring at the majors was slow. I had built up thousands of hours of flight experience, and had been through IOE more than once already, qualifying as a First Officer and as a Captain in one fleet, and again as a Captain in an entirely different fleet. Would IOE at a major airline be much different? Granted, the airplane was bigger and more complex in some ways, and certainly new to me as a new hire at the major, but was my IOE going to feel like I was starting all over again in the industry from scratch?

In some ways, yes. In some ways, no. IOE at any level, at any carrier, and in any flight operation theater is going to be new, different, and will swiftly whisk you away into the real-world operation. It's On-the-Job Training (OJT) like you will never experience anywhere in the world. Buckle in, get ready, keep your eyes and ears open, and your head on a swivel. You're going to have a blast!

WHAT EXACTLY IS IOE?

What sets IOE apart from other vocational examples of OJT, however, is the hands-on nature of the training. There will not be much that will be simply demonstrated to you by your check airman (the pilot who will be teaching, evaluating, and mentoring you), where you sit back and watch. "Over the shoulder" exercises don't actually work too well in a crew environment, after all.

Aside from a flight (also referred to as a leg) or two where you polish your pilot monitoring skills, you will be at the controls as pilot flying for most of your IOE. Takeoffs and landings are essential skills to be learned outside of the simulator world. But there will be so, so much more. Every aspect of routine flight operations—which you practiced in simulation—will be trained again in real-time exposure to the real operation. Here is a short list of the real things you will handle during IOE:

- Real airports, security, and ground operations
- Real dispatchers, gate agents, ramp agents, fuelers, and mechanics
- Real flight attendants
- Real passengers, with all their complaints, needs, and expectations
- Real weather
- Real maintenance issues, paperwork, non-normals, and supplementary procedures
- Real air traffic control, rapid fire transmissions, garbled transmissions, missed callsigns, bad frequency changes, re-routes, holding, ground delays
- Real flight traffic, controlled and uncontrolled, seen and unseen
- Real sounds, smells, and other sensations of flying
- REAL AIRPLANE!

Don't fret over the realities of IOE. At this level, you have already seen much of the real-world list above and more in your time as a pilot. It is the new frame of view, the new pace and feel, and the new experience of a new airplane in a new operational theater that you are acclimating to. It takes what cannot be possibly trained in simulation during the qualification syllabus and makes it available for training and proficiency.

Your Line Check Airman (LCA) will be the PIC during your IOE trip, even if you are qualifying as a Captain.[1] The LCA wears two hats. First and foremost, they are your flying partner; your Captain or First Officer as required. You and the LCA make up the flight crew (along with any relief pilots, if applicable for long-haul flights requiring them). You will function like any other flight crew would in any other flight operation. Second, the LCA serves as instructor, evaluator, and mentor. In wearing that hat, the LCA will teach you how to apply already known and evaluated flight procedures in the real operation. They will also demonstrate and teach techniques that will aid your airmanship and conduct of duties within the bounds of SOP. As you complete each leg of IOE, the LCA will debrief with feedback of your progress. Each carrier employs a set of standards that LCAs are looking for on IOE. Finally, they will serve as a mentor to you as you become acquainted with the airplane and the operation.

IOE is completed when a certain number of hours and/or flight cycles have been completed,[2] and when the LCA is satisfied that all standards have been met. For pilots qualifying as PIC in the aircraft, an FAA inspector (or FAA-designated check pilot from the carrier) will conduct an Initial Line Check where they will also affirm that standards for a newly-qualifying Captain have been met.

As mentioned in the previous chapter, toward the end of your qualification syllabus your crew scheduling or training scheduling department will be in touch with you to arrange your first trip or trips on IOE. In accordance with your pilot contract (where applicable) and scheduling rules and policies that allow the transition from the schoolhouse to the flight line, you will get scheduled for a trip that hopefully will efficiently and proficiently allow you to complete IOE in a minimal span of days over the calendar.

For the purpose of what is called "knowledge consolidation" you will want to complete IOE in as little time necessary both in terms of flight time and in terms of calendar days since you completed your LOE. From that date, you have 120 calendar days to accumulate 100 hours of flight experience in the actual airplane.[3] During this time frame, you will be considered a "high minimums" pilot. For Captains it is regulatory that instrument approach and landing weather minimums are increased.[4] For First Officers, depending on the carrier's operations specifications, other restrictions may apply when you have less than 100 hours.

Beyond the restriction on landing minima, however, is the prospect of additional training if you don't achieve 100 hours in 120 days since the LOE. The carrier's flight operations department doesn't want you to become non-qualified due to this, so it is common for pilots at risk of not meeting this requirement to be scheduled additional flying prospectively to make sure they can make the hours.

PREPARING FOR IOE

Once you receive a schedule for IOE, review it to ensure you understand the sequence of events before you. Scheduling software among carriers has more-or-less the same format and information available to a pilot. A typical trip or pairing (referring to the pairing of crewmembers together to conduct a series of flight segments) on paper includes more information than simple flight numbers, arrival and departure times, and aircraft assignments. It also includes report times, release times, pay information, layover details, and more. Here is an example from my carrier:

```
FF 03/28/20 THRU 03/28/20                                    ID F1052  - BASIC
      RPT: 0630
   19F    1777 SJC IAH 0730 1314    1.14 B      3.44  3.44
   19F    2256 IAH PHX 1428 1528   18.24        3.00  6.44   9.13      .00
      RLS: 1543      HTL: SHERATON GRAND DTWN          602-262-2500        OP=> 602-586-2221
                          DESERT COACH                 602-286-6161
      RPT: 0907
   19F     604 PHX DEN 0952 1237    3.04        1.45  1.45
   19F DH 2186 DEN SJC 1541 1721                2.40  1.45   8.29      2.40
      RLS: 1736
         DAYS- 2 CRD-11.09* FTM- 8.29* TAFB- 35.06 INT-   .00 NTE-   .00 M$- 87.75 T/C- 2.40    .13*
```

This cryptic clip of text, believe it or not, contains all the schedule detail a pilot would need to complete a two-day trip. It has flight numbers, city pairs, scheduled departure and arrival times, and report and release times. What this doesn't show is gate information and where you need to go when you get to the airport... more on figuring that out later.

After reviewing your schedule and understanding when you are expected to be at work, you should begin planning, or carrying out, a pre-trip routine. This is a basic set of actions you need to do to get ready for a trip. It's no different than anyone else who has a routine for getting ready for work each day—but there are some considerations a pilot needs to make that may be different than the average cubicle worker.

First and foremost, a pilot needs to report—and certify before operating a flight—that they are fit for duty. This includes, perhaps most significantly, a consideration of rest received prior to the trip along with overall health. So, a primary consideration of your pre-trip routine is how your sleep schedule looks prior to your report time. I cover this in detail later in this book (Part II, Chapter 12).

Next, your pre-trip routine should include packing. Consider not just clothing (uniform and off-duty wear included) but also what you need to bring for your flight duties. What is in your flight kit when you get to this level? Check out Part III, Chapter 18 on "Pilot Paraphernalia" for more considerations on this.

MEET THE AIRPLANE

Due to the varied nature of the pilot commute, especially with access to flight benefits, jumpseating, and other avenues to travel from home to the airport your trip starts at, I cannot do much justice in providing practical information for the subject. Your best resources for on how to get to work, as an airline pilot, are peers. Company websites, union websites, and even industry online forums and message boards always have a good amount of information on this subject.[5]

It is typical for the LCA who will be doing your IOE to reach out and contact you. They will often coordinate a meeting time and place, pre-flight, to do an appropriate briefing and cover any operational or training information in advance of your first flight together.

In lieu of such a meetup, your responsibility will likely be to report to a central location—a flight operations office, crew room, flight planning area, or similar. If that isn't the case, your only other option is to meet your LCA and crew at the airplane itself. Either way, give yourself plenty of time, arrive early, and come prepared!

Once you get to your assigned airplane, everything you have been preparing for is about to unfold. To be honest, it already has been unfolding—all the learning, preparation, briefing, and planning you have been doing will affect your first real, live flight.

One of the first things you should absolutely, positively, do is to make introductions with your fellow crewmembers. Make an effort to say hello and shake hands. Remember back in Part I, Chapter 4 on crew briefings, I wrote about making the best first impressions? It goes as much for First Officers as it does for Captains.

Once you get onboard the airplane, familiarize yourself as you walk through the cabin or climb into the flight deck. Your LCA may even give you a bit of an aircraft walkthrough as well during your preflight inspection. Pay attention and remember as much as you can, ask questions, and jot down any notes you might want to make to revisit or remember to ask about later.

As far as flight deck setup is concerned, I write about this later in the book in Part III, Chapter 11. But, as somebody who is new to the airplane, I want to add a few notes here. First, ensure you know and understand where all safety and emergency equipment is located in the flight deck. Most training programs train pilots on using this equipment in static trainers or classrooms. Here you will see exactly how fire extinguishers, crash axes, safety ropes, oxygen masks, protective breathing equipment (PBE), life vests, and more are stowed, secured, and accessible in the actual airplane. Second, pay attention to how the flight deck door operates, and how to secure it. Particularly after the tragic terrorist attacks of September 11, 2001, flight deck security is paramount to overall security of the flight.

DURING THE IOE TRIPS

Your time on IOE will go by in an eyeblink. Even a four-day trip will seem like it happened in less than two after it is done. The primary driver for this is the new pace of the real flight operation. Prior to IOE you worked in the safe, somewhat-pretend realm of the training center, sheltered from the hectic and unpredictable pace that is found on the flight line. In the simulator, your instructor had pace under their control, but you and your flying partner also had a lot to do with how the pace was set. That will remain very true on the flight line, but the pace gets dictated by more than just the flight deck. Other actors enter the scene from here on out—some with which you can interact and influence, and others who you cannot.

Your LCA knows that this change from the simulator world to the real world can be a shock to some pilots, especially those new to the industry as a whole. They will do their best to help you acclimate and adjust, but it will be on your shoulders to use appropriate workload management skills to make the adjustment happen. Lean on SOP, knowing and trusting that it has been developed by people with expertise on how every task necessary to fly your aircraft type needs to be carried out. Use your LCA as a resource to find techniques and actions that help those tasks fit with the pace of the operation. By the time you complete IOE, you will feel like you understand the pace through the sequence of events that occur every leg. From preflight to shutdown, and every phase of flight in between, you will have learned every step, made every possible radio call, performed all the aircraft system tasks, completed a successful flight, and experienced the flow, connectiveness, and continuity of the entire flight operation. If it begins to feel natural and routine to you, it means you have hit your stride. Congrats!

Chapter 8 Notes

1. You will still perform all duties and functions of a PIC; the LCA retains ultimate operational control as he or she is fully qualified to operate as PIC, and you will not be until you complete IOE.

2. See 14 CFR §121.434(c)(3)

3. See 14 CFR §121.434(g)

4. See 14 CFR §121.625

5. The Air Line Pilots Association, Int'l. has maintained jumpseatinfo.org as a great online resource for pilot commuters for several years.

9

Known Unknowns and the Challenges of Non-Normals

Every pilot is trained in how to handle abnormal situations. This chapter delves into what many refer to as "non-normals." But what exactly does "non-normal" mean?

In reality, there are so many extraordinary things happening during flight that it may be possible to classify several parts of the operation as non-normal. The spectrum of normal to non-normal all depend on a person's point of view. A layman passenger who doesn't understand the effects of frost on critical flight surfaces may consider a deicing procedure as non-normal. A ramp agent who is used to servicing a CRJ200 may consider the servicing activities for a charter B737 as non-normal. Likewise, a new-hire first officer may consider every non-critical system fault as non-normal, regardless of the fact that the faults have no impact on the safety of flight.

Pilot leaders have a well-developed perspective that "non-normal" does not mean the same thing to everybody. This is why well-developed procedures, including the appropriate usage of checklists, are paramount to handling what is defined by the operator or aircraft manufacturer as an abnormal situation.

RELAX. IT'S JUST A LIGHT...RIGHT?

It is amazing how far aircraft technology and refinements have come over the years. State-of-the-art aircraft in the twenty-first century practically manage themselves when it comes to mechanical discrepancies and system faults that are non-flight-critical. A "silent" message gets posted in an indicating system for the flight crew or maintenance personnel to rectify post-flight. But all pilots can't fly brand-new, state-of-the-art airplanes, and many will still have to make critical decisions about indications in the flight deck that in some cases lead down several possible paths of resolution. Therefore, many pilots are trained from the get-go to have a very immediate, and deliberate, reaction to an abnormal flight deck indication.

Realizing that every aircraft type is different, and realizing that some aircraft have abnormal situations that require expedited action to prevent further damage, protect life, and/or prevent an accident, there is a very simple rule of behavior to follow when an abnormal flight deck indication presents itself: Relax.

Relax—but don't snooze! I have heard many a "seasoned" pilot say the best thing to do is to cancel the indication (if it keeps sounding an aural alert), slide the seat back, take a deep breath (sip of coffee, thoughtful view out the window, etc.), and then make your decision on how to react.

Relax? When something could be going very wrong, and I don't have control of it? Are you kidding me?

Pilots—by their nature—have very little capacity for abnormal situations. Most pilots are "Type A" personalities, which crave order and control. So learning to first relax when something goes wrong is a lot to ask. But given the fact that your idea of abnormal may be different from another person's, it doesn't seem prudent to simply "shoot from the hip."

More importantly, the psychological and physiological responses to abnormal indications have the tendency to initiate the "fight or flight" response of our human nature. Adrenaline levels increase, which even in small amounts can cause us to take the path of least resistance, rather than the thoughtful, methodical, procedurally correct path.

Many operators develop what are known as "Quick Reference Handbooks" or "Quick Reference Checklists" for abnormal situations. The "QRH" or "QRC" gives procedural guidance for resolving a non-normal situation, typically involving a series of steps for the flight crew to follow. Over the years, pilots (again, being known for the Type A tendency to be in control) have developed the bad habit of "cowboying" the discrepancy, rather than "QRCing" it.

An example of this would be when a generator comes offline in an aircraft that has multiple generators (in which case the other generator(s) typically pick up the load of the offline generator). A pilot who "cowboys" an offline generator discrepancy may respond as follows:

[Aircraft Sound.]: "CHIME!"

Pilot Monitoring: "Uh, we have a left generator fault."

Pilot Flying: "Aw, stupid $&%& plane!" [He reaches up and selects the affected generator switch from "ON" to "Reset/OFF" and back to "ON."]

The pilot flying's cowboy response to the abnormal situation—even if the generator reset works to resolve the abnormal—comes with these major problems:

1. The pilot assumes that his response to the abnormal is appropriate because he just does it.

2. He takes no time to respond in a thoughtful, methodical, procedural manner.

3. He takes no time to inquire from the pilot monitoring if he thinks his reset attempt is the correct course of action.

The pilot in this scenario "shot from the hip," just like a cowboy would in a gunfight. Instead of reacting in that way, how about this alternative:

[Aircraft Sound.]: "CHIME!"

Pilot Monitoring: "Uh, we have a left generator fault."

Pilot Flying: [*Takes a deep breath, clicks his seat back a few notches.*] "I will continue to fly the airplane, and I will take the radios from you, if you would please look at the non-normal checklist: Electrics. I think I know what we will eventually do to resolve this, but let's make sure to follow the book."

This response by the pilot flying demonstrates that:

1. He is willing to take a calm, relaxed procedural approach to the problem.

2. He wants to share the load with the pilot monitoring, ensuring that while the abnormal is worked on, each pilot is focused on distinctive responsibilities.

3. Although his systems knowledge and "gut instinct" are urging him to respond with a quick fix, he wants to submit to the procedure.

The use of the checklist cannot be overlooked, or overemphasized, as the number one positive response to a non-normal. But along with the use of the checklist must be a positive attitude response. Despite the relatively simple nature of the non-normal, effective pilots will endeavor to keep within the bounds of SOP, and do so in a way that makes the non-normal routine painless, efficient, and effective.

CHECKLIST AND NON-NORMAL MANAGEMENT

While operators are good at developing checklists that cover as many scenarios as possible related to non-normal indications, not every indication or combination of indications can possibly be covered. More complex aircraft systems will typically incur more iterations of a checklist procedure in an attempt to tackle as many scenarios as possible.

Hydraulic systems are a typical example of this. With many modern aircraft utilizing a multiple-source hydraulic system, checklists need to be tailored based upon which system or system(s) are at fault. Operators are careful in instructing pilots to choose the appropriate checklist, especially when the non-normal involves a combination of systems. Within the checklist for a multi-system issue, guidance is typically provided for how to use the checklist. But what if there isn't?

This is where a good set of basic rules and practices come in handy for checklist management. While recognizing that every aircraft is different and every non-normal can be run differently, there are common guidelines everyone can follow when tackling a non-normal checklist. First, the rules:

Rule 1: Using a Checklist is Mandatory. There are no caveats to this rule. Even if *you know* that there is no checklist associated with the non-normal you are encountering, grab your book (QRH/QRC/Non-Normals, etc.) and head to the index. Look for the indication or situation, no matter what. Why? It is procedural habit, plain and simple. You may look in the index and come up with nothing, but at least you are giving due diligence to the non-normal.

Rule 2: Using Common Sense is Mandatory. This is where systems knowledge becomes paramount to the handling of non-normals. Essentially, pilots must be able to discern with common sense, and a bit of practical system knowledge application, that the procedure they are following will appropriately address the problem. This becomes highly important when tackling multiple indications, especially within the same (or related) aircraft system. A good example of this is electrical non-normals. Knowing how various busses are powered, or what relays are related or sequenced, will aid your decisions to use a particular procedure, and will also aid your assessment of whether or not the procedure is affecting the intended changes to the non-normal.

Rule 3: Use of TEM (Threat and Error Management) Skills is Mandatory. The handling of a non-normal is actually an active (rather than passive) application of TEM. Non-normals are born of either threats or errors. Your goal, of course, is to manage the threats and errors, and in doing so, prevent more from occurring that could lead to a UAS (undesired aircraft state). But specifically, you need to manage them by resolving any errors and trapping any additional threats. A great example of this is a flap failure that prevents fully-configured landing flaps from being selected. The non-normal procedures common among most transport-category aircraft include disabling related warning systems (EGPWS or some other aircraft system) from alerting crews that the flaps have not been extended to proper configuration for landing. At the same time, crews need to recalculate landing reference speeds appropriate for the flap malfunction. If these two steps are not accomplished, it can lead directly to inadvertent errors (e.g., a go-around maneuver in response to the configuration warning, or an aircraft instability error or stall from approaching at too low of an airspeed for the flap malfunction—both of which result in a UAS).

Rule 4: Use of CRM is Mandatory. It might seem odd that this is a rule. One would think that CRM would be something that should be naturally occurring during a non-normal. But anyone who has been through a CRM case study will tell you that it was precisely the degradation in CRM that led to the incident. Under the additional pressure of the non-normal, it is common to become over-absorbed in the tasks required by the situation. This is where crew roles, division of duties, and overall PIC management techniques pay off.

Non-Normal Best Practices

First and foremost, *fly the airplane!* This is emphasized in training centers everywhere, and is written in the preface of several flight manuals. It seems like a no-brainer, but when things get stressful and busy, especially when you become absorbed in complex checklists and procedures, it remains the number-one basic rule. Someone needs to fly the plane. After this *primary* best practice for handling non-normals, I offer the following list of four best practices to follow.

Best Practice #1: Establish Roles

Best practices for managing non-normals start with basic resource management skills. The topic of crew roles was covered back in Chapter 3, and it resurfaces here as the first best practice. Once a non-normal is discovered, effective PICs should immediately determine and assign roles. I recommend that for particularly complex non-normals (e.g., total system failure, inflight emergencies, or procedurally intense checklists), the PIC should assume the role of pilot monitoring (PM) and the SIC should fill the role of pilot flying (PF). This affords the PIC the best vantage point to manage the non-normal situation. Radio tasks related to air traffic control should mainly fall on the PF, as the PM will be saturated with handling checklists along with communicating with cabin crew, dispatch, maintenance, and other resources.

Best Practice #2: Share Information

As a non-normal procedure unfolds, the PM becomes task-saturated with the checklist and the ancillary communications. Meanwhile, the PF becomes task-saturated with aviating, navigating, and communicating. *Do not allow these roles to put up a communications barrier in the flight deck between PF and PM!* The best way to prevent that proverbial wall is to speak up. PMs should verbalize where they are in the checklist (if not already reading it aloud as it's executed). PFs should be verbalizing all confirmable flight path changes (new flight control/autoflight mode, altitude changes, heading changes, course changes, FMC programming, etc.). Even when either pilot is "heads down" and not paying direct attention to the actions of the other, verbalization is a primary method to prevent further errors from occurring. "Verbalize, verify, monitor" (VVM) has long been taught in CRM/TEM courses as the best practice for trapping automation errors. But it also proves useful in every aspect of flight deck management. Verbalize the step you are on, the switch you are throwing, the entry you are making, the decision you are contemplating. Make your inner pilot dialogue heard! Then verify that what you are doing makes sense—both with a self-assessment and by asking your flying partner. Once you make your move, monitor to verify that the action produces the expected result. It is simple due diligence, and it goes a long, long way.

Best Practice #3: Make Your Own "Global" Non–Normal Checklist

While some operators and checklists already include some global non-normal considerations, it is a good practice to develop your own, which may be dependent on the type of non-normal you are handling. Following is a setup that can be applied to most operations.

System Malfunction, Non-Emergency

✓ QRH/MEL and flight manual procedures complete

✓ ATC notified (if operational impact)

✓ Crew notified

✓ Dispatch notified

✓ Maintenance notified

✓ Passengers briefed (If needed; for example, if they might hear, feel, or see something that is abnormal.)

✓ Logbook entry made

System Malfunction, Emergency

In Flight:

✓ QRH/MEL and flight manual procedures complete

✓ ATC notified

✓ Crew notified

✓ Dispatch notified

✓ Passengers briefed

Post Flight:

✓ Maintenance notified

✓ Logbook entry made

✓ Required reports filed

Non-Systems Emergency

In Flight:

✓ Flight manual procedures complete

✓ ATC notified

✓ Crew notified

✓ Dispatch notified

✓ Passengers briefed

Post Flight:

✓ Required reports filed

You will likely pick up on the similarities between the above checklists. They all include notifications or briefings with everyone who isn't sitting in the flight deck with you (ATC, dispatch, maintenance, cabin crew, passengers). The upshot here: communicate. Make sure that all your resources are in the loop on the situation. And if at all possible, ask your resources to pass on information to others. For example, if your non-normal emergency will cause you to divert, why not ask dispatch to call the station personnel at the diversion airport to relay what you will need upon arrival? If you are time-critical on airborne tasks, why not have ATC contact your company if you have an immediate air return due to smoke or fire? There is no rule written anywhere that says that being PIC means making all the phone calls. You have full authority to delegate to, designate, and direct other resources in the administration of your duty as PIC.

Best Practice #4: Debrief, Debrief, Debrief

In Chapter 4, postflight debriefs were covered in the context of an average, everyday normal operation. When a non-normal event occurs, especially one which leads to either an emergency situation or a situation in which reporting would be required (or highly desirable), a full debrief of the event becomes mandatory.

While it may seem like debriefing is the last thing you want to do (reliving some non-normal scenarios doesn't always conjure up good memories and laughs), it will actually help you process the event in a healthy and professional manner. First and foremost, it will enable you to learn from the event. Whether it was a mistake, a malfunction, or mere happenstance, the occurrence of the non-normal means that at the very least some error occurred, and perhaps an undesired aircraft state resulted. Debriefing to understand the why and how of the event is important in so far as it enables you as a pilot to change behavior as a result of the experience (i.e., it enables you to learn from the event).

Secondary to learning from the event is the task of information control. For many pilots, the safety systems now in place at air carriers are driven by the collection of information. Whether it is the Aviation Safety Reporting System (also known as the "NASA Report"), Aviation Safety Action Program (ASAP), Flight Operations Quality Assurance (FOQA), or Line Operations Safety Audit (LOSA), the information that is provided to the safety program is paramount to the program's success. It is also crucial to your own voluntary participation in these programs.

What is meant by "information control"? It can mean many things, but very simply that as PIC, you need to ensure that the event as it happened is properly and accurately reported. The honesty and integrity of the information reported is key, even if it is an honest admission of guilt. Mistakes happen. Errors are made. We are human. Report the facts—nothing more, nothing less—and allow the safety programs and processes to take their course. These programs exist largely due to the confidential nature of the information shared. Most data is de-identified, and pilots can only be prosecuted for willful, negligent, or unlawful behavior. If you didn't intentionally break a FAR or other law, you have nothing to worry about when telling your story.

Therefore, in the debrief, make sure to cover how the information will be shared. Talk with your crewmembers about what reports will be made, who you will speak with (chief pilot, fleet manager, director of operations, etc.), and what reporting and information-sharing expectations you have of the crew. Get your stories straight (keeping them factual and honest) and ensure that the rumor mill doesn't ever become a factor.

10

Pilots (and Dispatchers) In Command of Operational Integrity

If working with dispatchers is an everyday occurrence for you (because you operate either for an airline or similar operation under 14 CFR Part 121, or as a charter or "on-demand" operator under Part 135 with a flight tracking/following protocol of some kind), this chapter is geared toward something you grapple with every workday. For those of you who don't or have yet to utilize dispatchers for your operations, this chapter is even more important.

Hypothetical scenarios sometimes can have an uncanny knack for replicating, if not recounting exactly, a real event. It just so happens that over the time span that this chapter was being drafted, Minnesota, North Dakota, and Wisconsin were encountering some of the most dense, lingering fog in years. Visibilities across the region were at or below approach minima for most airports, and lapses were few and far between. As a result, many operators were suffering delays and cancellations. To add insult to injury, much of the fog was *freezing fog*, coating every surface with elaborate blankets of hoar frost. While nature's paintbrush made beautiful front-page images, it also made news as the airlines suffered deicing delays, diversions, ATC congestions, and cancellations.

Flight crews were at the front line of the challenge, of course. I was operating on one of these days, as well. In the crew rooms, at the gates, and in the flight decks, the weather dominated the conversations, and briefings focused more intently on whether or not the flight plans had been legally filed, and the flights legally "released" by dispatch. Meanwhile at corporate headquarters—several hundred miles removed from the foggy, frosty reality of the upper Midwest—airline dispatchers were scratching their heads and trying to make the best of a complicated situation.

Tying together the crews and the dispatchers was a common question: Go or no go?

GO/NO-GO DECISIONS—IT'S MORE COMPLICATED NOW

The University of North Dakota (UND) has one of the largest and most well-known aerospace science schools in the world. UND has to maintain a vibrant in-house flight operations department to support all of the school's flight training needs. Students are actively taking flying lessons during the school year, with many of them continuing to fly in the summer months. The retention of flight student load over the summer months is attributable to UND's meteorological challenges. Located in Grand Forks, North Dakota, UND pilots deal with all kinds of weather, but the cold winter weather—fraught with blizzards, low ceilings, and bitter cold temperatures—posts the most flight cancellations for the school.

The traditional school year (early fall to early spring) sees the worst that aviation weather has to offer in Grand Forks. For UND students, the go/no-go decision is relatively simple, as they are bound to 14 CFR Part 91, with even stricter limits imposed by school policy for safety standards. UND instructors—the majority in the hunt to build hours to move on to another step in their own piloting careers—spend lots of time rescheduling students for cancelled lessons.

Embry-Riddle Aeronautical University (ERAU) is also world-renowned, particularly as the only university completely focused on aerospace sciences. However, with campuses in Daytona Beach, Florida, and Prescott, Arizona, they have far fewer "IMC" days in their school year than UND. The pilots at ERAU comply with the same rules under 14 CFR Part 91 and have protocols similar to UND's, but with some other challenges tossed in: hurricanes and tropical thunderstorm activity for the students in Florida; mountainous terrain considerations and high density altitude flying for the pilots in Arizona.

For many students, it can seem amazing that the airlines can "get in" when many others—especially general aviation flights—cannot. The airlines, however, have a great advantage in operating under 14 CFR Part 121: The rules under Part 121 are vastly different than Part 91. And while some will repeatedly argue that Part 121 offers much greater "protections" than Part 91, in fact the standards remain very much the same. Perhaps the simplest example of this is in 14 CFR §121.613, which prescribes the limitation for dispatch under IFR:

...no person may dispatch or release an aircraft for operations under IFR or over-the-top, unless appropriate weather reports or forecasts, or any combination thereof, indicate that the weather conditions will be at or above the authorized minimums at the estimated time of arrival at the airport or airports to which dispatched or released.

The key words in this regulation are "authorized minimums." For each individual certificated operator, the minima can be defined as "less than standard" under certain conditions and situations, under the operator's operations specifications (ops specs). But even if a carrier can, for example, dispatch to an airport when conditional language in the terminal forecast says that the visibility will be half of what is required to shoot an approach to the airport at ETA, there is still a limitation and a standard to which the conditions must apply.

I am not trying to digress into the finer points of instrument flight rules, but rather only to set the stage. The upshot is that the act of making a go/no-go flight decision *involves* several people, but only one person *acts*. Guess who that one person is?

This is where the worlds of dispatch, crew coordination, and PIC authority collide within the sphere of operational control. In the airline world, even though it is standard procedure (and just common sense good form) for the PIC to seek out the input and knowledge of his co-pilot(s) and dispatchers, the decision to operate remains the PIC's, and his alone. This isn't hard to understand, as there will always exist that over-arching standard that the FAA applies when it evaluates the prudence of a go/no-go decision: the role of the PIC, as defined by 14 CFR §91.3. (Remember, this is the regulation that says the pilot-in-command is "... *responsible for, and is the final authority as to, the operation...*")

So what is the point? If the PIC is still the final authority, why are dispatchers needed? Simply put, they offer the perspective, information, and tools that pilots don't necessarily have access to from the flight deck. The challenge for the pilot is to properly utilize the dispatcher as a resource. Unfortunately, many pilots either utilize dispatch as a crutch—relying too heavily on the dispatcher to make the decisions reserved for the PIC—or disregard dispatch altogether, choosing the attitude that the only perspective they need to operate safely is the view out the flight deck window.

In order to strike a balance, pilots-in-command need to remain focused on their overall role, while respecting the role of the dispatcher. While both are decision makers, the pilot-in-command remains the *ultimate* decision maker. While both have the ability to discern and consider alternatives, the pilot is held to the *higher* standard of accountability for that discernment and consideration. The remainder of this chapter exposes a straightforward approach for how to properly handle the pilot–dispatcher relationship.

PLANNING AND EXECUTING: EFFECTIVE DISPATCH RELEASE REVIEW

At most airlines, the dispatcher takes over the general flight-planning responsibilities that we became so familiar with as private pilots, or as single-pilot commercial or even Part 135 operators. Airline pilots simply show up at the gate and receive their paperwork, already prepared in advance by dispatch. Prescribed by 14 CFR §121.687, the "dispatch release" is the flight's playbook. Aircraft ID, flight number, airports, operation type (IFR or VFR), minimum fuel calculations, and weather all are mandatory per the regulation. In addition, a detailed route/flight path plan, performance calculations, weight and balance, weather, and other pertinent operational information for the flight are typically included.

The review of the release is one of the most important aspects of the PIC's preflight duties. In fact, the FARs require that both pilot and dispatcher put their names to it. 14 CFR §121.663 states, "The pilot in command and an authorized aircraft dispatcher shall sign the release only if they both believe that the flight can be made with safety." It is typical operational procedure to assume that if the dispatch release is sent out to the pilots by the dispatcher (with the dispatcher's name on the release) that the dispatcher has "signed off" on the release. And some operations even have procedures for electronic "acknowledgement" of the release which serves as the PIC's signoff, rather than the old school pen-and-ink signature on the flight papers. Regardless of the method, the pilot-in-command's signature is the "last vote" in accord with his role as final authority for the safety of the flight operation.

It can be very easy for pilots to fall into the complacent practice of giving the release a quick glance and scribbling out his or her John Hancock, especially when the skies are known or forecast to be clear, blue, and bright from takeoff to touchdown. However, safe and effective PICs know that it will be their ultimate responsibility to ensure that the flight can be made with safety, even if the dispatcher already thinks it to be the case. A thorough review of the release will almost certainly trap any errors that may have arisen, unbeknownst to the dispatcher, in the flight-planning process. But cutting to the chase: what specifically must PICs cover to ensure that basic safety criteria have been met?

SAMWISE—Your Trusted Companion

Here I would like to introduce another mnemonic for your consideration. *Lord of the Rings* fans will recognize the name of Frodo's closest companion: Samwise Gamgee. Samwise's advice and input was essential in choosing the right path for Frodo to take, and he served as Frodo's protector throughout the *Lord of the Rings* saga. So in honor of J.R.R. Tolkien's heroic character, here is the mnemonic device:

S Ship number

A Airports

M Minimum fuel

W Weather

I IFR procedures

S Secondary flight plan

E Equipment

The first item to look for on the dispatch release is the ship number or aircraft ID. This could be listed as the operator's ship number, the aircraft "N-Number", or both. Once you find it, look at the airplane (if possible) and confirm you have the right ship. If you don't, the entire release is worthless. The *flight number* could be considered important in this regard, as well, but flight numbers are simply a designation for tracking the flight or flight route. For example, Flight 1001 could operate several times a day, between different airports even. But it will be likely that several different aircraft will operate Flight 1001. More importantly, it is common for aircraft swaps to occur last minute to ensure operational continuity in the fleet. When the flight was originally dispatched and flight papers printed off, Flight 1001 may have been slated to be operated by aircraft 4901. But if a plane swap occurs, Flight 1001 could now be operated by aircraft 4977.

Next on the list are the airports, which are equally controlling for the validity of the entire release. If you are supposed to fly Flight 1001 from Billings (BIL) to Denver (DEN), and instead you see Baltimore (BWI) to Dallas (DFW) on the release, you have a clear problem.[1] But the validation of the airports listed on the release goes beyond the departure and destination airports. If any intermediate stops are to be made, or if there are any alternate airports (including all types of alternates: destination alternate, takeoff alternate, second destination alternate, ETOPS alternates, etc.), they all must be listed. At this point of the release review, PICs should become keenly aware of the circumstances that drive the selection of airports. The FARs and the operations specifications for each carrier dictate the selection criteria for destination and alternate airports. The review should include an analysis on whether the airports listed on the release are "legal" in accordance with all the applicable rules.

Minimum fuel calculations are typically the next place my eyes roam to on the release. The importance of "min fuel" cannot be overstated. That number is almost like a "magic number" for the flight. From it, all other fuel limitations can be derived, and from it we can determine during any phase of the flight operation—from initial taxi out to takeoff, climb, cruise, descent, and approach to landing—whether or not fuel is sufficient for the flight to make it safely back to terra firma. This number needs to seem reasonable given several factors; looking at flight time, alternates, reserves, contingency fuel, and other factors will give you a good sense on whether or not the calculation seems right. (And if it doesn't, you may as well stop right where you are and call your dispatcher.)

Many pilots may turn first to weather in the release, and I think it's fine to put weather first in your mind when conducting the entire release review. This may be a carryover habit from our single-pilot, non-commercial days of flying. A good majority of pilots were trained to get a weather briefing before developing and filing the flight plan. Take a good cue from that habit and remember what the weather briefings included and what things you looked at the closest. The "standard briefings" from Automated Flight Service Station briefers provide a good clue. After an overall synopsis, focus on current conditions, enroute weather, and destination forecasts, in that order. Likewise, and excepting the synopsis, many dispatch release weather packages are ordered in the same way. You will likely develop your own method for reviewing the weather package, but sticking to this basic order will keep you focused on the most important information pertinent to the flight planned on the release.

At this point, without going into the details of aircraft performance, weight and balance, and other items typically included in the release package, the SAMWISE mnemonic diverges from the paperwork itself. An effective review of the release should include a quick verification of the expected IFR procedures for the flight. There are a few ways to tackle this, but I recommend heading right to the section of your release or flight papers that includes either the flight plan itself or the "filed ATC flight plan," or similar. For example, here is a flight plan for a release from Newark (KEWR) to London-Heathrow (EGLL):

KEWR..EWR1.MERIT..HFD..PUT..WITCH..ALLEX.N93B.
CYMON..DENDU..

NATX..DOGAL..BEXET..LIFFY..WAL..NUGRA..BNN1B..EGLL

Many international flight plans commonly have point-to-point routing rather than point-route-point like we see normally on domestic routes. But even if there is a transition route (such as "N93B" in the above example) take note of it and make sure that the waypoints before and after make sense. Note that the plan shown above has both the departure SID procedure (the "EWR1") as well as the arrival or "STAR" procedure (the BNN1B). Reviewing both of these procedures, as well as any anticipated instrument approach procedures, could be crucial for determining alternate minimums, or even needing a "Plan B." Countless flights have left the gate with both the dispatcher and PIC not verifying that a particular approach will be available at an airport listed on the release. Take a moment to look at NOTAMs for your departure, destination, and alternate airports to determine whether an IAP is unavailable, and you will save yourself a lot of trouble once airborne.

It very well may be that by the time you get through the weather and NOTAMS, you could be thinking, "Boy, this may not go as planned." This is why the second "S" in SAMWISE reminds us to make a "secondary flight plan." This is really an opportunity to consider "Plan B" (or C—and hopefully not D, which typically results in flight cancellation). This secondary plan should be one that you can rely upon if the original flight plan cannot be completed. In other words, when the flight from AAA to BBB needs to change into a flight from AAA to CCC, the secondary plan will be ready to execute with confidence. Create the secondary plan yourself, including your crew if at all possible, and then contact the dispatcher to make them aware of it. This doesn't apply only to diversions; it can also apply to weather or airspace deviations. If the flight plan from AAA to BBB will potentially drive you right through a line of thunderstorms, a secondary plan is wise. Determine the best way to get around the storms safely, call dispatch, let them know, and have them take that information into consideration. It is likely such a deviation will require more fuel, so the release will likely be amended, which is the dispatcher's way of signing off on your secondary plan. The main point here is this: think carefully about Plan B. Do you need one? What is it? What will you need to execute this plan?

The final point in the mnemonic is equipment. As a final exercise of the release review, take into consideration the aircraft itself and any equipment that is deferred or inoperative. Does it affect the flight plan? Does it affect performance or procedures? You also may take time to verify the release against the aircraft maintenance logbook. Has something been deferred or has a configuration change taken place that has not been reflected on the release? What about equipment issues that are listed on the release but that have been resolved according to the logbook? Address these items carefully, reviewing the minimum equipment list (MEL) or aircraft-specific procedures where appropriate, as well.

THE BIG PICTURE: MAINTAINING OPERATIONAL RELIABILITY

During a line check I had several years ago I heard something pretty remarkable and unexpected from the check airman. During the debrief he said, "We are responsible to move people from Point A to Point B. So when people say we only need to focus on safety, they are falling short on not only the mission, but the full expectations of a professional operation. Because, let's be real, we need to make sure that we are doing everything we can to keep the operation moving. That is our *real job*."

It was refreshing to hear him say this. Common sense should always play a big role in our actions as pilots. Airlines have employed us to ensure that the flight operation can be conducted safely and efficiently. But so many pilots find it hard to strike the balance between safety and operational reliability. Why? Is it all just that difficult? Can't we get our heads around one concept without stepping on the rights of the other? Can these two concepts even co-exist in the pilot-in-command's world?

Of course they can. We can approach the challenge of getting safety and operational reliability to work together by having a flexible viewpoint on the operation as a whole. In other words, pilots need to shift from their own perspectives on situations posing safety and reliability/operational challenges to view the situations from other's perspectives. And they must do it quite often.

If a mechanical discrepancy is found that you know can be deferred by the flight crew, or can even wait until you reach a maintenance base (for example, a nonessential furnishing or décor accent in the cabin), your company may have a general procedure to follow. But for items which may require your discernment, especially when the general procedure may not directly apply, think about the perspectives of (1) your crew, (2) your passengers, (3) the dispatcher, (4) the mechanic, (5) the ramp and ops crew, and (6) any other entities that may be effected by your actions. Taking time to think through the different views on the situation may help you make the right decision, even if the views all comport or agree with what your gut feeling was in the first place!

You can use the same exercise in any circumstance that could cause you to consider delaying or even cancelling a flight operation. Whenever there may be "gray" areas, which call for your discernment as pilot-in-command, you should task yourself with a mental roundup of the different perspectives, viewpoints, inputs, and effects of the options you have to take action.

And when the mental picture of a perspective is unclear, by all means, ask someone! You have every right as a captain—and as an imperfect human being bound to make mistakes—to *ask* for an opinion. Nobody is requiring you to have all the answers, and particularly all the right answers. I challenge the pilots reading this now to think about how many times you, or a captain you flew with, asked another crewmember, "I'm thinking we will handle this in this way...what do you think of my plan?" or even, "What do you think we should do?" It happens every day, all across the world, and not even in our own vocation. Coworkers who value the benefits of teamwork, who stretch and push for cohesiveness between their crew, their team, and their resources, take the time to query, check, and test out ideas, plans, and consequences before taking action.

As a final conclusion to this discussion about operational reliability: To "see the big picture" doesn't require an omniscient ability to understand fully how your actions will impact other flights, other people, or the airline as whole. The metaphor is much more oriented to your local focus—the flight operation at hand, which you as PIC are ultimately responsible for. The "big picture" pilots need to see is the view seen not just through their own eyes, but through the eyes of fellow crewmembers, customers, and coworkers who have their hands on the flight operation. Their perspectives and their viewpoints will paint in the corners of the picture that lie outside a pilot's peripheral vision. They will fill in the details the pilot cannot see from the angle of the left seat. Bringing all of those viewpoints together creates the big picture of operational reliability.

Chapter 10 Notes

1. Take care to properly confirm IATA city codes with actual ICAO airport codes, as well. Particularly for non-U.S. destinations, these IATA codes look nothing like their ICAO match. A good example is Belfast International Airport, in Belfast, Northern Ireland, UK. The IATA code is "BFS" and the ICAO code is "EGAA".

11

You Can't Leave Home Without Them

Ask any professional pilot where they started in the industry and you will get a myriad of responses. But many of the answers will have commonalities. Setting aside the fliers who got their wings from the military, you will have a group of aviators who learned to fly in the private sector, either from a college or university, a flight school operator, or a fixed base operator. Besides attaining their certificates and ratings, most aviators also gained some experience working on and around airplanes. Whether it was adding gas and oil, towing, parking, or loading aircraft, many pilots can attest to their work on the ramps and in the hangars.

So it should come as no surprise to any aviator how important ground services are to the day-to-day, and really to the flight-to-flight, operations of the commercial aviation industry. Ground services extend behind the flight lines, as well, to maintenance, operations, and facilities.

DON'T LEAVE HOME WITHOUT IT

American Express® used to run a popular advertising campaign with the slogan, "Don't leave home without it." That same slogan really rings true for most ground services. Fuel and oil is a no-brainer, and one would hope that every pilot makes double, even triple-check, certain that they have adequate fuel or other consumables for flight. The fact of the matter is that aviation history is littered with accidents and incidents due to fuel exhaustion that could have been prevented with appropriate preflight action.

It doesn't seem that hard: You look down at the fuel gauges and see if there is enough fuel to make the trip, and if not you get more, right? Well that depends on two major factors: 1) how accurate is the fuel quantity reporting system, and 2) how much do you *really* need to make the trip? First, let's tackle the accuracy question.

The next time you engage in some hangar flying or shop talk with your flying buddies, run this question by them: "Who knows what the regs say about how accurate fuel gauges should be?" Invariably, somebody will answer with, "The regs require that the gauge be accurate only when reading empty." Think about that answer for a second. How unnerving is it? This misunderstanding of the FARs is prevalent; for some reason the concept that fuel gauges should only have to be accurate when empty was woven into our flight school urban legendry long ago. Some instructors will argue that since most piston aircraft have gauges that work on a float-sensor type system, accuracy is limited in turbulent air when the fuel is sloshing around in the tanks. It's true that the floats will hit bottom when the tanks are dry, and the gauge will definitely read zero, but guess what? There will be another very clear indication that fuel is gone!

14 CFR §23.1337 is very straightforward in its approach on the accuracy of fuel gauges. It reads,

> (b) Fuel quantity indication. There must be a means to indicate to the flightcrew members the quantity of usable fuel in each tank during flight. An indicator calibrated in appropriate units and clearly marked to indicate those units must be used. In addition: (1) Each fuel quantity indicator must be calibrated to read ''zero'' during level flight when the quantity of fuel remaining in the tank is equal to the unusable fuel supply...

So, the regulations *do* clearly require that the gauges are supposed to indicate usable fuel "during flight." Not just when on the ground when the tanks are being filled and the plane is still. Furthermore, the subparagraph that gave rise to the hangar talk of "only accurate when at zero" has a much more distinctive purpose. Every aircraft has some amount of "unusable fuel"—fuel caught in the bottom of the tanks, fuel in lines, etc. When the amount in the tanks equals the amount of unusable fuel—in level flight—then the gauges must read "zero."

So have we solved the accuracy problem? Not by a long shot. Notwithstanding the FARs and the hangar talk, aviators shouldn't completely rely on fuel gauges. This is because fuel gauges (like any aircraft component) can, and will, fail. Pilots are taught to compute fuel quantities (both fuel required and fuel used) by multiplying the fuel burn and the time. Modern flight management systems (FMS/FMC) do the same thing. The fuel quantity inputted to some FMS comes from pilot input, not directly from a gauge. In the name of redundancy and double-cross-checks, savvy pilots utilize the fully computed flight plan, the FMS calculations, *and* the fuel quantity indications to keep track of how much gas they have at any point in time. Going by the gauges alone simply is not enough.

Rewinding a bit, this chapter focuses on ground services. In terms of fuel, it's important to discuss what to be vigilant about when your plane needs to be refueled. First off, I'm going to assume that you as a pilot-in-command will require fueling at every stop you make, and that cost is no object to you (and truthfully, it shouldn't factor much in your decision of where to buy fuel, since pricing is pretty consistent within a market). You should be 100-percent interested in two things from your fueler: safety and accuracy.

Safety includes paying attention to little things that could become big things if there is a malfunction, mistake, or accident. Is equipment properly maintained, marked, and operated? Is there a spill kit or station? Does the operator use the kill or "dead man's" switch when fueling? Is the aircraft being properly bonded during the refueling process? There are numerous regulations and specifications that aircraft refuelers must adhere to. Safe pilots know the basics and remain vigilant for any deviation from the norm during refueling procedures.

For the sake of accuracy, ask your refueler for a fuel slip or fuel report upon completion of the refuel. The fuel slip is a simple report showing the starting fuel and ending fuel indications, as well as the dispenser meter start and stop readouts. The values can be easily compared to show that an accurate fuel load was dispensed into the aircraft. If you need some anecdotal evidence on why fuel slips are crucial in verifying accuracy, read about the crash of Tuninter Flight 1153.[1] The captain was sentenced to ten years in prison for manslaughter because (among other failures) he never got a fuel slip!

NOT YOUR AIRPLANE, STILL YOUR BABY!

If you have ever been around a birthing center or a hospital's newborn wing, you know how the nurses act when handling other people's babies. They hold, caress, feed, bathe, and care for the children as if they are their own. (If you have had a different observation, you probably need to switch hospitals!) The concept—and really the human instinct—is natural and straightforward. Infants are delicate and need protection. Therefore, people who are entrusted by an infant's parent to care for the child are extremely protective and careful when carrying out their charges. They sometimes do a better job than the parents! It is not uncommon to hear nurses call someone else's child "their baby" in the course of their duties.

The majority of commercial aviators are flying aircraft that they do not own. In fact, most airlines themselves don't even "own" their aircraft, but rather lease them from the banks who are the true owners of the ships. Some airlines lease airplanes from other airlines. But regardless of who owns the airplane, safe pilots operate much like the nurses do. They treat the aircraft they are operating as their own—their baby.

Believe it or not, such a manner of operating is not natural for many aviators. This could be for many reasons. Perhaps the plane isn't the pilot's "favorite" to fly, or maybe they are unhappy with their job in the first place. It could even be that they just don't have a great deal of respect for property. In any case, the fact remains that not only is treating the airplane with that level of respect a common courtesy to the actual owner, but it is also a matter of safety.

One of the most relevant situations in which this attitude can literally save the day is during ground handling operations. Loading and unloading, fueling, catering, servicing, and pushback operations present a unique hazard to the PIC. None of these tasks are the PIC's to accomplish, but the safety of flight is the PIC's responsibility. Just as the nurses go into overly protective mode with other people's infants, pilots must also become overly protective of their ship when it's being handled by others. If you see someone kicking a tow bar into place, stop them. If you see bag handlers tossing bags into the cargo bin, stop them. If you see a caterer driving up to the service door without a wingwalker, stop them. If your pushback crew is about to jackknife the nose gear—stop them!

Some pilots are content to allow mishaps to occur so that the guilty party can "learn a lesson." Is that safe or right? Of course not, and the ramifications of inaction can be severe. When others lack professionalism, pilots are looked upon to pick up the slack and set a proper example. Pilots are responsible. They are *pilots-in-command* and are counted on for leadership by their coworkers and customers—onboard, above wing, and below wing.

LEAVING MAINTENANCE TO THE PROS

Pilots are, for the most part, mechanically inclined. Not only is it a part of their training to have a basic understanding of mechanics and aircraft maintenance, it is just part of their nature. Pilots tend to be gear heads, grease jockeys, and techies. There are many things that they technically understand in the myriad of aircraft systems, but without the proper training and certification, they are not aircraft mechanics.

So many times, however, the line between mechanic and pilot gets blurry. 14 CFR Part 121 carriers with turboprop and turbojet aircraft, and all Part 135 and Part 125 operators, are required to utilize "master minimum equipment lists" (MMEL) under the operations specifications for their carrier. Approved by the FAA, the MMEL allows the carrier to operate aircraft with certain equipment deferred due to inoperability. Many MMEL items require some procedure for the inoperative equipment to be secured and deferred, and that is where sometimes pilots go into "mechanic mode."

The fact is that MMELs are not designed with the intent that air crew become substitute wrench turners. Crew and maintenance procedures should be clearly delineated in the MMEL, and the responsibilities are distinct. For a pilot to utilize a maintenance-only procedure in the MMEL would be akin to a fisherman doing a self-appendectomy while out at sea. Unless expressly allowed under a carrier's operations specifications, and under strict adherence to SOPs, pilots should not conduct maintenance procedures.

I once had an interesting scenario happen in a rural outstation in northwestern Minnesota. The armrest on the captain's seat became jammed into an upright position. Though it was out of the way (it didn't interfere with any flight controls, and flight deck egress was still possible), deferring an armrest on a flight deck seat is a maintenance-only procedure. The armrest is to be "secured" into an upright position that does not interfere with flight controls and egress, and must be acceptable to the crewmember occupying that seat. Ironically, the armrest was already secured in an upright position—it became jammed that way! But we, the flight crew, had no authority in handling the MMEL deferral of that arm rest. Instead, we had to call outstation contract maintenance. Since we were at a rural airport, and it was a Sunday when the local contract mechanics had the day off, getting a mechanic to the airplane just seemed impractical. Our outbound flight was delayed for over two hours to have that armrest deferred, just because it wasn't a crew procedure.

Such a story raises a good question: Why even write it up? Why squawk the airplane for something as innocuous as an armrest? Why not just wait until you can get the airplane into a maintenance base and then write it up?

The answer depends on where you want to blur that line between pilot and mechanic—and where you want your worth to be measured as a true pilot-in-command. As PIC, the captain must balance the whole operation when considering whether or not an inoperative piece of equipment will jeopardize the safety of flight. This includes certain passenger cabin items. How about a seat back that won't stay upright, or a tray table that won't stay locked? What if the exit row placard is degraded? Do you have placards on your boarding stairs that get scuffed to a point of becoming unreadable? When is the best time to get those things fixed—before or after a possible aircraft evacuation (which could be at any time)?

In the end, all pilots should agree upon these three points when it comes to aircraft maintenance:

1. When something is broken, degraded, or in need of replacement, it should happen sooner rather than later, and when possible, should be rectified immediately.

2. Aircraft maintenance procedures should be performed by qualified maintenance personnel at all times. No exceptions. "Paperwork deferrals" should be reviewed appropriately to ensure that no physical or mechanical type of procedure is required for the deferral. If you encounter an MMEL procedure that has you doing something you don't typically do (or have not been trained to do) as a pilot, *don't do it.*

3. If aircraft safety is ever in doubt—even if it is something that you think is easily remedied—follow procedure, squawk the plane, and leave it to the pros.

THE SURPRISINGLY ESSENTIAL NATURE OF GATE AGENTS

Once you become a seasoned air traveler or have worked in the airline industry for several years, you gain an appreciation for the often over-looked, often scorned, and clearly overworked gate agent. These professionals work long days, attending to the boarding and deplaning of several flights each day and ensuring customer needs are being addressed by acting as a crucial link to the airline. These people need to operate in a capacity that supports several tough roles.

In the eye of the general public, and many airline executives, pilots, and other industry professionals, their job seems trivial, even unnecessary. Airlines have researched alternatives to the venerable gate agent, trying to leverage automation to facilitate boarding.

Surprisingly enough, though we try to minimize their role from the point of view of the flight deck, gate agents are an essential resource for pilots-in-command. First and foremost, they are an important "hinge pin" kind of link for the entire flight operation. Here is a brief, non-exhaustive list of what these employees provide during a normal flight sequence (normal meaning a flight without some sort of emergency or non-emergency situation that interrupts the normal operation):

- Access to dispatch paperwork, airline resources
- Link to operations (above and below wing) to coordinate servicing
- Serve as last line of aircraft security pre-boarding
- Verify and board passengers, provide final count to crew
- Assist with special passenger needs/arrange and coordinate for special passenger services
- Jetbridge operator

And perhaps one of the most overlooked, but most vital role in airline executive's eyes, gate agents are very much responsible for on-time departures (which beget on-time arrivals, on which the airline industry gets rated for performance). Their actions at the gate determine the "countdown" to departure time where all loading and servicing tasks have to be completed both above and below wing before the aircraft can depart.

If an emergency or other abnormal situation—and in particular a security issue—occurs at the gate, the gate agent becomes a vital point person. Without going into another list here, let's suffice it to say that without their help, summoning emergency resources in an urgent manner can be challenging.[2]

Chapter 11 Notes

1. Agenzia Nazionale per la Sicurezza del Volo. *Final Report, Accident Involving ATR-72 Aircraft Registration Marks TS-LBB.*

2. Foreign carriers will often contract gate and ramp services to local airport service companies. This is highly prevalent in the European Union. What is remarkable about these contract providers is that they do *everything*. They run the gate, cleaning crew, loading crew, servicing crew, and oftentimes technical crew as well. And more often than not, there is a single person (oftentimes called a "dispatcher") who is in charge as the single point of contact between the flight crew and the operation services they provide.

12

Up in the Air—Understanding and Managing Your Schedule

Did you see the movie *Up In the Air,* starring George Clooney and Anna Kendrick? Clooney plays Ryan Bingham, a corporate downsizing specialist who travels around the country, hardly ever spending more than a single day out of each month in his own home. As a loyal American Airlines customer, he crosses the 10-million-mile mark over Dubuque, IA during one of his trips. American's Chief Pilot, Capt. Maynard Finch (superbly played by Sam Elliot), is aboard to honor him and present him with a special membership card—only the seventh ever made, he says. During their conversation, Capt. Finch asks Bingham where he is from. "I'm from here," Bingham pensively replies.

When pilots go to work, their world becomes much different from that of the ordinary, everyday, 9 to 5 worker. Due to the nature of the job, the airline pilot work schedule can become very non-traditional. Long stretches of time away from home, extended flights across multiple time zones, operations at all hours of the day, all in a high stress environment can make a pilot feel a long way away from home.

Additionally, the rules and regulations that govern how pilots are scheduled, rescheduled in cases of operational issues, and how much time they can be working overall come into play. If you are a newcomer to the industry, it is going to seem extremely complicated. If you are a veteran, you know you can never say "I've seen it all" because of the dynamic nature of the airline schedule. What you should be able to do, however, is have at least a basic understanding of how pilot schedules are constructed, develop a system, method, or routine to help you fly by the rules and maintain the quality of life you desire.

THE BASICS OF THE PILOT SCHEDULE

Most airline pilots today work under the terms of either a collective bargaining agreement, or under a similar non-union handbook, that stipulates flight and duty time limitations on pilot schedules. Because the rules under these agreements vary from carrier to carrier, it is important to learn your contract as best as you can. Your experiences from previous employers may be similar, but the variance between them is likely very large. And while reading legalese may not suit you so much, you owe it to yourself to read as much as you can, including various guides, manuals, newsletters, and the like, that the union or the carrier publishes to aid your understanding.

Underlying any workplace agreements is federal law. Part 117 is the part of the FARs that govern pilot schedules. I will give you a primer on Part 117 later on in this chapter, but for now, as we acquaint with the basics, understand that the rules in Part 117 are a backstop to anything in your contract, employee handbook, or scheduling guidelines, and compliance with them is mandatory. Therefore, I also encourage you to read Part 117 (it's not terribly long and you can keep a copy of it in your flight kit for good measure).

As we head into the nuts and bolts of scheduling, we need to have some common terminology available to us. Here are some terms you need to know:[1]

- *Trip, Pairing, ID, Rotation*—all of these words mean a combined set of duty periods, flights, and off duty periods that a crewmember is assigned to over the course of a day or several days.

- *Duty*—means any task that a flight crewmember performs as required by the airline, including but not limited to flight duty period, flight duty, pre- and post-flight duties, administrative work, training, deadhead transportation, aircraft positioning on the ground, aircraft loading, and aircraft servicing.

- *Flight Duty Period*—this is a period that begins when a flight crewmember is required to report for duty with the intention of conducting a flight, a series of flights, or positioning or ferrying flights, and ends when the aircraft is parked after the last flight and there is no intention for further aircraft movement by the same flight crewmember.

- *Line*—a schedule consisting of either Trips and/or Reserve Availability Periods, typically spanning a month.

- *Lineholder*—a pilot who has been awarded a Line consisting of Trips and days off.

- *Reserve*—a pilot who has been awarded a Line consisting of Reserve days and days off.

- *Reserve Availability Period*—a duty period during which an airline requires a pilot on short call reserve to be available to receive an assignment for a flight duty period.

- *Rest Period*—a continuous period determined prospectively during which a crew member is free from all duty. A rest period is scheduled for the purpose of rest, including sleep, but the rules don't dictate activity during a rest period (more on this later).

There are more terms, both informal and defined, that your carrier may use. But when we talk about how a pilot is scheduled, the above are the basic terms that describe the building blocks of a pilot schedule.

GETTING SCHEDULED

The first step in understanding your schedule is to know how you get a schedule assigned to you in the first place. Most operators today use some sort of bidding software for crewmembers to enter their selections or *bids* for a schedule. In the United States, airline crew rosters are typically sorted in seniority order, and a pilot's seniority governs practically everything they are afforded under the terms of their employment— rate of pay, schedule, vacation, advancement, and even some benefits are all dictated by a pilot's seniority.

In the case of scheduling, the most senior pilot is awarded their choice(s) first, then the next most senior pilot, and so on. Some carriers have what is called Line Bidding where pilots select pre-constructed schedules without input on what actual trips, flights, or duty periods are on the schedule. More common, however, is bidding via a Preferential Bidding System (PBS). Schedules awarded with PBS take into consideration the preferences of a pilot for flights, duty, days off, pay, layover length, and more. The PBS software builds and awards lines in accordance with the pilot's preference to the maximum extent possible. PBS is popular with pilots who like to have more control over what their schedule consists of, and is popular with airline management because the software maximizes the efficiency of the roster.

PBS can be hard to understand, unfortunately. Because you enter into the computer your preferences, it sometimes can be frustrating when somebody else gets what *you* asked for, and you didn't! In order to fully understand why PBS would do something like that in building a schedule, I would have to write a separate book. Instead, for our purposes here, I have five tips that will help you understand the basics of PBS – and this goes for any PBS system out there today.[35]

Tip 1: You are not the only bidder.

And this goes for you, too, number-one-most-senior person out there! In fact, the most interesting call I ever received when working at the PBS help desk was from the number-one-most-senior bidder in the airline at the time. He was having a fit about not getting exactly what he asked for. His problem, I pointed out, was that he wasn't bidding his preference based on what he didn't want (more on this later). But there was another concept he needed to grasp. PBS ensures that a legal scheduling solution can be built for every pilot out there—reserves too! This means that if your preferences (requests) are too constraining for the solution to be created, your preferences could get bypassed for the sake of the whole thing working.

This same advice can go for every bidder. This is called *solution constraint* or *global constraint*. An individual bidder's seniority allows their schedule to be built prior to someone who is junior to them, but their preferences will only be satisfied if the entire solution remains solvable with all contract and FAR legalities in compliance *for every pilot on the roster*. And, yes, once it gets down to the most junior bidder, the ability to satisfy that person's requests is quite narrow.

Tip 2: At the end of the day, the airline still has to have operational integrity.

Unfortunately, there will always be ugly trips out there. In fact, schedule quality has much more to do with the quality of each trip rather than the outcome of a PBS solution. I always refer to this as "garbage in, garbage out" when talking to crew planners. In other words, if the trips are undesirable, the schedules will be too, and pilots will end up bidding with more preferences to restrict the placement of garbage trips on their lines, bogging down the solver (the PBS software) on solution run-time.

But the thing is, even the garbage trips need to get assigned. Most PBS rulesets or contractual provisions require a *zero open time* solution, meaning that every trip gets assigned to a schedule. Some pilot groups enjoy the flexibility of allowing PBS to leave out some unassigned trips with the goal being a higher quality of schedules for the pilot group. It is a tricky balance, however, because those unassigned trips will likely be undesirable (hence why they don't get assigned). Open trips of a certain amount require heavier reserve staffing to cover if they are not picked up or assigned voluntarily to line holders.

The point is this: you are likely, especially if you are in the lower one-third of line holders, to have a trip awarded to you by PBS that you think is garbage. This isn't because PBS is horrible, but rather because the airline needs *someone* to fly those trips.

Tip 3: The PBS wants you to fly as much as you legally can!

Mathematically speaking (which is how PBS speaks), you score more points for getting a schedule that meets the parameters set out by the crew planners and the rules your PBS is governed by. These parameters include assigning all (if not most) of the flying for the month. So, it is pre-wired to give you trips you may not want. This is important to remember not only for maximizing days off, but also minimizing the award of undesired trips.

Tip 4: You need to say what you DON'T want first.

Because of the variety of PBS software being used today, I can't get into bidding details here, but this is an important point to make regardless of the system being used. When you bid, you need to express what you don't want to do before you ask for things you do want. This approach matches up with the overall problem PBS has to solve pretty well. PBS will assign you any legal trip you haven't ruled out with your preferences.

As a practical example, it is quite easy for a bidder who only wants to fly to Honolulu (HNL) to simply place that preference in their bid and nothing else. However, the bid needs to include the times the bidder doesn't want to fly to HNL. Said another way, make your priority in bidding the things you absolutely want to avoid. Let's take a look at an example wish list for this HNL flier:

- Only HNL trips
- Weekends off
- The 23rd of this month off for a wedding I'm in
- Max days off
- Only trips that get me home before 1400

Okay, with this list, we need to have some priority of must haves versus "I could let that slide." Let's say we ask this bidder to prioritize the list for us a bit, and she comes up with:

1. The 23rd of this month off for a wedding I'm in
2. Only HNL trips
3. Weekends off
4. Only trips that get me home before 1400
5. Max days off

Now we have a good template from which to build out our preferences. The bidder has clearly indicated with her ranking that the wedding she is in is a non-negotiable. Next is only HNL trips, weekends, commutability, and days off. What this means is that her bid should be constructed with preferences that are ranked in this manner: So long as she can get the 23rd off for that wedding, she is ok with a non-HNL trip, a weekend workday, a non-commutable trip, or an additional work day. Whether your system allows you to express this with points, ranking, or the ordering of avoid versus award statements, target your preferences in this manner.

Tip 5: Bid according to your seniority and WIN.

I think I have heard PBS trainers and help desk volunteers say "You have to be realistic" to disgruntled bidders hundreds of times. When they say it, they are speaking with bidders who are shooting for pie in the sky with their bids. When you bid for something that is unattainable at your level of seniority, and then have nothing to show for it, or worse end up with something you really didn't want, well…you're just wasting your bid.

Instead, figure out what is attainable at your level of seniority and aim for the best to be had there. Many PBS interfaces are able to provide you with good data on how your bid worked out in the grand scheme of things. Most carriers also publish the category reports for the bid (which shows how everyone else's schedule ended up). Use these reports and tools to your advantage. If you can't have all weekends off, how many per month can you get? What about partial weekends mixed with full weekends? What are bidders just senior to you getting? How about the bidders just junior to you? If any of them are getting trips or days off you didn't bid for but would have been happy with, there is a 99 percent chance you need to change your bidding strategy.

* * *

Once you get your schedule for the month, it is a good time to start thinking and planning ahead. Where will you be flying? If your time off balanced with your time at work? If you commute, does your schedule allow for you to make it to work in time to start your trips? Most importantly, is there adequate time to rest and recharge between trips – or during the trips themselves?

REST IS KING—THE ADVENT OF 14 CFR PART 117

It cannot be stressed enough: Layovers are created to provide crew rest. The new Flight and Duty Limitations and Rest Requirements recently codified in the Federal Aviation Regulations (14 CFR Part 117)—also known as "Flight Time/Duty Time" regs—target the mitigation of crew fatigue directly.1 The first section following the definitions is "Fitness for Duty", and it says:

> "Each flightcrew member must report for any flight duty period rested and prepared to perform his or her assigned duties." —14 CFR §117.5(a)

While common sense may dictate that crew members naturally should want to fly when well rested and prepared, the FAA's rule-makers wanted a headline rule that demonstrated the importance of being rested and prepared for duty as a shared concern of both pilots and operators. To wit, when the final rule language rolled out, the FAA said in their explanatory documentation:

> Section 117.5(a), in conjunction with the other provisions of this rule, places a joint responsibility on the certificate holder and each flightcrew member. In order for the flightcrew member to report for a [Flight Duty Period] properly rested as required by this section, the certificate holder must provide the flightcrew member with a meaningful rest opportunity that will allow the flightcrew

member to get the proper amount of sleep. Likewise, the flight-crew member bears the responsibility of actually sleeping during the rest opportunity provided by the certificate holder instead of using that time to do other things.

So practically speaking, what does this mean for you when you check in for a layover? Prior to January 4, 2014, crews operating under Part 121 had very little guidance, protection, or rights when it came to getting a good night's sleep while out on a trip. In fact, even the most liberal union contract provisions, which several airline pilot groups negotiated to cover the wide gaps in rest and duty limits under the FARs, still did not fully protect a pilot from disruptions to a natural sleep cycle that were completely out of the pilot's control.

If a pilot was scheduled for a minimum "reduced rest" overnight of eight hours, and arrived just in time to get in about seven hours of actual sleep, the pilot was lucky...unless of course a fire alarm goes off, or there is a tornado warning, or the heat goes out in the middle of the night, etc. In these cases, the pilot's sleep was disrupted with only one recourse, taken reluctantly: the fatigue call.

Calling in fatigued was a hard sell for the airlines and the pilots. Pilots are mission-oriented. They want to get passengers to their destinations. In that quest for mission completion, however, fatigue had become all-too-often ignored. Pilots, sure of their ability to dump copious amounts of coffee or energy drinks down their throats in an effort to combat fatigue, have *for decades* been flying airplanes when not properly rested.

Then on February 12, 2009, a Q-400 operated by Colgan Air aerodynamically stalled and crashed into a house while on approach to Buffalo, New York, killing all 49 occupants and one person on the ground. One of the findings of the NTSB (which put the entire accident cause on pilot error) was that "The pilots' performance was likely impaired because of fatigue." Colgan 3407 certainly was not the first, or the last, flight to be operated by pilots struggling with fatigue. However, it was the flight that made everyone "wake up" to the severe problems of fatigue and the lack of sensible regulations regarding crew rest that exist in the United States.

Due to tremendous pressure from the families of Colgan 3407 victims, and efforts of the Air Line Pilots Association, International (ALPA), the NTSB, and the FAA, Congress enacted law under House Bill H.R.

5900 and Public Law P.L.111-216 that have now fundamentally changed the way the airline industry handles fatigue. The rules matter now.

14 CFR PART 117: THE BASICS OF FATIGUE MANAGEMENT (I.E., GET SOME SLEEP!)

There really is no better way to describe the FARs governing crew rest, duty limits, and fatigue than this: *It is against the law to not get a decent amount of sleep prior to any flight duty period.* As mentioned above, one of the most paramount parts of 14 CFR Part 117 is section 117.5—Fitness for Duty. It's worth repeating this extremely important code that all pilots need to take special heed of:

> *Each flightcrew member must report for any flight duty period rested and prepared to perform his/her assigned duties.*

It can't be said any more plainly than that, but just to be sure, the rule makers also added these sections to 117.5:

(b) No certificate holder may assign and no flightcrew member may accept assignment to a flight duty period if the flightcrew member has reported for a flight duty period too fatigued to safely perform his or her assigned duties.

(c) No certificate holder may permit a flightcrew member to continue a flight duty period if the flightcrew member has reported him or herself too fatigued to continue the assigned flight duty period.

(d) As part of the dispatch or flight release, as applicable, each flightcrew member must affirmatively state he or she is fit for duty prior to commencing flight.

Parts b, c, and d are where the rubber meets the road for the airlines regarding fitness for duty. A fatigued pilot cannot work a flight duty period (meaning, they can't even report with the intention of moving an airplane) if the level of fatigue mitigates safe performance of duties. Nobody should be trying to split hairs with §117.5(b) and (c). Instead, if a crewmember is fatigued, that pilot must (1) not report for flight duty, and (2) the airline must not assign the pilot flight duty. That's it. No quibbles over, "well maybe just one more leg to get home," or "please do us a favor and get the plane to a hub." If a pilot is fatigued, end of story—they must *go to bed.*

The rule makers wanted to make fitness for duty something so important, so vital to safety, that a pilot is now required to "affirmatively state he or she is fit for duty" when accepting the dispatch or flight release. Each carrier will have their own procedure to comply with this provision, but no matter the mechanics or techniques used, the essence of §117.5(d) is that each pilot is now required to sign off on their own fitness for duty. Even if the procedure each pilot uses is somehow automated or computerized, think of it this way: *for each flight they conduct, pilots must sign their name to a statement affirming they are fit for duty.*

14 CFR §117.25 (Rest Period) requires that a pilot has a minimum of 10 hours of rest prior to commencing a reserve or flight duty period (FDP), and the 10-hour rest period must provide the flightcrew member with a minimum of 8 uninterrupted hours of sleep opportunity. *The upshot is to make sure you know how much rest you are supposed to get when you start the layover.* If you aren't getting enough time to rest, rectify the matter with your crew scheduling resources immediately.

THE REST OF THE REST RULES: 14 CFR PART 117 FATIGUE MITIGATION AND RISK MANAGEMENT

Moving on through 14 CFR Part 117, it contains whole host of requirements and limitations that are designed to specifically mitigate pilot fatigue. Highlights include:

- Each carrier must have a Fatigue Risk Management Plan (FRMP) that includes crew education and awareness training, a reporting system, a system for monitoring crew fatigue, and systems in place for reporting and performance evaluation of the overall Fatigue Risk Management System (FRMS).

- The crew education program on fatigue must be updated (and approved by the FAA) every 2 years.

- Daily flight time limits are based on whether or not a crew is augmented (i.e., no differences between domestic, flag, and supplemental), and depend on what time of day the pilot begins the flight duty period.

- Cumulative flight time limits are now calculated on a rolling basis: 100 hours flight time in any consecutive 672 hours;

1,000 hours flight time in any consecutive 365 calendar day period.

- Cumulative limits on duty time (in conjunction with the new FAR-defined "Flight Duty Period"): 60 FDP hours in any consecutive 168 hours; 190 FDP hours in any consecutive 672 hours.

- Rest periods are protected with a minimum duration of 10 hours between FDPs. That 10-hour period must provide a pilot an opportunity to get a minimum of 8 hours of uninterrupted sleep. (There are additional rest provisions that protect how much minimum rest is required if the pilot travels more than 60° longitude [i.e., a change in "theatre"] under different circumstances.)

- Regulation of "Consecutive Nighttime Operations"—also known as "high-speeds", "stand-ups", or "continuous duty overnights"—in terms of limits (no more than 5 if given at least a 2-hour rest period in suitable accommodations, otherwise no more than 3).

The balance of Part 117 puts together the regulatory framework intended to mitigate fatigue risk. From the cumulative flight time and duty time limits, to the training curriculum, to the monitoring and reporting systems, the rule makers took direct aim at the fatigue problem from key angles.

Evident to many pilots who operated pre-Part 117 was the lack of truly "hard" limits on flight and duty times. All the limitations entailed in 14 CFR Part 121 were applied on a "scheduled" basis. Legality was an exercise in academic theory rather than practical reality. Thus, the industry became accustomed to the phrase, "legal to start, legal to finish," meaning that if a pilot could look at his schedule prior to releasing the parking brake and determine that on a scheduled basis, he would be within legal limits for flight and duty under 14 CFR Part 121, he could continue with the flight assignment.

Part 117 doesn't just relegate "legal to start, legal to finish" to the history books; rather, it turns the whole idea on its head. A pilot, even before entering the flight deck in most cases, will now be required to determine legality on a prospective, hard-limits-applied approach to the operation as it will occur. Specifically for flight time limits, 14 CFR §117.11(a) states:

No certificate holder may schedule and no flightcrew member may accept an assignment or continue an assigned flight duty period if the total flight time:

(1) Will exceed the limits specified in Table A of this part if the operation is conducted with the minimum required flightcrew.

(2) Will exceed 13 hours if the operation is conducted with a 3-pilot flightcrew.

(3) Will exceed 17 hours if the operation is conducted with a 4-pilot flightcrew.

When Part 117 rolled out, several questions were raised to the FAA's rule makers about how this looks from an operational perspective. The FAA's response was generalized as follows:

> ...if a flightcrew member finds out before takeoff that the flight segment that he/she is about to fly will cause him/her to exceed the flight time limits, that flightcrew member may not take off. It does not matter if the flightcrew member acquires this knowledge after taxi out because, as the preamble to the final rule explains, until the flightcrew member actually takes off from the airport, that flightcrew member is still able to return to the gate without a diversion. Accordingly, if a flightcrew member finds out after taxi out but before takeoff that the flight segment that he or she is about to fly will cause him/her to exceed the pertinent flighttime limit, that flightcrew member must return to the gate.[2]

Of interesting note here is the care and attention to the point-of-time in the flight operation sequence that the FAA gave in their answer. If something changes while the crew is moving the aircraft under its own power (ground delay programs, weather, mechanical, etc.) that will cause a crewmember to exceed their limit, it's game over and a gate return is required for a re-crew. This explanation puts the final dagger to "legal to start, legal to finish."

This same clarity can be applied to the duty limitations as well. It can be reasonably said that there will be many instances where pilots will be required to "think again" about their legality under the new rules. The flight time limit can be exceeded per 14 CFR 117.11(b), which stipulates that once the pilot reaches the destination or destination alternate, they are done. While that may give some pilots the idea that an air carrier will schedule crews right up to the "foreseeable minute" of the limitations, the FARs have the flight crewmember's back. In order to keep the rules in check and ensure enforcement, any exceedances are required to be reported to the FAA. Specifically, 14 CFR §117.11(c) states:

> (c) Each certificate holder must report to the Administrator within 10 days any flight time that exceeded the maximum flight time limits permitted by this section or §117.23(b). The report must contain a description of the extended flight time limitation and the circumstances surrounding the need for the extension.

These "teethy" requirements burdened upon the airlines lead down an even more regulated and supervised program road: the Fatigue Rest Management System (FRMS). Airlines that request exemptions or changes in how their flight crews operate under Part 117 rules must develop an FRMS through data collection and research. Through cooperation of pilot groups and labor leaders, FRMS development across the industry is quickly and positively taking shape.

The FRMS for each carrier will be unique and likely will be driven by the carrier's culture. Although each FRMS will be customized to the carrier's culture and operations, the FAA has spelled out requirements for the FRMS. Under 14 CFR §117.7, the FRMS must include:

(1) A fatigue risk management policy.

(2) An education and awareness training program.

(3) A fatigue reporting system.

(4) A system for monitoring flightcrew fatigue.

(5) An incident reporting process.

(6) A performance evaluation.

And of course, the FRMS must be approved by the FAA. Perhaps the most important portion of a FRMS is the education and awareness training program, which has its own set of requirements. 14 CFR §117.9 provides that carriers must provide annual training to their employees who work under Part 117. This includes crews, schedulers, dispatchers, operational control workers, and flight operations management. Naturally, the rule has curriculum requirements, including fatigue awareness, the effects of fatigue, and fatigue countermeasures (i.e., how to get a good night's sleep).

Airline FRMS have been taking shape as Part 117 has become the new normal for operators. In the global aviation marketplace, U.S. carriers have employed FRMS to obtain certain exemptions for long-haul and ultra-long-haul flight segments. Utilizing research assistance from universities and cooperative input from pilot group representatives, the successful outcomes from FRMS can generally be summarized as follows:

- *Fatigue Awareness Improves*—Under 14 CFR Part 117 we expect crews to become more aware of fatigue. This will be due not so much to the awareness training as to the impact of operational constraints versus rest opportunity. In other words, pilots will become more aware of their fatigue when, despite getting appropriate opportunities to rest, they become fatigued during operationally demanding flight duty periods.

- *Flight Safety Improves*—The requirement of each pilot to sign off on each flight segment will cause pilots to track their own limits more directly and accurately. This should drive pilots to fine-tune preflight planning in order to trap and mitigate errors or factors that could cause a flight time or duty limit to be exceeded. The elimination of the "legal to start, legal to finish" mantra puts a stop to "pilot pushing"—whether the push comes from the pilot himself or from the operator.

- *Schedule Efficiency Improves*—Operators will need to stretch crew resources under Part 117 in ways that have not been previously contemplated, but as staffing rightsizes to the operational constraints under the rules, schedules will become more efficient.

Under this part, an FRMS does not just give operators automatic relief from the standard flight, duty, and rest limits. The FAA has said that such applications have to "[provide] at least an equivalent level of safety against fatigue-related accidents or incidents as the other provisions of this part." The FAA has said, therefore, a "broad [request] will likely be more difficult to obtain than a narrow [request]."[3]

Since the implementation of Part 117, several pilots, organizations, and operators have written to the FAA seeking clarification and interpretation of these rules. Part of the inquiries have to do with the "newness" of the rules themselves. As pilots started operating under Part 117, the new terms, calculations, and functions that were required needed some backup for true understanding of the rulemakers' intent. Another focus of the inquiries was on the fact that operationally speaking, not all rules perfectly fit every flight. FRMS has proven helpful in these cases, as well. In conjunction with the FAA, operators can seek operational feasibility when an interpretation could possibly stand in the way of how a segment has traditionally operated, and done so safely.

Keep up to speed on these interpretations by visiting the FAA's website and downloading the interpretation letters. However, don't make the mistake of re-interpreting the interpretations. Even though the FAA's lawyers write the letters, they do seek technical and operational input from experts. You will find that if you read the letters carefully, explicit instruction on how to read and interpret different rules in Part 117 are clearly provided.

SCHEDULE MANAGEMENT

I want to share a framework I use to manage my schedule. It is very straightforward and helps me achieve the best quality of life I can be afforded by my schedule, maximize my compensation, and maintain my health.

- Step 1: Analyze
- Step 2: Modify
- Step 3: Plan
- Step 4: Operate

Step 1: Analyze

When I get my schedule, the first thing I do is look it over as a whole. How many days off was I awarded? How many days off between work spans are there? Is the schedule constructed with a regular pattern (e.g., four days of work followed by three days off, followed by another four days of work, and so forth)? What about my specific day off requests for my personal life commitments—were those requests honored? How much pay credit is it worth and how much actual flying will I do?

After that overview, I dig into the individual trips. I look at the cities I will fly to, the layovers, the time between flights, and the equipment I will fly. Every pilot has specific likes and dislikes, so this review is very personalized. Do I want trips that are efficient (six to eight hour flying days followed by 12 hour layovers) or do I want trips that offer less flying with long layovers? I also look for possible conflicts with my personal schedule, my commutes to and from base prior to and following each trip, and my opportunities for rest.

Taking all of this into consideration, I make the decision to try to modify the schedule by entering the trip-trade process, or to be satisfied with what I have been awarded.

Step 2: Modify

Trip trading is a scheduling benefit that is offered everywhere. It is not any different from trading shifts in other vocations, but the regulatory nature of flight time and duty limits can create obstacles. Each airline operates their own version of trip trading, and it will be incumbent upon you to learn the system yours offers. But one thing remains common among all trip trade procedures—it is the *only* way to affect changes to your schedule after the bid award.

For me, I try to work out several ways to enhance and improve my schedule every month. I look for combinations of trading trips on the same days, different days, dropping trips, and adding trips—and I engage in this process most fervently in the weeks leading up to the start of the bid month in hopes of settling my schedule once-and-for-all before the month commences.

As the month progresses, I take a more relaxed approach, typically only trading vertically (i.e., trading one trip for another on the same span of days) to improve trip quality or pay, as I likely have made personal commitments on my days off. Some pilots, however, remain aggressive through the month, always trading for better quality of life, pay, or both. It can be a lot of work, and you have to be engaged nearly constantly with open trip alerts, and the trading system itself. The choice is yours, and the opportunities can be fantastic at times, particularly when new trips (like charters, special ferry segments, or reassigned flying from irregular operations) become available to trade with.

Step 3: Plan

For each trip I intend to keep and operate, I pre-game plan the way life surrounding and during the trip will look like. This includes my rest prior to the trip, my commute to base, my activities during layovers, eating schedule, exercise, and sleep times.

Some might say this is a bit much. But there is a wise adage that says if you don't schedule something, it won't get done. Scheduling things like when I eat, exercise, or sleep might seem odd. There are many pilots who, rather than taking time to schedule their layover routine, simply have a regular sequence of events in mind. For example:

1. Arrive at layover hotel
2. Get a "quick" workout in
3. Get some food
4. Watch something on Netflix
5. Go to bed when I get tired
6. Wake up around two hours before shuttle pickup
7. Shower, morning routine, etc.
8. Grab a coffee and a light breakfast at coffee shop if I have time
9. Head to airport

Putting that plan on repeat on every layover makes it, by definition, a routine. There is nothing wrong with said routine, but when I look at a scheduled layover, I want to make sure I am prioritizing proper exercise, eating, and sleeping. That requires me to be more precise with my layover schedule. Here is a sample for a 14 hour 30 minute layover (released from duty 15 minutes after arrival and reporting 45 minutes prior to departure):

1. 1530—Flight scheduled to arrive
2. 1600—Arrive hotel, check in, settle in
3. 1630-1730—In hotel gym for workout 16:30-17:30
4. 1800-1930—Eat
5. 2000-2200—Netflix/wind down/evening routine
6. 2200—Lights out
7. 0600—Wake, morning routine, shower, etc.
8. 0700—Coffee, breakfast
9. 0800—Shuttle to airport
10. 0815—Report time
11. 0900—Departure

Now I have a *planned layover*. The times ensure I have adequate margin in my 14:30 of freedom to hit my priorities—exercise, food, and rest. Instead of a "quick" workout, I schedule myself an hour. Rather than getting to sleep when I get tired, I commit in the plan to have lights out by 22:00 and wake by 6:00. Eight hours—just what Part 117 requires.

Will I sleep the whole time? Not likely, as I am more a seven hours of sleep person. But I have to give myself the opportunity to get that eight hours. Eating wise, I again have carved out sufficient time to eat healthy, without rush, and not right before I am going to sleep.

Step 4: Operate

During a trip I continually re-evaluate my schedule given how the trip is working out. If I experience delays, have a flight cancel or reschedule, or otherwise have my plans from the previous step disrupted, I need to adapt. Any changes that are forced upon me and that affect my big three priorities (sleeping, eating, and exercise) need to be addressed with a revised plan. Typically when time during a layover is reduced, my eight-hour window for sleep takes precedence over anything else. Once I get that locked into my schedule, other items can fall into place depending on how the delay or reschedule maps out. For example, if the flight to my layover is delayed 2 hours, I could decide to eat prior to my flight rather than waiting for the layover. The point here is that during the Operate step in this framework, everything remains dynamic.

YOUR "PERSONAL" FATIGUE RISK MANAGEMENT PLAN

As we've seen, Part 117 has put the onus on both pilots and management to manage the risks associated with fatigue. While carriers are required to have more structure and scrutiny under the rules, pilots simply check a box (or sign the release, or otherwise certify) that they are "fit for duty." Just because the FARs don't prescribe the steps pilots must take to manage their fatigue, pilots should not think they are immune to the scrutiny of the FAA. Therefore, why not develop your own "personal" Fatigue Risk Management Plan (FRMP)?

The pilots-in-command personal FRMP has four main components:

1. Learn how to sleep properly.
2. Keep track of your flight and duty times.
3. Schedule work (and life) with an eye on fatigue.
4. Pass on your knowledge and learn from others.

Learn How to Sleep Properly

We have heard of and read about studies on our sleep habits across the Western world. The National Sleep Foundation (NSF), in its 2011 Sleep Survey, found that "43% of Americans between the ages of 13 and 64 say they rarely or never get a good night's sleep on weeknights. More than half (60%) say that they experience a sleep problem every night or almost every night (i.e., snoring, waking in the night, waking up too early, or feeling un-refreshed when they get up in the morning.) About two-thirds (63%) of Americans say their sleep needs are not being met during the week."[4]

Pilots know that sleeping at home is tough enough. Sleeping on the road, however, is a monumentally difficult task. The National Sleep Foundation surveyed transportation workers, pilots included, in 2012 and confirmed this:

About one-fourth of train operators (26%) and pilots (23%) admit that sleepiness has affected their job performance at least once a week, compared to about one in six non-transportation workers (17%). Perhaps more disturbingly, a significant number say that sleepiness has caused safety problems on the job. One in five pilots (20%) admit that they have made a serious error...due to sleepiness.

The NSF goes on to report that 50 percent of the pilots they surveyed said they were dissatisfied with their sleep, and rarely or never get a good night of sleep while at work.[5]

Despite the fact that these statistics were from surveys prior to 14 CFR Part 117 rest rules for pilots, the challenges to being able to sleep while on the road (and at home) remain the same. Part 117 gives pilots the time to sleep. It is up to the pilot to make the best of it!

Here are some simple steps you can take to improve your sleep habits:

1. Plan your bedtimes ahead of time—and stick to the plan!

Many pilots receive their flight assignments well enough in advance that they will know when to reasonably expect to be in a position to sleep. Plan your layover activities so that you get at least eight hours of uninterrupted sleep. Studies show that pilots receiving less than eight hours of sleep are more at risk for fatigue.

If you get into a layover at 1700, and will show for duty the next day at 0600, you have to be disciplined to make sure to get to bed no later than 2100. (This assumes you will rise at 0500 and give yourself an hour to get ready in the morning.) But add in dinner upon arrival and breakfast in the morning, and perhaps a quick run on the treadmill in the hotel workout room, and now you are pushing things.

Furthermore, if you end up on a "reduced rest" overnight, or if due to circumstances beyond your control will end up with your planned sleep time more than four hours delayed (or eliminated), you are at high risk for fatigue. This is important to remember under Part 117: the rules are there to make sure you get the sleep you need. Let's say, for example, that a fire alarm goes off in the middle of your sleep period. That sleep period just got eliminated. Contact scheduling to let them know.

Another consideration that must be factored in is that of time zone changes. While Part 117 does not stipulate that you enter into a new "theater" of operation until traveling more than 60° of latitude, you can still travel just under that distance and traverse at least six time zones. Without the chance to get "acclimated" to the new time zone (for example, if you have less than 36 hours of rest period in the time zone), you need to be highly cognizant of how the traversing of time zones take a toll on sleep habits and threatens fatigue. Naps are essential if you plan to schedule other events during your layover. For example, if you fly from New York to Dublin, you will arrive five hours ahead of New York time. If that arrival time is 0800 in Dublin, it is 0300 is New York, and your body is smack-dab in the middle of its primary "Window of Circadian Low" (WOCL) and it thinks it should be sleeping! You have a 25-hour layover, with your flight back scheduled to push back at 0900 the next day. The problem is, if you hit the rack for 8 or 9 hours, you wake up at dinnertime and will have trouble sleeping later that night to rise the next day to fly back. Your WOCL hasn't changed. But your work schedule has!

This problem can be tackled in several different ways. A nap plus a long sleep seems to be a common technique. The trick is timing the nap correctly so as to get enough REM-based sleep to cover the WOCL gap, be able to wake, and then commit to a normal-length sleep (eight hours or so). So long as you make a sensible plan and stick to it, you should have no problem getting adequate rest prior to the next flight duty period.

2. Make sure your sleep space is comfortable.

Make a habit when you are checking into your hotel room to ensure that your bed will be clean and comfortable, that the room temperature and humidity level is going to be conducive to your sleeping preference, and that it is quiet. If not, lose no time in rectifying the situation with hotel management. When sleeping away from home, you are typically behind the power curve when it comes to the level of comfort you are used to during your most restful sleep. Every hotel has different beds, feel, sounds, smells, and overall aesthetic that can distract you during sleep. In other words, even if you fall asleep, your mind can be kept "awake" by aesthetic distractions. If you wake up after eight hours of sleep feeling tired, or if you have trouble falling asleep, something is distracting you!

For many people, the biggest distraction is light. It has become more and more the norm, rather than the exception, for good hotels to be aware of the need for complete darkness in order for their patrons to sleep well. This is why such hotels will have blackout curtains, and perhaps clips or other devices to cover windows. Some air carriers have contracted with their hotel vendors to ensure dark rooms. But don't count on always having a dark space. Carry a sleep mask with you, and use it.

3. Don't go to bed hungry, thirsty, or overfull.

In addition to planning your bedtime, plan your meals accordingly, too. Trying to sleep on an empty stomach, or too soon after you eat, can keep you from having a comfortable sleep period. It is also important to go to bed hydrated, not thirsty. If you already subscribe to the formula of "eight glasses of eight ounces of water per day," you are on the right track. But remember, flying up at altitude, in the sun, causes flight crewmembers to need more water—so if you already had your eight glasses, have one more before turning in for the night.

4. Try to wind down.

If your schedule can muster it, have at least one hour before you go to sleep in which you engage in a quiet, relaxing activity. Exercise is the opposite of relaxing, so save the workout for the next day. Try to avoid computer and TV activity in the last 30 minutes before you fall asleep. Read a book, pray, meditate, or listen to some quiet, relaxing music. And please don't sleep with the TV on. Even though you may be asleep, your subconscious mind is still processing the noise and flicker of the TV.

5. Track your sleep habits and learn when your best sleep happens.

Several sleep specialists and medical professionals recommend keeping a logbook, diary, or journal of your sleep habits while in the quest for better sleep. Simply track the time you lay down, the time you rise (even if you wake up in the middle of your sleep), the total time in bed (i.e., attempting to sleep), and the factors that may (or may not) be affecting the quality of your sleep. This includes whatever food, caffeine, or alcohol you consumed prior to your sleep time; drugs or medications; and stress and emotions. Finally, track how well rested you felt when you awoke. Review the journal to find patterns that work and target habits that don't.

If you want to get more detailed, you can try tracking your actual sleep cycles—the rhythms of sleep that you go through after your eyes close and your conscience slips away. This will help pinpoint the details of what "good sleep" is for you. Particularly, you will be able to know when your deepest sleep occurs, or how long it takes you to enter into deep sleep and subsequent REM sleep cycles. Our most restorative sleep occurs just before the REM cycle, and occurs anywhere from 70–90 minutes after falling asleep.

Tim Ferriss, in his book *The 4-Hour Body,* experimented with tracking and recording his sleep cycles in order to fine-tune and "engineer" perfect nights of sleep.[6] One of his findings was that his "good sleep" nights were ones that were eight to ten hours in length, and were "most dependent on the ratio of REM-to-total sleep, not total REM duration." Our REM sleep stages lengthen as we continue on through our sleep. While the most restorative sleep occurs via deep sleep stages, to Ferriss more REM seemed to correlate to more restful sleep, and he also cited "better recall of skills or data acquired in the previous 24-hours."

While his experiments are not hard-core sleep research done by a physician, they do give a lot of credence to the idea that investigating and recording your sleep habits, stages, cycles, and results can give you an edge. I have tried it myself, and I am a believer. If you need the gadgets and apps to help you, there are several on the market. Just search online for "sleep trackers" and you will find them. I have found the most helpful ones not only track your sleep, but also can be set to wake you at the most opportune time to maximize restfulness and wakefulness.

6. Follow ALL of these tips at home!

If you follow a good sleep and rest routine at home, it will come naturally for you to do the same while on the road. Additionally, remember that the night prior to leaving for a trip is just as crucial for getting rest as while on the trip. Make sure you get all of your packing and preparation for the trip completed in time to have a full night of sleep prior to heading to the airport in the morning.

Keep Track of Your Flight and Duty Times

Some pilots keep a logbook regularly, others irregularly, and many not at all. Logbook apathy happens when we get settled in with a good employer and know that our flight histories are all being tracked by the employer anyway. So why bother?

14 CFR Part 117 has put a new emphasis on the personal accountability of pilots and their statement before every flight that they are fit for duty. This is not just a proclamation of being "not fatigued"— it is also a declaration that you have determined, personally, that you are legal to accept the flight assignment. You can argue all you want that your carrier's crew scheduling department should be looking out for you, or that the computer programs they use should prevent illegal flight assignments from happening. These are all great assumptions, but in the end, you are still in charge of your own assessment.

It is time to start up the logbook habits again if you have stopped. As a pilot, you once logged time to track currency, attain new certificates and ratings, move towards upgrade, get to another job, etc. Now you need to log more than just time—you need to track flight duty periods and rest periods, and keep track on cumulative rolling timeframes rather than months, days, and years. The pocket-sized logbooks available throughout the industry will work for most of your needs. However, the available twenty-first century technology has become very useful. Consider using logbook software, or a smartphone logbook app. Recent versions of the most popular programs on the market have been adapted for 14 CFR Part 117, and some standalone "legality" calculators are already available, as well.

Keeping track of your flight and duty times will keep you safe, legal, and able to rest assured that you are in compliance with the FARs when you say you are fit to fly.

Schedule Work (and Life) With an Eye on Fatigue

In the U.S. airline industry, most schedules are awarded on a seniority basis. This allows the crewmember to exercise their seniority to bid for the flying they want to perform. Some pilots bid for work, and some bid for time off. Others focus on the quality of the flying and layovers, and others for overall quality of life.

Perhaps now with 14 CFR Part 117 bringing fatigue risk mitigation to the forefront, pilots will begin bidding trips and schedule characteristics for their rest qualities. Look for trips that give you appropriate times to rest given your personal sleep habits and cycles. Build schedule bids that maximize your time at home to recoup following trips that may leave you behind the rest curve.

The same can be said with your non-work related schedule. When returning home from long trips, you'll obviously want to maximize your time with family and friends, and take care of your personal life outside of the flight deck. Just make sure that your time at home doesn't leave you with a sleep or rest deficit prior to reporting for the next trip.

Pass On Your Knowledge and Learn From Others

I will never forget it. My first Atlantic crossing was Newark, New Jersey, to Shannon, Ireland. As we started talking about the layover ahead of us, one of the first things I asked my line check airman was, "What is the best way to deal with the time change and sleep?" He gladly answered my question, and lent some great advice. I continued to ask the same question of other pilots as I became more accustomed to trans-oceanic and trans-continental flying on the B757 and B767. I continue to learn more and more each day. It is no different than when I started flying "high-speeds"—continuous-duty overnight trips common in the regional airlines. I needed to learn how to fly late at night, sleep for four to five hours, fly at dawn, sleep more at home, and then repeat the sequence again the next night. As I became used to the cycles, the techniques, and how to balance them out with all other kinds of flying, I passed on what I learned to others.

I encourage you, as part of your Personal FRMP, to trade your best practices with fellow pilots. Learn what works and what doesn't through recommendations, augmented by your own experiences.

A Note on "Extracurriculars"

Pilots oftentimes get layovers that provide ample time for rest as well as leisure, and with the new Part 117 rules, it is believed that longer layovers will become more common. Arriving early afternoon for a twenty-hour layover is a choice opportunity to get together socially with your crewmembers, and as I said above, there certainly are times and places to do this appropriately. Exercise leadership and discernment when you head out with the crew. Be wise about transportation, location, and safety at all times. Hiking through back lots and down alleys to get to hole-in-the-wall local watering holes is less preferable to finding well-known and recommended establishments that the hotel can provide transportation to.

While you are out, be mindful of your actions. Locals can spot out-of-towners a mile away, and they are keen to wonder who you are and what brings you to town. Remember that you represent your employer at all times while on layovers. In addition, your crew will look to you for leadership, and your employer is counting on it. We all know how to have a good time without getting carried away, but if someone in your crew is having trouble knowing when to say when, it is your duty to step up and be both a leader and a friend to them.

SLAM, CLICK! CREW INTERACTIONS ON LAYOVERS

There are some workers in other professions that make a nightly habit of hitting the bar or coffee shop with a coworker after work. It is pretty common in today's society for business trips to turn into semi-tourist excursions. And when you think about the interpersonal dynamics of a flight crew—especially one that has "chemistry" and gets along wonderfully on the job—it should come as no surprise that layovers become prime times to have a little social interaction and unwind. It is human nature and is a good thing, when it happens at the right place, at the right time, and responsibly.

It happens every trip, every day, all over the world. A flight crew checks into a hotel, and the most important question (after, "What time is the van tomorrow?") seems to always be, "what are (we) (you) doing the rest of (today) (tonight)?" Some crewmembers have no problem handing a question like this, while others may feel pressured. No matter what your viewpoint, it seems impolite not to answer—and to some it seems impolite not to ask. But the reasons for these responsorial feelings are sometimes not so much personality-based as they are practicality-based.

Crew overnights are not the same as office workers' time after work. Crew overnights are intended for crews to rest and get recharged for the next duty day. So oftentimes, it truly is an evaluation of practicality that drives a crewmember's response to an invitation to get out of the hotel room for a bit. There is nothing wrong with this; actually, there is a whole ton of things right about it.

Over my years of experience as an airline pilot, the pejorative term "slam clicker" has been used time and time again to describe a crewmember known for being somewhat anti-social. The term is coined from two onomatopoeias—words that are made up of the sounds associated with them—in this case, the "slam" of the hotel room door and the "click" of the door's deadbolt lock.

Responsible, leadership-oriented pilots and crewmembers learn to recognize that "slam click" is not a term of necessary shame. Instead, they recognize that there is a time and place for social layovers. The key is setting your own personal boundaries and maintaining them. Here are some points to remember in setting those boundaries:

- Layovers are created to provide rest, not recreation.
- Activities you partake in on layovers will reflect both on you as a professional and on your employer.
- Taking a leadership role in setting the tone for the layover is key.

IN SUMMARY

Pilots have a love-hate relationship with layovers. When there is sufficient time to enjoy the locale, eat properly, rest, and feel prepared to head back to the airport, layovers are enjoyable. When time is scarce, sleep is difficult, and we feel the pressure of the job, we simply wish we were back at home. Either way, we are still at work. Keep a professional mindset about your layovers: take care of yourself, get appropriate rest, and you will remain ahead of the game.

Chapter 12 Notes

1. I have adopted (and slightly modified for clarity) most of these terms from 14 CFR §117.3. Some contracts, depending on how and when they were written, may have similar terms that are used colloquially at the carrier.

2. AD OPT, NAVBLUE, Jeppesen, SmartPref, AOS, and others have been around the industry for a long time, and all use practically the same logic and rulesets when it comes to building and awarding schedules.

3. Federal Register, Vol. 78, No. 43, 14 CFR Parts 117 and 121, Clarification of Flight, Duty, and Rest Requirements. (March 5, 2013)

4. Ibid.

5. National Sleep Foundation. "Annual Sleep in America Poll Exploring Connections with Communications Technology Use and Sleep," (press release): March 7, 2011. Retrieved at sleepfoundation.org/article/press-release/annual-sleep-america-poll-exploring-connections-communications-technology-use-

6. National Sleep Foundation. "Sleepy Pilots, Train Operators and Drivers," (press release): March 1, 2012. Retrieved at sleepfoundation.org/article/press-release/sleepy-pilots-train-operators-and-drivers

7. Ferriss, Timothy, The 4-hour Body (New York: Crown Archetype/Random House, 2010).

13

Safety

It may almost seem unnecessary for this book to contain a chapter dedicated to safety. Nearly everything here, cover-to-cover, points back to the practicality of operating safely. If you are a collegiate aviation student reading this book, you more than likely have taken (or will soon take) a class all about safety. If you are already in the airline industry, you know that safety is job number one simply by being a part of the operation. It is inescapable, for one simple and obvious reason: operating airplanes is dangerous work!

That may seem counterintuitive when you factor in the data on airplane accidents and incidents versus other land-based modes of transportation. It's commonly known that you have a higher risk of an accident or incident while driving to the airport than you do flying in an airplane. Not only is this currently a statistical fact, but as the years go on, the number of airplane accidents and incidents continues to decrease. Amazingly, even though demand for air travel continues to grow at a tremendous rate, and although the skies are becoming increasingly busier, and despite the twenty-first-century threats to air safety (drones, lasers, aging infrastructure), the statistics show flying is *getting safer.*

The International Civil Aviation Organization (ICAO) reported that in 2009, there were 4.1 accidents per million departures worldwide. That number dropped to 2.8 accidents per million departures in 2013. More exactly, the Flight Safety Foundation reported that 29 fatal airliner accidents occurred in 2013, resulting in 265 fatalities.[1]

These are big-sounding numbers, to be sure. However, comparing airliner fatality rates to automobile fatalities is a bit like comparing apples to oranges when you consider the number of vehicles on the road and the nature of driving itself. The comparison is also difficult because of the statistical measure used. Automobile fatalities in the United States in 2013 were 1.1 per 100 million vehicle miles traveled.[2] Airliners flew about 53 million hours in 2013, or about 21 billion miles. I'll spare you the math, but let's suffice it to say that when you start thinking this through, and trying to extrapolate various data points for comparison, it becomes clear: air travel, mile for mile, is indeed safer.

Where pilots-in-command can particularly excel in the craft of airmanship is the intentional focus on safety. To do so, you need to focus not only on the out-of-the ordinary things that can affect safety of flight, but on the normal everyday challenges that pose the most potential of harboring latent threats. In other words, an intentional focus on air safety doesn't mean training to dead-stick into the Hudson like Sully, but employing safe practices each moment on the flight line. Every phase of a flight operation, from preflight planning to engine shutdown and postflight, has the potential for threats and errors.

PREFLIGHT PLANNING

When you are a student pilot, especially one working on private, instrument, or commercial certifications, flight planning is huge. There is so much to think about and consider. You must pore over pages of charts, briefings, weather data, flight plans, pilot operating handbooks, and more with the simple intent to fly safely from Point A to Point B. Preflight planning was a big deal for me back in my "old days" of learning to fly. It continues to be so today.

14 CFR §91.103, "Preflight Action," says that "each pilot in command shall, before beginning a flight, become familiar with all available information concerning that flight." This paints a picture of the preflight planning operation using a pretty broad brush. The regulation goes into specifics for IFR flights and takeoff and landing distance performance.

In the airline environment, the requirements become much more detailed and specific. Several FARs outline different aspects of it, but practically speaking, it all comes down to what information is available to the pilot-in-command and the dispatcher. 14 CFR §121.533(b) states explicitly that, "The pilot in command and the aircraft dispatcher are jointly responsible for the preflight planning, delay, and dispatch release of a flight in compliance with this chapter and operations specifications."

Get into the habit of using a preflight planning process. Depending on where and when you do this, you could use some physical elements in your methodology. Many operators provide their pilots with a flight planning area with access to the Internet, charts, and other flight planning tools. Sometimes I do my preflight planning from the layover hotel, as I have access to weather briefing tools and have the ability to download my dispatch release and flight plan (if it has been prepared).

Prior to every flight, I have a consistent chain of tasks that I complete to prepare for the flight. For me, this starts with looking up pertinent flight status information: is the inbound flight on time, at what gate can I expect to meet the plane, what will the load be like, etc. Next, I do a high-level weather overview. I look at the general weather synopsis for the route, the current conditions at the departure airport, and the forecast for the arrival. From there, I can log into my company's pilot information app on my EFB and review additional flight information, certify my fitness for duty, and download the dispatch release and flight plan if it is ready. After I do my release review, I do a more detailed weather briefing using the weather app installed on my EFB. Lastly, I start setting up my EFB and chart selection in anticipation of the flight.

In Chapter 10, we covered dispatch release review, using the "SAMWISE" mnemonic to aid us in that task. But outside of the dispatch release and flight plan, what else can pilots effectively look at in the preflight process? Viewing it from the standpoint of safety (the subject of this chapter), additional considerations may come to mind. We can even employ the SEA-ICE mnemonic as we think it through:

- *Safety and Security*—What threats are present for this flight that directly impact safety and security? Are they being acknowledged and dealt with through your preflight plan? What is your plan to brief the other crewmembers about any of these threats? What responsibilities will you charge them with to deal with these issues?

- *Equipment*—If there are equipment deferrals for your flight, do operational requirements in the minimum equipment list (MEL) now become threats to the operation? This seems odd, as the MEL exists to ensure safe operations. So why would it be a threat? First, you have to ensure that MEL procedures have been properly complied with. If a piece of equipment is deferred under the MEL, actions will be listed in that particular deferral that crew need to be aware of and comply with. The same is true with the mechanics. Second, a particular deferral will prohibit certain flight operations. A great example is a deferred weather radar preventing flight into known or forecast areas of thunderstorms. In addition, some deferrals can impact performance. I recently flew a B767 that had a flap fairing missing, which gave us a single engine performance hit of 611 feet. It gave me pause for consideration...was that performance hit important? That day it was pouring rain in London, and although I was fairly certain the runway clear zones were free and clear of 611-foot obstacles, it was worth noting as a threat during my preflight briefing with the crew.

- *Abnormals*—Air carriers provide crews with memos or bulletins that highlight threats of an operational nature. These range from a sudden change in an approach procedure that didn't make the revision, to locations of staff security screening, to ground transportation considerations. At my airline, we receive bulletins about abnormal operation information all the time, and our dispatch release system is "rigged" so that we have to read and accept them before we can download our dispatch release and flight plan. When you read these memos, or become aware of an abnormal operational consideration, remember to properly check that your fellow crewmembers are in receipt of, or know about them, as well.

- *ICE (In case of emergency)*—How do we preflight plan for emergencies? There is not much we can plan for, other than ensuring that all other known threats are dealt with responsibly. Taking into consideration all the available information will aid significantly in uncovering latent threats and trapping errors. And we can do this from the comfort of a desk, before we head out to the aircraft.

WEATHER SAFETY

I don't know of many professions, other than meteorologists, that have the type of vocationally intimate relationship to the weather that pilots do. Some pilots get an instinct for weather as they get more experienced, and I have met several who could give any local weatherman a run for their money on predictions. I guess at some point pilots developed the talent to just read the skies.

Until each one of us gets to that level of weather acumen, we need to have a plan in place to properly review, understand, and respond to weather in the name of safety. This begins with waking up the morning of the flight and turning on the TV. Honestly, don't we get the best "big picture" weather briefing simply from watching the news or the Weather Channel? There is a reason that local news stations often do a "first look" weather report at the top of the newscast. People of all vocations, from mail carrier to stay-at-home parent, like to know what the weather will be in order to plan their day. Pilots should be Grade-A weather junkies, constantly looking for updates and refining the big meteorological picture that surrounds their flight operations.

The next important piece involves understanding what kinds of weather can become threats to the operation. This can vary depending on the type of flying you do, and the equipment you fly. Icing, low visibilities and obscuration, turbulence, and convective activity are often the chief culprits of these threats. And what's more, they affect your operations as much on the ground as they do in the air. You also must be wary of the rare occurrence of microburst activity and low-level wind shear.

But what about the "latent threats" posed by seemingly innocent meteorological phenomena? What about things like wind shifts, unique cloud patterns, temperature inversions, and the like? We see them happen and sometimes don't pay close enough attention to what they are telling us about the weather. An airborne wind shift can foretell turbulence, but it can also threaten our fuel endurance plan (or improve it). The appearance of altocumulus standing lenticular clouds on the horizon indicates possible performance-killing wave activity, or it can be the precursor to leeward-side convection. If we find a temperature inversion during climb or descent, we can almost always count on a change in the local weather, as well as the potential for turbulence, icing, and sudden sky condition changes to show up for the party, even if they weren't in the forecast.

This chapter will not be diving in depth into the adverse weather conditions listed above, except for turbulence (discussed in the following section). Understanding weather, especially adverse weather, and respecting the power contained in meteorological phenomena will make you a safer pilot. Many airline operators grant pilots excellent weather information, especially with the advent of EFB technology that allows access through high-quality apps. Much of this information comes from private and customized services from third-party and internal meteorological reporting and forecasting services. But even if you don't have access to good weather products via your employer, you have the wonderful resource of the Internet at your fingertips.

Turbulence

It should go without saying that a "smooth ride" is the goal of every aviator and the desire of every passenger. Light chop is annoying, moderate
turbulence is unnerving, and anything worse is absolutely dangerous.
Turbulence remains perhaps the most prevalent and concerning adverse
weather phenomena for pilots. Turbulence injuries continue to plague
air carriers, and their frequency will only decrease with pilot action.
Following are simple steps you can take with every flight to identify the
threat of turbulence and mitigate its impact.

1. *Get a Turbulence Forecast.* The issuance of an AIRMET for turbulence over your route of flight is a great start. But now there
   are good, real-time turbulence reporting and forecast products
   available. Several use advanced forecast products like the RPM
   model to give updates to the turbulence forecast plots every few
   hours.

2. *Be Proactive About Turbulence Avoidance.* On the ground, use your
   best efforts to route around, above, or below turbulence that
   is known or forecast. When dealing with convective weather,
   ensure you have the ability to give growing thunderstorms a
   wide berth. Whether you will be looking to avoid clear-air turbulence or convective turbulence, proper preflight planning
   action includes ensuring proper fuel for altitude and route flexibility. Once you are en route, check with ATC—every sector
   or region, if necessary—for turbulence reports (i.e., "ride reports"). Listen up for other aircraft nearby reporting turbulence. Make tactical changes in altitude to find not just a better
   ride, but a safer one.

3. *Brief Your Crew On What to Expect.* If your carrier has a specific protocol for alerting cabin crew to turbulence, brief it as a
   reminder to everyone, and follow it. If not, create one that is
   practical and gets crewmembers into safe positions quickly. For
   example, you could tell flight attendants that if moderate or
   worse turbulence is immediately expected, the pilots will make
   a PA stating, "Flight attendants take your seats." This command
   will direct them to suspend service, return to their jump seats,
   and fasten their safety belts. Tell them once they are safely
   seated to call the flight deck for a briefing on what to expect
   thereafter.

AIRPORT SAFETY

As air traffic increases with increased passenger and cargo demand worldwide, airports will become more crowded and complex. The statistics continue to show an increasing trend of runway and airport surface incursions. Some of this has been linked to the seemingly constant state of airport construction and refurbishment. At the time of this writing, all of the top 30 busiest U.S. airports had some sort of runway or taxiway construction or closure. And as the infrastructure continues to age, this probably will not change.

The best line of defense to the threat of an incursion is, again, information. NOTAMS are so incredibly important, but all too often get glossed over because they are printed off in long weather packages. Instead of trying to weed through pages and pages of FDC and enroute NOTAMS to find what is pertinent to your flight, use an online tool or an app. The most readily available one is the FAA's NOTAM retrieval website at notams.aim.faa.gov. You can filter down to the most pertinent NOTAM you need for your flight.

If you see that there are closed taxiways, runways, or construction areas, you can plan your taxi routing and brief the expectations given the situation. That's really the goal: to enhance situational awareness. By pairing proper situational awareness with clear communications, safety takes a step up. Brief taxi plans with airport diagrams out and in front of all eyes in the flight deck. Locate "hot spots" (now standard markings on all airport diagrams) where intersecting runways and taxiways have proven to be incursion-prone. Ensure that everyone feels comfortable with the plan, and that everyone has been given full authority to speak up and say "STOP!" or use the brakes if needed if they feel that an incursion is imminent. Encourage your fellow pilots to call "heads down" if they will be taking their eyes off the taxi progression at any time.

Finally, remember that incursions and safety issues don't just occur on active taxiways and runways. Non-movement areas are just as prone to incursion threats. Keep an eye out for vehicles, carts, foreign objects, and personnel as you taxi in and out of ramp and gate areas. Utilize guidelines and clear zone markings, and follow marshalling commands closely.

TAKEOFF SAFETY

Remember 14 CFR §91.103 covered earlier in the chapter? It gives particular weight to the analysis of takeoff and landing performance, and for good reason. According to Boeing, 16 percent of fatal accidents occur during takeoff and initial climb, while 29 percent occur during the approach and landing.[3] Therefore, it behooves us as safe pilots to truly take into consideration all factors for these phases of flight.

Any takeoff maneuver for a transport-category, multi-engine aircraft can result in a rejected or aborted maneuver. Our goal is to first minimize the possibility of a rejected takeoff and, if we have to reject, to maximize the safety of the abort and recovery. This starts with actually utilizing appropriate runway analysis.

For any particular airplane, manufacturer specifications and performance recommendations will comply with the performance standards in 14 CFR §25.111. This regulation describes the takeoff path, the various segments, and the requirements for each. However, pilots must ensure they can *perform* the takeoff per 14 CFR §25.111 safely and within the standard.

This is where the runway analysis comes into play. In the twenty-first century, most operators have invested in performance-computing software and other technology to quickly aid the flight crew in determining takeoff performance data. At the touch of a button, you can get the numbers you need: takeoff speeds (V_1, V_R, V_2, and others), distance for the takeoff roll, engine thrust settings, flap settings, trim settings, engine failure procedures, and more. Here are a few tips to ensure that you consider all information when getting takeoff performance data:

1. *Be as Restrictive as You Can.* When computing takeoff data, think through all the mitigating factors to performance. Wind, temperature, pressure, runway conditions, runway slope, engine limits, and weight and balance are all in the mix. If any of these elements become a limiting factor, signal to yourself that others may be close to limits, as well.

2. *Be as Efficient as You Can.* Depending on the operating technique of a carrier or a fleet, takeoff performance becomes essentially an exercise in efficiency. After all, the goal is to get the airplane safely airborne, preferably in the least amount of runway possible. Use your best combination of judgement and technique

when selecting your takeoff data if you have a choice. Keep in mind the difference between, and especially the benefits versus risks of using, a balanced or unbalanced field length method for computing takeoff data.[4]

3. *Understand the Runway Environment.* Takeoff performance may often come down to the unique environment the runway physically lies within. Geography, nearby structures that cause wind to veer, obstacles in proximity to the takeoff path, intersecting or converging runway paths, and other factors may exist and play a role in how you consider your takeoff performance and profile.

Next, let's discuss the actual takeoff. As you are holding short of the active runway, and receive the "line up and wait" clearance from tower, you then move the aircraft into position. As soon as you do, *the runway belongs to you.* Someone may be on a three-mile final, and someone else could be holding short waiting to cross. It is time to commit to the departure phase of flight, and all eyes are literally on you. Is this any time to decide when you will reject the takeoff if something goes awry? Absolutely not!

Effective and safe pilots-in-command will have already fully briefed the crew, *at the gate,* on what will instigate a rejected takeoff, and how the reject maneuver will be handled. Those briefs should be clear and specific, and sagely, they should not allow for the possibility of a reject to occur in the "high speed regime" of the takeoff roll for anything but engine fire, engine failure, loss of controllability, or another abnormality that would make it dangerously unsafe to take the plane airborne.

Pilots often struggle with the temptation to reject a takeoff in the high speed regime (typically 100 knots or more) when something as "simple" as a generator bus coming offline occurs. The struggle is natural and real. It has been ingrained into pilots, from their first days as student pilots, not to take off with a broken plane. But things are much different now. Now you are accelerating down the runway with a much more intense amount of energy; for heavy-category aircraft, more than 100 metric tons are being accelerated from zero to 160 knots in about 30 seconds! Reversing that trend and fully stopping such a beast in half the time and distance is dangerous, and should be avoided. Boeing quotes a great example in their studies on rejected takeoff (RTO) procedures.

The incident occurred at Evergreen International Airlines after revising RTO procedures:

> A DC-9 was departing Portland International Airport on runway 10L. Conditions included a crosswind, wet runway, and the airplane at balanced-field maximum weight. Near 100 knots during the takeoff roll, the captain felt something strange occur in the nose area. Because he was not sure if a tire had blown or failed in another manner, he elected to continue takeoff. A noise similar to a deflated tire thump was heard as the airplane accelerated. The takeoff continued uneventfully, however, and the airplane diverted to Seattle-Tacoma International Airport. After landing, it was discovered that the left nose tire had come apart and deflated. This incident could have had other consequences had the captain attempted an RTO from high speed. Given the conditions of the runway, and the fact that the tire was deflated, the airplane could have been very difficult to stop on the available runway.[5]

Undoubtedly, RTOs between 100 knots and V_1 speed can occur. But when they do, they will result in an extreme threat level. Pilots need to resist the urge, trust the research of Boeing, NASA, the NTSB, and ICAO, and understand that unless a catastrophic failure has occurred, the safest course of action is to continue and get the aircraft off of the confines of the shrinking runway. Dealing with a warning light, a mechanical issue, or the unknown is easier, and safer, in the open sky.

One final note on takeoff safety to consider is the ever-debated definition of V_1, or rather, what happens at V_1. For years, pilots treated V_1 as a "decision speed." However, the definition has been refined based on research, and V_1 is now purely considered to be a performance marker. The decision to either reject a takeoff or continue a takeoff should occur *prior to V_1*. Most operators now utilize a procedure to make the V_1 callout 5 to 10 knots prior to V_1 in order to trigger the decision to take the plane airborne with a catastrophic failure before it accelerates past V_1. This is significant for the same reasons that high-speed RTOs need to be avoided—the end of the runway is coming quickly. Stopping an airplane with a catastrophic failure after V_1 has proven in most cases to cause more damage than continuing the takeoff, and sometimes fatalities. Be restrictive, conservative, and safe. Taking a limping plane into the sky using proper technique and then getting it cleaned up for a successful landing will save lives and airframes.

SAFETY IN CRUISE

It is surprising to many people that most aviation fatalities occur due to loss of control in flight, specifically in the cruise phase rather than during takeoff or landing. It truly sounds like a horror because it is. The International Air Transport Association (IATA) reported that 37 fatal accidents were caused by loss of control in flight between 2010 and 2014, resulting in a total of 1,242 fatalities.[6] The majority of these accidents occurred with both meteorology and aircraft malfunction as significant contributing factors. In almost all cases, crew performance was also cited as a contributing factor.

So as a pilot, what can you do? First and foremost, you *must* commit to SOP compliance. This is especially true when things outside of your control pose a threat. SOPs are designed to mitigate threats and trap errors. Stick to them, and survive.

Secondly, employ flight deck discipline when it comes to vertical and lateral navigation and the use of automation. This is a nice way of saying, "Don't misuse the autopilot!" Again, SOPs should be able to trap any errors made when using (or not using) automation. But take extra time and care to actually verify and monitor the inputs made to flight controls, whether through automation or manual manipulation. Constantly ask yourself, "Is the plane going where I want it to go?" At my carrier we call this "VVM," which stands for "Verbalize, Verify, Monitor." We are encouraged by our SOPs to verbalize any changes to automation when a mode or control input is changed. We then verify that the mode or input is producing the desired result. Finally, we monitor the aircraft to ensure that the desired result continues.

Empirically, we know that misuse of automation comes in two basic forms. The first is the pilot who simply does not know or understand proper use of the autoflight system or related components. The second is the pilot who uses the autoflight system too much, almost as a crutch. In the first case, training will remedy the pilot's misuse of automation. In the second, a re-establishment of hand flying skills will need to occur over time.

Increasing focus has been placed on whether "hand flying" skills are taking a hit as pilots are becoming more reliant on automation. Granted, some operators require a higher level of automation than others, and in some aircraft types, automation use is mandated. Safe pilots will make specific efforts to find a healthy balance between the required use of automation and the need to keep their basic airmanship skill of hand flying up to standards. Use appropriate opportunities to hand fly the airplane, and if you anticipate such opportunities, include them in your preflight briefing.

Automation becomes the norm at cruise. Unfortunately, this also introduces the temptation for complacency. Gross navigational errors have become problematic as this complacency seeps in. However, these navigational errors are not a direct result of the automation or pilots' complacency, but rather result from the prevalent expectation bias pilots have towards automation. Modern flight management systems have the capability to be programmed to navigate from wheels up to wheels down. Pilots put an immense amount of trust in these systems to accurately guide them waypoint to waypoint. However, like any other computer, the resultant output of flight guidance from an FMS is only as good as the accuracy of the input. Once again, SOP saves the day here. Flight deck procedures that verify and monitor the inputs to the FMS and the autoflight system may seem mundane, but they serve a critical purpose.

Gross navigational errors are not just confined to lateral deviations. Vertical (altitude) deviations are also prevalent, and are also mainly due to complacent flight deck procedures. Altimeter settings, particularly when crossing transition levels/altitudes, routinely get missed. SOPs, typically in the form of climb checks or descent checks, are structured to capture altimeter setting errors. Planning ahead in briefings (i.e., briefing what the transition altitude will be on departure and what the transition level will be on arrival) primes the memory of the crew to anticipate setting the altimeter at the appropriate points. Some flight management systems will even allow pilots to plot a fix at a predicted altitude, and I know many pilots use this function as a helpful memory aid by plotting these transitions on their nav display. Beyond that, many next gen modern autoflight systems will automatically alert the pilots for these transitions, and allow presetting QNH for quick one-button switches between the settings. Use these tools to your advantage!

APPROACH AND LANDING

The accident rate increases again during the descent phase of flight. As aircraft start down and enter into an environment where pilots' workload increases exponentially, the threats start stacking up. The very best way to trim the stack is to plan ahead. Many operators have implemented an SOP that dictates the latest point by which a descent or approach briefing should occur. Knowing that not every flight is the same length or has the same challenges and considerations, crews typically will get a feel for when to conduct a meaningful approach brief and checklist and not simply wait until the very last minute it is required.

When I transitioned as a captain from turboprop to jet aircraft, a big focus of the check airmen corps at our carrier was to acclimate the pilot to the expediency of the flight. After flying around at 250 knots for several years, I formed habits as to when and where to do things like an approach brief, and suffice it to say that we did it very close to the actual flying of the approach. Typically, it happened during initial descent with the first altitude change below cruise triggering the checklist. It was suggested to me and many other pilots transitioning from props to jets to brief the descent and approach as soon as possible—as in right after the cruise check is completed! It was only a suggestion, but it is one that I took to heart and carry with me today, even when initial descent may be six or more hours down the road. We may not run the actual descent or approach checklist six hours out, but it doesn't hurt to anticipate it and discuss it. It doesn't hurt to talk about the approach and landing even back at the gate during preflight!

Once again, the idea here is to enhance situational awareness and foster communication. We prime our operational minds well in advance for the most complex portion of the flight. Here is how to do it:

1. Look at the weather forecast; anticipate the arrival and approach. What kind of navigational requirements exist? Will you have legal weather minimums for the approach? How about any NOTAMs that need to be considered? SEA-ICE comes in handy for the initial analysis.

2. Look at landing data and analysis, if possible. At a minimum, consider maximum gross landing weight. Remembering that preflight action requirements compel pilots to consider runway lengths and distances required, it doesn't hurt to review predicted landing performance both at the gate and again up at cruise. Fuel burn is a large variable, and your numbers may very well have changed. Case in point: I have flown short legs in a CRJ900 several times with the APU on and spoilers out in cruise just to make sure we would not land overweight.

3. Review the approach plate and visualize the sequence of events that will occur between the cruise phase and the landing. Thinking through this will help you catch latent threats and decide on actions to mitigate them.

4. To the extent possible, set up navigation aids, FMS, and automation well in advance in anticipation of the approach plan. When it comes time to brief and recheck these items, you can utilize a definitive form of verbalization and verification.

Stay ahead of the airplane to keep safety at a high level. Don't be afraid to rethink, recheck, and verbalize any changes that may come your way as you head downline in cruise flight. Safe pilots know that flying is a dynamic practice of dynamic variables. Anticipate changes and adjust your plans and technique accordingly.

21ST-CENTURY THREATS

The FAA reported that in 2014, pilots filed 238 reports of near-misses or proximity sightings of unmanned aircraft. That number increased dramatically the following year. By August 9, 2015, 650 sightings had been reported by pilots year-to-date, with some reports occurring at altitudes as high as 10,000 feet. Drones were interfering with wildfire containment operations in the western United States in the summer of 2015, triggering a "If You Fly, We Can't" information campaign by the National Interagency Fire Center. In December 2015, the FAA started requiring drones to be registered, and by March 2016, more than 400,000 people had done so. In the spring of 2016, the FBI and FAA began testing UAV detection systems at New York's John F. Kennedy International Airport.[7]

Another threat is lasers, which can be purchased for as little as fifty dollars and can render a person momentarily blind, or potentially permanently blind, if the laser light is viewed directly. This can impact pilots while operating aircraft, and the nature of flight deck windows can actually magnify the intensity of a laser strike. Unfortunately, over the last decade, some people have decided it would be fun to shine lasers at airplanes and helicopters. In 2012, after over 3,500 reports of laser incidents in 2011 alone, a new federal law was passed in the United States making it a federal offense to shine a laser beam at an operating aircraft. A California man was sentenced to fourteen years in prison for pointing a beam at a police helicopter in 2014. Between January and October 2015, the FAA recorded more than 5,400 laser strikes, showing that despite the stiff penalties involved (up to 20 years in prison and a $250,000 fine), people are still threatening the safety of flight with lasers.[8]

Every four years, U.S. lawmakers haggle over funding for the aviation and aerospace infrastructure of the country. Airports, air traffic control technology, navigational aids, and other crucial pieces of the airspace system need constant renewal and refurbishment. What's more, the entire system needs to keep up with market demand, busier skies, and the advancing technology of the airplanes themselves.

Advanced technology, touched on earlier in this chapter, bears mentioning again. Automation in the flight deck is a great tool. The management of aircraft systems becomes easier and more intuitive, aircraft control becomes more precise, and the planes fly more efficiently. Regardless, pilots are still responsible for superb airmanship. This means not only the appropriate use of automation, but the effective use of decision-making skills. No matter what level of automation is used, there is still a pilot-in-command that is responsible for it. Automation does not release pilots-in-command from their duty to be the safest pilots they can be.

Drones, lasers, infrastructure, and automation are threats that are, for the most part, out of your control. Latent threats sometimes present themselves that way. But you can still do something about these threats. Being vigilant is the first and foremost action to take. Next, it is important to remain educated about these threats and how they can be mitigated. Finally, contribute to the safety culture of the twenty-first century, which focuses on data collection and non-punitive participation in safety reporting programs for pilots, mechanics, flight attendants, dispatchers, air traffic specialists, and other aviation workers. Modern safety management systems in the industry are moving the ball down the playing field in terms of safety advancements. As professional pilots, we need to be contributing members of the winning team.

SMS AND SAFETY REPORTING

While accident rates continue to drop, we still need a way to assess the threats to aviation safety that exist. A safety management systems (SMS) is a formal approach being used across the industry today. Just like other quality assurance systems used in all kinds of business, SMS uses a data-driven approach to drive safety policy, identify risks and risk-mitigation strategies, evaluate the effectiveness of those strategies, and promote training, communication, and a positive safety culture.

Pilots are on the operational side of the SMS structure. They are the ones actually working through and benefiting from the policies, strategies, and training that results from SMS. But pilots also play a huge role in providing the data that underpins the entire system. The Aviation Safety Action Program (ASAP), Flight Operations Quality Assurance (FOQA) program, and Line Operations Safety Audit (LOSA) program at most carriers not only provide for that data input from flight crews, but also assist SMS managers and safety specialists in developing the education and safety communication components. Flight departments also benefit from SMS by being able to identify the need for new procedures and operating practices.

Safe, effective pilots-in-command actively participate in safety programs. As humans, pilots are not perfect. But you can work towards the betterment of your airmanship and professionalism by reporting when things go wrong and learning from the threats you encounter and the errors you commit. You owe it to your profession, your employers, and especially your passengers to be the safest possible pilot. Understanding SMS programs and joining your fellow pilots in utilizing the reporting process, digesting the data and reports they issue back to you, and enhancing your own level of safety, airmanship, and performance as a professional is key to the success of your overall career as an airline pilot.

Chapter 13 Notes

1. A treasure trove of accident data, reports, and stats can be accessed from the Aviation Safety Network, a service of the Flight Safety Foundation, at aviation-safety.net.

2. Per the National Highway Traffic Safety Administration, nhtsa.gov

3. boeing.com/resources/boeingdotcom/company/about_bca/pdf/statsum.pdf

4. You may not have a choice here, but it is worth mentioning that operators are increasingly using dynamic performance models that will optimize takeoff performance depending on all common factors plus whether or not there is a benefit to using balanced versus unbalanced field length.

5. The Boeing Company, "Practical Applications for Rejected Takeoff Studies," *Aero 11* (2000). Retrieved at boeing.com/commercial/aeromagazine/aero_11/takeoff_story.html

6. International Air Transport Association (IATA), *Loss of Control In-Flight Accident Analysis Report, 2010–2014*. Retrieved at iata.org/whatwedo/safety/Pages/loss-of-control-inflight.aspx

7. faa.gov/uas

8. Federal Aviation Administration (FAA), "Laser News, Laws, and Civil Penalties." Retrieved at faa.gov/about/initiatives/lasers/laws

PART III:
Professional Excellence

14

Pride in Professionalism—The PIC Leadership Model

Throughout the book, I have covered many aspects of the job of a pilot-in-command. There is a central theme that runs throughout the topics in this book, and if it isn't yet obvious, this chapter should cement that theme in place. In every career setting, professionalism is important. But in professions that are very closely scrutinized by the public, professionalism is essential. There is no better example of this than the airline industry.

A professional, as defined by Merriam-Webster, is someone who is "(1) characterized by or conforming to the technical or ethical standards of a profession, (2) exhibiting a courteous, conscientious, and generally businesslike manner in the workplace." The question for pilots is this: How they can rise to the standards set out by this definition, and even exceed the basic standards, in their professionalism?

The answer to this question, and the key to becoming a consummate professional, centers on leadership. Plain and simple, leaders cannot lead without being:

- Ethical
- Courteous
- Conscientious
- Businesslike

All of these qualities from the definition of the word "professional" are cornerstones of leadership for pilots-in-command. This chapter looks more closely at these cornerstones and how they enable pilots to become good leaders—ones who develop the skill to lead naturally and who become intrinsically driven to constantly improve in their leadership role.

ON LEADERSHIP

If you imagine a prospector panning for gold in a mountain stream, you can visualize the process of dipping the pan into the streambed and sifting through the rubble in hopes of finding even the smallest bits of precious metal. More often than not, all that is found is gold dust. Finding a nugget was considered "striking it rich." The nuggets were more commonly lost among the rubble.

People who are naturally and intrinsically driven to lead are like golden nuggets. Golden nugget leaders are people who already feel "called" into their leadership role. A "call" is an internal, intrinsic, contemplated pull towards service that only the individual can discern.

The question for pilots is whether they wish to be a golden nugget, or simply a flash in the pan. Interestingly enough, there are plenty of people out there who, despite their type-A, left-brain-dominant personalities, can develop into a leader. You don't have to have an innate ability to lead, but you do need to make an effort to become *influential* and *transformational* to your crew.

Many experts define leadership as the ability to influence others. But increasingly, leaders are called upon to influence behavior changes; they are called upon to be transformational. The airline flight crew environment is a perfect crucible for all of the factors of transformational leadership to come together.

Professor Mark McCloskey at Bethel University in St. Paul, Minnesota, developed a model of transformational leadership that is easy to understand and apply in many business settings.[1] Applying his model to flight deck leadership is relatively simple, as the construct uses four categorical elements to picture leadership: Relationships, Roles, Responsibilities, and Results. Thus, the model is called the "4R" model. This approach has been developed and deployed across the business spectrum, and is being used by several leadership consulting firms to determine leadership capabilities within an organization, and coach clients to maximize the potential of transformational leadership to foster organizational change. The 4R model is straightforward, scalable, and customizable, and is a great fit for the purpose of understanding, teaching, and exercising transformational leadership from the flight deck.

THE PIC LEADERSHIP MODEL: AN APPLICATION OF THE "4R" APPROACH

Much like the "New CRM" model presented earlier in this book, the *Pilots In Command* leadership model presents a new way of looking at aspects of leadership we already have heard of. With the "4Rs" (Relationships, Roles, Responsibilities, and Results), constructing the model begins with the development of *relationships*—constructive interactions between the pilot leader and the crewmembers and co-workers he is leading. Relationships don't always come easy, however. Pilot leaders must first work on their own persona, cultivating a special set of virtues that enable leaders to lead. The PIC Leadership Model builds a platform of virtues similar to other deployments of the 4R model, which serve to "anchor" relationships among crewmembers. Once the virtues are in place and exercised, relationships can be built and strengthened.

Picturing transformational leadership through virtue-based relationships leads us to see the *roles* that the pilot leader has, in contexts of vocational place and time. Pilot leaders serve leadership roles both inside and outside of the flight deck, in points of time that involve the present flight operation, and the future of the flight operation. Like the 4R model, the PIC Leadership Model pictures the pilot leader utilizing his virtue-based relationships to apply leadership in these roles, which connect through efforts of communication and mentoring.

The pilot-in-command, ever cognizant of his charges under 14 CFR §91.3, has specific, primary, flight-operation-based *responsibilities* that are used to practically apply transformational leadership across the flight operation. This application across the roles and relationships pictured in the PIC Leadership Model produces the *results* of transformational leadership. Results under McCloskey's 4R model are qualitative, quantitative, and contextual, and the same is true under the PIC Leadership Model.

Let's step through the PIC Leadership Model, developing the model and picturing each "R" from both the viewpoint of McCloskey's original model and the viewpoint of the PIC model.

Relationships

Relationships serve as the core category of the 4R model, and as such the virtues and characteristics that pilot leaders need to both possess and exhibit directly relate to how crewmembers interact with each other.

The group of virtues that anchor the relationships category of the PIC Leadership Model are:

- Effective communications
- Honest discernment
- Sole-sourced integrity
- Commitment to duty
- Promotion of teamwork

Concisely, in order to build, strengthen, and perpetuate relationships as PIC, you must be able to communicate effectively, have an honest approach of discernment, display integrity that comes "sole-sourced" from your own persona, remain committed to the duty you have before you, and promote teamwork among your crew. That final virtue of "promotion of teamwork" truly ties together the relationships that transformational leaders need to foster. But before the team can come together, the preceding four virtues must be in full force and effect. Let's look more closely at each one.

Effective Communications

Previous chapters of this book already focused on effective communications. In fact, because so much of being a pilot and crewmember really hinges on communication, it should be obvious that effective communication should be an anchor point for relationship building. To spotlight some of the points covered in previous chapters, pilots who are effective communicators keep the lines of communication open. They understand that the exchange of information needs a clear path. Whether the communication is between two pilots in the flight deck, among and between pilots and cabin crewmembers, or between flight crewmembers and persons external to the airplane and flight operation, information must be exchanged with clarity, completeness, brevity, and timeliness. Good communicators allow for appropriate feedback (e.g., they listen to responses) and then affirm, correct, or counter when needed.

Honest Discernment

Discernment is the virtue of being able to determine the accuracy, value, quality, and efficacy of an action or plan of action. It includes the ability to make detailed judgments about an action or plan of action. For the purposes of the PIC Leadership Model, discernment is supported by direct honesty. The wisdom often ascribed to high levels of discernment truly is a manifestation of honesty and objectivity. This is especially true of honest discernment when overlooked viewpoints, subjects, or details are brought again to light by the discerner. Being honest about the facts and then taking each fact at its inherent value in the situation at hand enables wise discernment and good decisive outcomes. Reading weather reports is a fantastic illustration of honest discernment. It is hard to read a current-conditions (METAR) report and make an honest decision on what the weather will accurately be several hours later. It becomes easier to read a forecast (TAF) report to decide what the weather will be, specifically within a finite timeframe given in the report. But a wise, honest discerner will look at more than even the current METAR or TAF reports. Such a person will read previous METARs leading up to the present time, look at significant weather prognosis charts, area forecast discussions, and many other reports, graphics, satellite imagery, and even live radar to make an informed judgment of what the weather will be. This same process of information gathering and processing—taking in all the facts—is employed by leaders who possess the virtue of honest discernment in every decision and judgment they undertake.

Sole-Sourced Integrity

In looking at what integrity is and what it involves, it comes down to *consistency* in ethical values. The root of the word integrity is the same as the word "integer," which means something is whole; intact; consistent. Transformational leaders, including those who are safe and effective pilots, do not allow their integrity to be compromised. They are consistent in carrying out their responsibilities. Sole-sourced integrity, for the purposes of our model, emphasizes the necessity that a leader's integrity comes from within. True leaders do not obtain or utilize the integrity of others. Rather, they "own" their integrity independently. This is because each individual's level of integrity is a direct result of the choices the individual makes. This includes our "bad choices." To have integrity means to "keep it together"—for better or for worse, but in the hopes that even in the worse times, maintaining a high level of integrity leads us to the better.

Commitment to Duty

Pilots have an inherent sense of duty. Duty is also an important element to effective leadership, and since it seems to come naturally to many in the flight deck it should be employed with the right sense of the word in mind. As I discussed in Chapter 6, the true meaning of duty is to have debt. In this context, a pilot-leader has to have a sense that their passengers and crew are counting on them to come through on the task at hand. A PIC has the *duty* of being ultimately responsible for the operation of the aircraft. Realizing that this duty is something that they truly *owe* to their passengers, crew, employers—and quite frankly everyone who may be impacted by the operation of that flight—keeps a pilot leader centered on appropriate airmanship, safety, decision making, CRM, TEM, and all aspects of the flight operation in a responsible way.

Promotion of Teamwork

When transformational flight deck leaders promote teamwork, it happens organically after the leader has embraced the virtues of effective communications, honest discernment, sole-sourced integrity, and commitment to duty. This is because human behavior is keen to gravitate towards virtuous personalities. There are many other basic virtues, even more rudimentary than what are prescribed here in the PIC Leadership Model, particularly the cardinal virtues of character: Plato described these virtues as temperance, fortitude, prudence, and justice. But without the virtuous "setup," teamwork simply doesn't occur. We all know the saying, "there is no 'I' in 'team.'" The word "team" originated to describe a group of animals, such as a team of horses, that was harnessed together to pull something. Now the word describes any group of persons or animals that has come together to collaborate on a work project. Through their loyalty to one another, team members bond in order to do their best work together rather than separately. Airline crews, in order to operate safely, effectively, and efficiently, must engage in loyal teamwork. Effective pilots-in-command will step up to foster and promote teamwork, leading their crew to accomplishment.

Bringing together all of these virtuous elements—communication, discernment, integrity, duty, and teamwork—will enable you to positively influence those you are *required* to lead and even those who are not reporting directly to you. Remember, as pilot-in-command you are responsible for the entire operation, so your influence needs to impact not just your immediate crew, but also the people who surround the operation. Gate agents, ramp workers, dispatchers, mechanics—even passengers, who become useful in emergency situations affecting cabin safety—can all be led through your influence. This brings us to the next "R" in the "4R" approach: roles.

Roles

McCloskey's 4R Model defines four different roles that "*every* leader *must* play to lead well over time in and on behalf of the organization."[2] These include spokesperson, direction setter, coach, and change agent. Each of these roles is designated in a context of application either "inside" or "outside" the organization being led by the leader, and also in a context of roles being carried out today (inclusive of present and past realities) or tomorrow (future plans and aspirations). Outlined in a grid, the roles look like this:

Outside of Organization

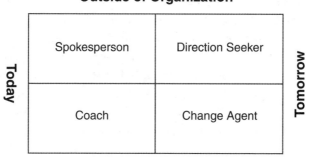

	Spokesperson	Direction Seeker	
Today			Tomorrow
	Coach	Change Agent	

Inside of Organization

These are simplified roles, and as such are to be globally applied to the organizational situation the leader is in, and not necessarily the "micro role" of the leader (such as CEO, manager, team leader, etc.). The placement and time contexts of these roles can also be viewed globally. But for the purposes of the PIC Leadership Model, some modifications to this construct will help apply it to the flight operations leadership environment.

The roles can be applied consistently: Pilots-in-command serve in leadership capacities in all of these roles. They are—by nature—the spokespersons, directions setters, coaches, and change agents for each and every flight they are responsible for. However, in the context of flight operations, the place and time contexts should be renamed. The better labels for the places are "Inside the Flight Deck" and "Outside the Flight Deck", and for the time, "Present Ops" and "Future Ops."

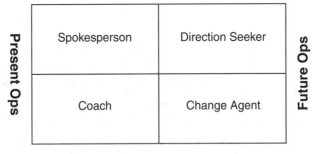

Outside the Flight Deck

Spokesperson	Direction Seeker
Coach	Change Agent

Present Ops (left side) · Future Ops (right side)

Inside the Flight Deck

Relabeling these contexts provides us with a better feel for the roles in the PIC Leadership Model. First, we will look at the roles in the Present Ops time context. Pilots-in-command are working very much as "coaches" from inside the flight deck, insomuch as they are fostering and developing the leadership capabilities of their team—the crew. By directing the flight operation with the mindset that all crewmembers have leadership potential, PICs can efficiently delegate tasks and responsibilities within the scope of standard operating procedures. But, also like a coach, the PIC makes the ultimate decisions on the play calls. When a direction of the present operation requires a change, the PIC "coach" can take suggestions in from the crew and make informed decisions. This couples directly with the "core truths" of the New CRM that was presented in Chapter 6. Those truths focused on what makes (or doesn't make) a crew work together. The PIC as coach makes sure those core truths are managed, and coaches the crew so that they work together.

The PIC as spokesperson is a straightforward role that has pilot leaders engaging with several external parties. The passengers are the first and most obvious group of people the PIC engages with under this role. Passengers expect to hear from their captain, and they want to hear truthful information being passed on to them. The PIC spokesperson is also responsible for the customer service aspect of the operation in this role, going beyond cabin announcements and ensuring passenger needs are being handled. As spokesperson, the PIC also engages with ground personnel, operations personnel, maintenance coworkers, dispatchers, and others who have a direct impact on the present operation.

Moving on to the roles in the Future Ops time context, the PIC Leadership Model roles serve situations that are both known and unknown. Moreover, we see direct links between the roles from the Present Ops context:

Outside the Flight Deck

Inside the Flight Deck

The PIC spokesperson of the present operation becomes the direction setter of the future operation through *communicating*. The PIC coach becomes a change agent for future operations through *mentoring*.

As a direction setter, the PIC has communicated how the operation needs to proceed. The PIC's decisions are communicated to his crew, the passengers, ramp, ops, dispatch, maintenance, ATC, and airport personnel in an effort to coordinate and set the direction of the operation. The virtue of effective communications is, therefore, essential for the PIC. Since we have previously discussed virtue in the 4R framework as something that is crucial to building and strengthening relationships, we can see how important the virtue is for the direction setter. Leaders simply cannot set course for their followers if these relationships are not established.

As a change agent, the PIC's role as a coach not only sets forth CRM and teamwork, it also instills the ability to change, improve, and advance the crew's leadership potential and capabilities. The link between coach and change agent can be best described as "mentoring." Mentoring is such an important activity and action of PIC leaders that new regulations now mandate mentoring programs at air carriers. The airline industry is ripe with the expectation that naturally occurring mentorship will take place in every flight deck, since the majority of captains are more senior than first officers.

Effective pilots-in-command should consider the role of mentor as one that is symbiotic with their role as leader. If a captain looks upon each of their first officers as a mentee, he or she can apply some of the most natural habits of effective mentoring during every trip: teaching, representing, and motivating.

Teaching

What nugget of experience can you pass on to someone in each trip you fly? Perhaps it is a technique you use, something you yourself learned from a recent experience, or even something you have seen someone else do. Try to find opportunities to bring up a subject when you may learn something from the person with whom you are flying. Sometimes the best teaching has its beginning in something you learn from your student!

Representing

Also termed "modeling," a good mentor (and an effective pilot) will always represent the appropriate behaviors of a pilot. Adherence to standard operating procedures is a must, but you should also consider good representations of ethics, beliefs and attitudes. Your crewmembers follow your lead, and they will oftentimes make adjustments to their own behaviors based on your example. Help your fellow pilot feel confidence through their affiliation with you as their leader. They want you to represent!

Motivating

Perhaps one of the best tools a captain has at their disposal for establishing motivation right off the bat is the first crew brief of the trip. Pilots-in-command need to set the tone in a positive, motivating manner—despite the circumstances! Remember, despite weather, mechanical discrepancies, rude passengers, and long duty days, a job still needs to be accomplished. Captains can motivate first officers, who in turn can also assist in passing on the same motivation to the rest of the crew.

Remember that mentoring is a two-way street. The person being mentored needs to be receptive and interested in your input. A good, healthy mentor—mentee exchange also includes feedback from the mentee to the mentor. Keeping the lines of communication open will always result in positive outcomes. Focusing on professionalism and taking pride in your professionalism will underscore those outcomes. Crewmember habits will change positively as a result of proper teaching, representing, and motivating. Through those improved habits, PIC leaders as change agents will have fostered a new generation of leaders in the flight deck.

Responsibilities

The next part of the 4R model is responsibilities, which McCloskey describes as "the effective practice of leadership—the *being* of leadership, translated into the *doing* of leadership in the organizational *context* of leadership."[3] The responsibilities are (1) vision casting, (2) strategy making, (3) aligning, and (4) encouraging. Again, in order to format the 4R model to the flight operations environment, these responsibilities need to be translated to the realm of the pilot. The best way to do this is to return to 14 CFR §91.3: Responsibility and Authority of the Pilot In Command.

While §91.3 doesn't break down specifics of PIC "responsibilities," we can use the 4R model to develop some definitive responsibilities. Where the 4R model is useful globally in several business areas, the PIC Leadership Model narrows the scope of the leader to the confines of the flight operation. For each "4R" responsibility, the "PIC" responsibility has a related aspect:

4R Model Responsibilities	PIC Leadership Model Responsibilities
Vision casting	Safety of the operation
Strategy making	Efficiency of the operation
Aligning	Crew dynamics of the operation
Encouraging	Duty to the operation

Safety of the Operation

Pilots focus first and foremost on safety. It's very hard to picture any flight operation that doesn't. Therefore, safety is also the first responsibility of the PIC. *Safety of the operation* relates to the 4R-model responsibility of "vision casting" in the aspect of every flight operation being set with the vision of "safety first." McCloskey quoted leadership experts John Kotter and Burt Nanus in his 4R model's description of vision casting: "Vision Casting is a process of (1) crafting, (2) communicating and (3) continually revising an intellectually credible and emotionally engaging picture of a preferable future."[4] Envisaging a safety oriented operation meets this definition head on.

Efficiency of the Operation

Along with safety, a pilot has a very important and primary responsibility to operate the flight as efficiently as possible. In fact, as it relates to fuel consumption, efficiency is actually an effort made in the name of safety. So, we link up efficiency to the 4R Model's strategy making responsibility. The PIC is called upon to create strategies as the flight operation progresses—strategies to keep the operation safe, comfortable, and on-time, all while balancing the constraints of procedures, traffic, aircraft limitations, weather, crew legalities, etc. All of those strategies are exercises in *efficiency*. Efficiency begets safety, comfort, and timeliness, and it conquers the challenges of the restraints to the operation. The practice of threat and error management is an exercise in efficiency. In most cases, the efficient way to fly is the best way to fly.

Crew Dynamics of the Operation

Time and time again we return to the concepts of CRM in this book. And like the responsibilities of safety and efficiency, *crew dynamics* is a responsibility that cannot be overlooked, and it is primary to operational responsibility as viewed through the lens of the FARs. The PIC role is defined by the FARs because of crew dynamics.[5] Everything points back to the PIC as the leader—the coach, the spokesperson, the change agent, and the direction setter. Through effective communications and mentoring, PICs manage, direct, and promote teamwork among their crews. They inspire crewmembers to lead one another, and inspire them to be agents of change themselves. The PIC is responsible for the crew and the way the crew interacts and understands, both individually and corporately, their responsibilities and how they affect the flight operation. That interaction and understanding of mission is what the 4R model espouses as the responsibility of aligning. This includes the leader's ability to "[find] practical ways for organization members to accomplish valued ends."[6]

Duty to the Operation

Flying an airplane is an amazing task. Especially for complex, large, transport-category aircraft, it is not a small task. The operation that surrounds and supports every flight is also complex. To operate a typical airline flight requires anywhere from 20–30 workers, not including the flight deck or cabin crew. Dispatchers, schedulers, ramp personnel, fuelers, gate agents, mechanics—the list goes on and on, and we know who they all are in their task-oriented roles. PICs have a primary responsibility of duty to the operation as a whole, because all of these other coworkers have that same duty as well. *Duty to the operation* can be linked to the 4R-model responsibility of encouraging because of the nature of the virtue of duty. Knowing they have a duty—that debt owed to their passengers, crew, and coworkers—PICs can be encouraging to crewmembers and others they lead. For if PICs instill hope, courage, and optimism in their coworkers, their commitment to duty increases and strengthens.

These responsibilities of the PIC—safety, efficiency, crew dynamics, and duty—make the PIC Leadership Model work. They are applied directly in each of the PIC's roles as a leader—whether as coach, change agent, spokesperson, or direction setter. Keep in mind that these responsibilities are *primary*. They encapsulate the most basic interpretation of the responsibility of the PIC as taken from the FARs. Other responsibilities may be evident in a particular operation, but only to the extent that they are ancillary to these primary responsibilities, and likely they are useful in a custom role or capability that the PIC may possess. (A good example is a PIC serving as a check airman. The PIC still has the primary responsibilities described here, but may also have additional responsibilities such as teaching or evaluating.)

Results

Relationships + Roles + Responsibilities = Results. Transformational leadership under the PIC Leadership Model, like the original 4R model, produces results that are qualitative, quantitative, and contextual. The results of transformational leadership are manifested in both the objectives of the flight operation as well as the enhancement of teamwork and crew resource management.

Qualitatively, pilot leaders who exhibit transformational leadership skills should be able to operate a safer and more efficient flight, and exhibit and elicit (from both themselves and their co-workers) a high level of customer service, crew cohesiveness, and job performance.

Quantitatively, pilot leaders working under this model should be capable of maintaining the schedule of the operation; hit cost performance targets with maximized efficiencies as much as possible given flight environment constraints; and be empowered to influence their crew to perform in the same way.

Contextually, however, the PIC Leadership Model has its best benefits in the development of the pilot leader, and the subsequent transformation of the pilot leader's crew members into effective and transformational leaders in their own right. Pointing back to the virtues of the pilot leader, we see promotion of teamwork capping the list; reviewing the roles, we see leadership efforts of effective communication and mentorship; surveying the responsibilities, we find safety, efficiency, duty, and again, communications. All of these elements combine to create pilot leaders who can overcome difficulties, spearhead strategies, delegate appropriately, and establish a work environment in which crewmembers thrive.

In summary, the PIC Leadership Model takes a very academic approach to leadership. Simply put, we can say it is well to focus on what is required to do the job right, communicate your plans and intentions clearly, make decisions wisely with the advice and input of your resources, and stand firm on your decisions with a high level of ethical value. But to develop dynamic transformational pilot leaders, the model serves to meet the demand for such leaders across an ever-changing, advancing, and growing airline industry.

PUTTING THE PIC LEADERSHIP MODEL TO WORK RIGHT NOW

If you have read through the last several pages and find the PIC Leadership Model to be a bit daunting, you are having a natural reaction. Even though it is a theoretical and academic approach to flight deck leadership, it can be easily applied in a practical way. And you can begin doing so right now.

To get started in the right direction, *don't* overthink this. Instead, simply go about your everyday routine. As you encounter situations where you know your leadership abilities are being put to the test, find your place within the leadership model; use it like a map at a big shopping mall where you need to find the "You Are Here" label.

For a good example, let's revisit Capt. Jones from Chapter 3. You will recall that Jones was having a rough morning getting his first flight off the ground. He was likely fighting the onset of fatigue, headed out for a trip with weather issues along the way, encountering a broken plane on the first leg, and answering questions from fellow crewmembers and coworkers. The account of Capt. Jones was used to explore the threats present in a TEM scenario. Here we will look for Capt. Jones in the PIC Leadership Model.

Recall that after Capt. Jones approached the departure gate, there was a flurry of activity with the gate agent, mechanic, and others trying to determine the status of the flight. Coworkers were attempting to contact operations ("OPS") to see if they had a definitive delay time and status, and First Officer Essex was dryly insinuating that OPS would not have the answer. Capt. Jones assured co-workers that answers were on the way, and led FO Essex out of the situation. Perhaps we can place Jones on the PIC Leadership Model map at that instant:

Outside the Flight Deck

Inside the Flight Deck

Notice that the star is placed between spokesperson and direction setter. That's alright; this simply represents that Jones is filling both roles in this situation. Since the place context is outside of the flight deck (at the gate), the relevant focus is on his roles shown on the top half of the model/map. He clearly is acting as the spokesperson for the crew and the flight operation in the present time context of "Present Ops." Through his communications to the crew, crew scheduler, dispatcher, and others, he becomes a direction setter.

The following section will help you if you are ready to dig a little deeper into the practical application of the model. A good way to unpack these concepts is to run through exercises that will bring your view of the model into focus. These are simple exercises, but by working through the questions and challenges, you can start thinking about how to be a transformational leader in the flight deck. During each day you will be headed to the flight deck, try to envision what elements of the PIC Leadership Model you will be operating with most. Will today's flights challenge you to be more of a spokesperson or a coach? Which one of your virtues will be tried-and-true as you manage your relationships among the crew? Be intentional in thinking it through, and each day that you employ the model, it will become easier to learn it.

Exercise 1—Inventory and Rate Your Virtues

Review the list of the core virtues of the PIC Leadership Model. On a scale of one to five, with "one" being never, and "five" being always, rate the amount of time you feel you embody each virtue when you interact with other crewmembers:

	never ..... always				
Effective communications	1	2	3	4	5
Honest discernment	1	2	3	4	5
Sole-sourced integrity	1	2	3	4	5
Commitment to duty	1	2	3	4	5
Promotion of teamwork	1	2	3	4	5

For each virtue you rated three or less, write down two sentences that will help you improve. For example, let's say you scored yourself "2" on promotion of teamwork. You might write, "I will work harder to promote teamwork among my crew by encouraging them to work together during my crew brief. I will engage with my crew to find out how I can make their job easier, and ask them to be helpful to one another."

Exercise 2—Seeing Your Roles in Action by Reviewing the Past

Look back over the last four trips you have flown. Pick up a logbook or crew calendar and take a walk down memory lane. Do a bit of armchair flying, if you will. Instead of focusing on the flying, however, focus on the crew interactions. When were you a coach, or a spokesperson? Did you have interactions where you were a direction setter, or were there moments when you were a change agent? Think about times when things went well, all normal ops, and also focus on flights where things weren't so smooth. How did different levels of operational difficulty and challenge trigger you into fulfilling different roles?

Exercise 3—Talk to Someone Who Mentored You About Responsibility

Find someone who you view as a pilot mentor, and take them out for coffee. Ask them these questions (verbatim):

1. When you are leading a crew, what are the best practices you have to encourage a safe operation?
2. How do you seek efficiency during your flights?
3. Tell me about a time when it was an absolute challenge to achieve a positive crew dynamic.
4. How do you see yourself as a leader when it comes to duty?

Your mentor's answers will aid you in seeing the responsibilities defined in the PIC Leadership Model in action from another viewpoint. Use the answers to better your understanding of the responsibilities you have as a pilot leader.

Hopefully you can see the PIC Leadership Model in action presently in your job. With practice and time, you will be fully functioning as a transformational leader, able to picture yourself in the model, working all aspects of it.

ON PROFESSIONALISM

Taking pride in your professionalism means that you live out the definition of the word in every aspect of life, both while at work and away. Now that you are familiar with the PIC Leadership Model and how to use it to hone your ability to be a transformational leader, let's drill down a bit more on professionalism itself.

Early on in this chapter, we looked at the basic definition of a professional. Ethical, courteous, conscientious, and businesslike characteristics of oneself are borne of careful personal evaluation. In fact, it is a "soft skill" that regulators are now finally placing as a certification requirement for pilots operating in the air carrier segment of the aviation industry. In the fall of 2016, one of the biggest cornerstones of the Airline Safety and Federal Aviation Administration Extension Act of 2010 was moved forward toward regulatory codification through a notice of proposed rulemaking (NPRM). The regulations, which will affect pilots for scheduled and on-demand commercial air carriers, have been crafted to drive a deeper level of professional development in airline pilots. To understand why this was a necessary step, regulators highlighted two important accidents that occurred in the early part of the twenty-first century that shaped the way both the general public and the airline industry have focused new training, certification, and hiring standards for pilots.

The first of these accidents was Pinnacle Airlines 3701, a Bombardier CRJ200 ferry flight that experienced a dual engine failure at a high cruise altitude and subsequent crash at Jefferson City, Missouri, on October 14, 2004. The second accident was Colgan Air 3407, a Bombardier DHC-Q400 revenue flight from Newark, New Jersey, to Buffalo, New York, which experienced an aerodynamic stall during the approach to Buffalo on February 12, 2009. In both of these completely fatal accidents, pilot error was cited by the NTSB as the probable cause, with mitigating factors connected to professionalism and leadership skills.

For the purposes of this book, we will review the big picture of what happened in each accident, and also take a more focused look at how professionalism and mentorship issues are related to each one of them. To be clear, this is not intended to be a subsequent analysis of what happened in these accidents, nor a commentary on either as matters of fact. Rather, my sobering approach in describing these accidents is meant to set an important stage for understanding why professionalism, leadership, and airmanship is so very important to a pilot.

Pinnacle Flight 3701

Ferrying an empty airplane from point A to B is one of the most rewarding and "fun" types of flying airline pilots get to do in their careers. For many pilots, the reward of ferry flights comes from being able to harken back to the good old days that preceded their airline careers, when flying was not only to build experience, but for fun. A two-pilot crew with no one else on board to worry about—no passengers or cabin crew—makes the job that much less stressful. The airplane performs like a rocket ship: light, nimble, and seemingly overpowered with empty seats.

However, the opportunity to fly such a trip is not an excuse for pilots to forget that they are professionals. The crew of Flight 3701, shortly after departure, tested the limits of their airplane—just for fun. At 450 feet AGL, literally just after takeoff, the crew aggressively pitched to 22 degrees nose up, pulling 1.8 g, activating both the stick shaker and stick pusher of the stall warning system. At 15,000 feet, they tried some more fun, again pulling 2.3 g in another abrupt pitch up climb angle of 17 degrees. During this climb segment, the rudder was abruptly deflected left and right in excess of 7 degrees. Climbing through 24,600 feet, another aggressive climb maneuver was executed at 1.8 g. The NTSB says in the accident report, "The pilot's intentional maneuvers, which were not required for any operational reason or safety consideration, placed the airplane in a flight regime that likely exceeded the airplane's certificated flight envelope."

But, it wasn't these maneuvers that pushed the operational envelope to the brink of disaster. For "personal and not operational reasons," the NTSB concluded, the pilots decided that the ferry flight's filed cruise altitude of 33,000 feet was less preferable than seeing if the aircraft could make the leg at its service ceiling of 41,000 feet. The climb to FL410 was performed not only outside of SOP, but dangerously on the back side of the lift/drag curve. The pilots began the climb with an airspeed of only 203 knots, transitioned to Mach 0.63, and slowed to Mach 0.57 once they leveled off at FL410. (The prescribed climb speed in Pinnacle's SOP was to climb at no less than 250 KIAS/Mach 0.70, regardless of climb rate.) At FL410, the flight deck voice recorder captured both pilots' excitement and awe of their accomplishment. Despite noting that their airspeed was nearing stall advisory indications, they continued at FL410, and one crewmember left the flight deck to get sodas out of the galley.

The fun lasted only for another two and a half minutes. The Kansas City Center air traffic controller remarked that he hadn't seen a CRJ200 up at FL410 before. The captain responded that they "decided to have a little fun" with an empty plane. But after the words left his lips he realized that the plane was behind the power curve:

Captain (CA): "###'ing thing's losing it…"

First officer (F/O): *[laughing in nervousness and surprise]*

CA: "…we're losing here. We're gonna be ###ing coming down in a second here, dude."

F/O: *[still laughing…but maybe now more incredulously]*

CA: "This thing ain't gonna ###ing hold altitude, is it?"

F/O: "Dude, it's losing it!" *[a nervous chuckle]*

The captain called up Kansas City Center to ask for a lower altitude, but as Center told them to standby, it was too late. The stall warning system of the CRJ activated as the airspeed had deteriorated to 150 knots, or Mach 0.53, and the aircraft's angle of attack continued to increase.

The first automatic response of the stall warning system is to activate the stick shaker. Motorized counterweights shake the control columns to alert the pilot into a recovery action. This happened *five times* without response from the crew. As the aircraft angle of attack continues to increase, the stick pusher, a mechanical push on the control column to force the nose over, activates concurrently with the stick shaker. This happened four times, each time with the crew *pulling back* on the control column. The aircraft pitched up to 29 degrees, at which point the wing stopped flying. Then, in full aerodynamic stall, the nose sliced down to a negative 32 degrees as the plane violently rolled into a 82-degree left bank.

As the airplane fell out of the sky, the negative airflow to the twin GE turbofans caused both engines to flameout. The crew struggled to regain control in the pitch-black night sky over Missouri. As they fumbled for flashlights, the airplane's warning system chimed and annunciated system failure after system failure as the engines spooled down. The crew re-established a controlled descent, but not before the cores on both engines locked up. Their attempts to restart each powerplant failed, and despite efforts to glide to the Jefferson City Memorial Airport, their aircraft crashed into a residential area 2½ miles short of the airfield. The last words heard on the flight deck voice recorder from the captain were indicative, in the very least, of regret and resignation.

"Aw, ####. We are gonna hit houses, dude."

Colgan Air Flight 3407

Sometimes, flying is just not that fun. It's all work. Weather, ATC delays, maintenance issues, grumpy passengers, and other unexpected issues can crop up unexpectedly and completely ruin everyone's attitude. If you add non-flying issues into the situation—fatigue because you slept poorly, struggles to make ends meet on a new-hire salary, stress at home, stress getting to work, stress about your career—well, it isn't hard to see the threat to a safe flight operation. It's on "one of those days" that pilots need to step up their vigilance and identify the threats.

The crew of Colgan 3407 was having "one of those days." On February 12, 2009, a low-pressure system was sweeping through the New York City area, bringing high winds from the northwest and forcing delays at Liberty International Airport in Newark, New Jersey. The captain, having finished a two-day trip the prior day, slept in the airport crew room the night before. The first officer, fighting a head cold, commuted from Seattle, Washington, to Newark via Memphis on cargo flights. She was witnessed to have only slept three to four hours over the span of the sixteen-hour commute process. After learning that the initial out-and-back flights of their trip had been canceled, the captain spent time doing office work, and the first officer napped on and off in the crew room.

Once they entered the realm of operating their flight to Buffalo, New York, Newark was entering a period of extended ground delays, which meant long taxi times from the departure gate to the runway.

Since 1981, 14 CFR §121.542 has made it illegal for flight crews to engage in "non-essential conversation" while in critical phases of flight, including taxi, takeoff, landing, and flight below 10,000 feet MSL. Because humans are social creatures, this "sterile flight deck rule" is routinely bent, if not broken. After the crash of Pinnacle 3701 (and Corporate Air 5966, which crashed in Kirksville, Missouri, five days prior to Pinnacle 3701, killing 13), the NTSB issued a safety recommendation to the FAA that principal operating inspectors at air carriers operating under 14 CFR Parts 121 and 135 should re-emphasize the importance of strict compliance with the sterile flight deck rule.

However, five years after the Pinnacle and Corporate Air accidents, the crew of Colgan 3407 acted almost like the rule didn't exist. Beginning from the time they left the gate area, the pilots were in constant conversation, including during critical phases of flight, about topics that were not pertinent to flying the airplane. The chatter during their 90-minute taxi to the runway covered topics ranging from the first officer's head cold and the captain's background ("What did you do before Colgan?") to commuting pressures and costs, payroll problems, schedule and vacation dissatisfaction ("You feel like you're getting walked all over..."), and comments on the landing traffic as they progressed along the taxi route.

En route, and above 10,000 feet MSL, the crew turned their attention to filling in the aircraft logbook, talking about maintenance issues, and discussing their future career paths. From the start of their descent into Buffalo, except for during the approach briefing, they continued to chat. The first officer remarked about the ice accretion during the descent, and as the workload increased, they continued to talk about their experiences with icing.

During their initial descent, the flight deck voice recorder transcript reads like any other February night on approach to Buffalo. The crew worked through their final checklists as they finished off their stories of icing experiences. The captain, who was the pilot flying for the leg, got his seat "situated" for the approach. They started configuring—selecting flaps, putting landing gear down—and received a radio handoff to Buffalo Tower with a friendly "good night" call from Approach.

But the last 30 seconds of the CVR transcript reads like a nightmare. As the aircraft leveled off at the glideslope intercept altitude, the captain failed to add thrust as the airplane's drag increased with the configuration changes. The airspeed deteriorated and an aerodynamic stall occurred. Rather than reacting to the stall warning (stick shaker) as they had been trained, the crew exacerbated the stall through a series of fatal errors. The aircraft banked left and right as the captain continued to pull back on the control column rather than breaking the stall with nose-down pitch. The first officer, for unknown reasons, retracted the flaps. The Q400 continued to stall out, and eventually "spun in" to the earth below, impacting a house and killing everyone on board as well as an occupant of the house. Like the Pinnacle crash four years prior, the captain's last words were one of resignation: "We're down."

Accident Aftermath

In both of these tragic accidents, the pilots at the controls—and specifically the pilots-in-command, the captains—were blamed for their lack of professional behavior. In order to fully understand the context for these charges, I encourage you to read the accident reports and particularly the CVR transcripts of each accident, which are available on the NTSB website. The CVR recordings allow investigators to in essence get inside the flight deck, sit on the jump seat, and from what they hear, gauge not only the level of SOP compliance but also the interpersonal interaction between the crew.

Reading through the transcripts will plunge you right into the conversations, attitudes, reactions, and overall tone of the operation. It is precisely the tone of both Pinnacle 3701 and Colgan 3407 that caused investigators concern and gave rise to calls for training in professional development, leadership skills, and mentoring.

The trouble is that we must be careful when defining what the right tone is to foster a safe flight operation. We can certainly point out that getting along with one another aids CRM, and therefore increases the likelihood of a safe operation. However, nobody has blamed these crews for not getting along with one another. These pilots have not been accused of lacking camaraderie. They have received neither blame for their work ethic nor critique for their willingness to step up to the plate when their jobs were hard. Nobody will say that they didn't have a tone that fostered a drive to get the job done.

Problematically, the tone that was lacking was that of professionalism. Remember the basic definition? Did these pilots meet that definition? Unfortunately, they had no sense of seriousness when it came to technical or ethical standards. As we read through the transcripts, we are hard-pressed to identify the conscientious or businesslike attitudes that mark professionals. These crews got along just fine. But nobody spoke up and said, "Hey, let's be professional."

Instead, we glean some other, all-too-common attitudes from these crews. They bent the rules for fun, to show off, or just because they didn't think the rules were necessary. They did things they knew were wrong. They allowed threats to professionalism to become errors—and using the TEM approach here is completely fair. The errors manifested into the complete disregard for SOP causing undesired aircraft states.

Threats to Professionalism

Indeed, because of the variety of people's backgrounds, societal influences and pressures, and other elements that could be considered "latent threats," certain direct threats to professionalism are more prevalent, and thus easier to detect, than others.

The FAA's longstanding guidance for aviators on aeronautical decision making, Advisory Circular (AC) 60-22, *Aeronautical Decision Making*, has taught pilots about hazardous attitudes. Pilots learn about these attitudes as early as private pilot ground school, and the reason is that the hazardous attitudes remain the most common elements of human nature that get in the way of effective decision making. These same attitudes, along with some others I will highlight, are also direct threats to professionalism.

Machismo

An age-old part of human nature is that we tend to want to impress one another. Proving (when we really don't need to) that we can do something better than somebody else is a self-indulgent personality trait that is referred to as "machismo." Being "macho" includes acting tough, bending the rules for fun, acting out in one-upmanship, pushing limits, and trying to prove a point without being asked to do so in the first place.

Who knows what motivated the crew of Pinnacle 3701 to get to FL410. Was it machismo? What were they trying to prove when they attempted to fly a CRJ like a stunt plane?

Professionals don't allow themselves to get into macho-mode. They understand that all they have to prove is that they can follow SOPs and get the job done right. When considering that professional attitudes have a "businesslike" characteristic, machismo will have no place among them.

Rebel/Anti-Authority

Closely linked to machismo is another threat to professionalism that manifests itself in very strong, sometimes visceral ways. Some people thrive on being known as "rebels"—they see their value in their ability to go against the grain, and they do so by taking an anti-authority approach to everything they do. When I was a first officer, I flew with several captains who thought it was OK to skip briefings, checklists, and simply fly by the seat of their own pants. They were rebels, and they demanded respect for it. Unfortunately, they were mistaken in thinking their anti-authority attitude would garner much more than an eye roll.

Blatant SOP non-compliance is a hallmark of a pilot with a rebel attitude. Knowing that something is wrong and doing it anyway is flat out dangerous in the operating environment of the pilot. Professional pilots, however, don't need to be rebels, because they are ethical, courteous, and conscientious. As transformational leaders, they set a tone and direction in how they operate that drowns out the rebel tendencies of others.

Resignation

As discussed earlier about the crew of Colgan 3407, "they were having one of those days." I have operated in and out of the Newark Liberty International Airport for several years, and in and out of hubs all day long (sometimes up to eight legs a day back in the "old days"), so I really do get it. It can be fatiguing when the delays, the weather, the maintenance issues, the bad passenger attitudes, and everything else you have no control over mount up flight after flight. However, it's not professional to let threats to safe flight linger in existence just because it seems like it's the "same crap, different day." The dangerous attitude here is called resignation. And, just like the main definition of the word, this attitude basically means you quit! But what pilots with this attitude are doing is quitting at being standard, and quitting the quest to do their best.

Professionals know that sometimes the going gets tough. But in the face of a challenge, they strive to rise up to meet it rather than slump into a pity party. Sticking to SOPs, ensuring that everything has been checked and re-checked, and pushing themselves to be the best they can be, professional pilots conquer resignation.

Laziness

Laziness is similar to resignation, but not exactly the same. An attitude of laziness seeps into our everyday lives very subtly at times. Around my house, it tends to be the aversion to house chores that gets tagged with an appraisal of laziness. But in the flight deck, laziness is often seen as a pilot's lack of motivation to fly proficiently.

We will undoubtedly encounter pilots who aren't up to speed on a certain procedural change. If the change happened just a couple of days to a few weeks ago, it is possible the pilot just isn't aware that the change was made. But if the change was made a month or more ago, then the pilot is simply being lazy about not learning the new procedure.

Taking your proficiency seriously is the habit of a professional. Working hard to find and learn the details of how a system works, or how to practically carry out a task, keeps laziness at bay. Finding opportunities to become more proficient through learning and practice not only shows proactivity on the part of a professional pilot, it proves to others that you take your job seriously.

Apathy

Laziness and apathy can go hand in hand. But for an aviator, apathy takes on a dark color that becomes deadly in the flight deck. Apathy is the attitude of indifference—the "I just don't care anymore" mindset. For many pilots, it may stem from feeling like they are constantly being wronged, undervalued, or ignored. The antagonist of wrongdoing, undervaluation, or ignorance can sometimes be the pilot sitting right next to them! But in many cases, the antagonist tends to be the employer themselves. On this point I can agree, having survived two bankruptcies and being paid slack wages to fly airplanes to the point I needed a second job. Pilots can and do feel these things. But having an apathetic attitude doesn't alleviate the situation. Deciding that because you are getting "walked on" you don't need to do the job right doesn't prove anything other than your selfish stupidity. Two wrongs don't make a right.

Professionals will counter attitudes of apathy, indifference, and dispiritedness with an attitude of appreciation toward the responsibilities they carry as pilot leaders. The safety, efficiency, crew dynamics, and duty to the operation keep these professionals above water when the stormy seas of feeling wronged come rolling in.

Impulsivity

Flying high-performance airliners takes speed and efficiency to a whole new level. Just before writing this, I was in a jump seat observing an initial operating experience (IOE) flight. The newly hired first officer had flown single-engine Cessnas as an instructor, and had only the minimum required hours of multi-engine time, all in reciprocating-engine airplanes. As we cruised over the upper Midwest, he related that he couldn't believe how fast things were going. Naturally, flying at 550 mph gives us an unnatural sense that we have to rush things. As ground-dwelling humans, we have a tendency to become impulsive when we take to the skies. The only problem is that when we think we need to do tasks quickly, and rush to get them done without allowing time to stop and think through the tasks as we complete them, we make mistakes.

Investigators look at the behaviors of crews, like those of Pinnacle 3701 and Colgan 3407, and wonder why SOPs get botched up. Do the flight deck voice recorders show signs of impulsivity, rushing, and blatant "cowboying" of procedures (when a person makes up their own procedure or remedy for a non-normal situation)? Did they run procedures methodically?

Professional pilots combat impulsivity by leaning into honest discernment, which is one of the virtues found in PIC Leadership Model. For example, when running a checklist, professional pilots take their time to carefully read and think through the meaning of each item. *Has it really been checked? How do we check it? Did we do it that way?* As a professional pilot, this quick mental quality analysis will help you slow down and ensure you are doing things right.

Invulnerability

Air travel is statistically the safest way to get from place to place across the globe. On average, approximately 110,000 commercial flights are conducted each day. The accident and incident rate is incredibly low: the odds of being killed in an airline flight are *1 in 29 million*. So, it shouldn't surprise us that pilots can be susceptible to attitudes of invulnerability. Quite frankly, it happens more often than one would think. There are many examples: an invulnerable attitude could result in a pilot not following the necessary deviation and cutting too close around a severe thunderstorm. Or a pilot may decide to intentionally take a large shortcut without considering downline winds, betting that the fuel will be sufficient. Or as a final example, how about getting slam dunked on approach, not attaining full configuration or a stabilized approach to landing, and then *not going around?*

These are real-life examples that have happened repeatedly. In fact, it is highly probable that they have occurred somewhere today. But why? Don't pilots know better? As pilots, we get trained to do better. We get admonished time and time again with accident reports, safety alerts and memos, and simple word of mouth ("Did ya hear about so-and-so's botched landing and tailstrike the other day?"). Pilots cannot ignore the wealth of information in front of them that proves they are most certainly not invulnerable. They are completely vulnerable, and pilot error is responsible for a full third of all accidents.

Counteracting an attitude of invulnerability is as simple as remembering to respect what you are doing as a professional pilot. Flying is an amazing feat of science and skill, quite unnatural to humankind. By tapping into the commitment to duty that is required (another PIC Leadership Model Virtue), a professional pilot is mindful of how their flying affects passengers, crew, and employers.

LIVING THE PART

This chapter is entitled "Pride in Professionalism" very purposefully. It is a common motto and is worded similarly to the motto "Pride and Professionalism." The two are vastly different, however, in intended meaning. Pride can certainly be separated from professionalism into bilateral virtues. Pride as a virtue (rather than a vice, or even sin) is a celebration of ability and a feeling of accomplishment. Sometimes we feel pride for the things we accomplish with others. Oftentimes the motto "Pride *and* Professionalism" is therefore used for a group of people working together as professionals, such as a police force or a business.

An individual leader must take pride *in* their professionalism. That is the motto that pilots-in-command should plaster on their flight cases. It means living out the aspects of professionalism in every thought, word, and deed. Really, everything a pilot does needs to reflect that he or she honestly feels accomplished, and fully able, as a professional pilot.

While I don't want this section to segue, or even morph, into a bit of "charm-school" type preachiness, I do want to give you some good tips on how to truly feel that pride and accomplishment as you live the life of a professional pilot. The tips are simple and focus a lot on appearance.

First, wear your uniform with pride. For some reason, the casual and cavalier nature of American society has created an environment where many pilots just throw on their uniform without proper care, and oftentimes in opposition to company policy. No different than the business executives who take time and effort to look sharp in suit and tie, pilots are viewed by the public as professionals. They are expected to look the part. Your company may have selected a uniform that you don't like. Perhaps you feel more like a fancy doorman or a ship captain in formal dress. It really doesn't matter, because it is your *duty* and your *responsibility* to wear that uniform properly and with *pride*.

Second, remember that the public image of the professional airline pilot goes deeper than just the threads. Carry yourself with confidence and a positive attitude. Honestly, there are things surrounding our everyday lives—both at home and work—that can bring us down, and the weight of that emotion and stress can become visible. I am not recommending you walk through the airport with a giant smile on your face. But I am certainly saying that a scowl, lack of eye contact, and general malaise in attitude is not very professional.

Finally, I think having pride in your professionalism requires that you exemplify it by teaching and inspiring others. When it comes down to it, every PIC is a mentor. Effective mentors apply their leadership skills to teach, represent, and motivate the people they work with. Mentoring is very much the practical application of the influence that leaders have.

Chapter 14 Notes

1. McCloskey, Mark, "The 4R Model of Leadership: A Virtue-Based Curricular Model For Business Education In A Global Context." (St. Paul, Minnesota: Bethel University, 2009)

2. Ibid.

3. Ibid.

4. Kotter, J.P. *A Force for Change* (New York: The Free Press, 1990); Nanus, B. *Visionary Leadership* (San Francisco: Jossey-Bass, 1992).

5. 14 CFR §1.1—General Definitions: Pilot in command means the person who:
   (1) Has final authority and responsibility for the operation and safety of the flight;
   (2) Has been designated as pilot in command before or during the flight; and
   (3) Holds the appropriate category, class, and type rating, if appropriate, for the conduct of the flight.

6. McCloskey, "The 4R Model of Leadership"

15

Customers Care that You Care

Some people, if not the majority of them, can remember their first flight on a commercial airliner. For some of us it was at a young age, where the impression left an indelible mark upon our lives that started the fascination which grew into a flying career. For others, their first flight was later in life when perhaps it wasn't as eye-popping exciting as if it had happened at a younger age. Regardless of the time frame or the emotional impact, most people were probably drawn to some common experiences and observations from their maiden voyage on an airliner.

To begin with, we all likely took stock of the airplane itself. Was it clean and well maintained? How did it look on the outside and the inside? We also likely did a mental assessment of the crewmembers we encountered: Were they kind and cordial? Did they seem confident? Did they make us feel assured in our safety?

While in flight, human senses are elevated to levels of awareness they aren't used to if the individual is unaccustomed to flight. So every twitch, bump, turn, acceleration, and deceleration is blatant, especially to the new flier. And every sound the airplane makes is evaluated more closely than common sounds they are accustomed to.

The grand finale—the descent, approach, and landing—are perhaps the most critical memories imparted to people on every flight, and again particularly to first-timers. But the funny thing about air travel and the general public's impressions of their flight experiences is that the impressions are only lasting if they were *remarkable*. And by remarkable I mean experiences that were beyond compare to the best, and beyond compare to the worst. Ask most people how the landing was, even a week after their flight, and they will likely recall absolutely nothing unless something unusual happened, typically for the worse. I was commuting just the other day when one of these landings happened. The pilot flying applied the brakes so hard at high speed that several passengers found themselves bracing against the seats in front of them, or smacking their faces into the seats.

But the vast majority—99 percent—of all phases of flight operations are unremarkable. Nobody will remember the "greaser" landings. Nobody will remember if they heard the cabin announcement about flying over Denver on the way to Salt Lake City. And why should they? Our customers simply want to get from Point A to Point B in one piece. And that is indeed the key to customer service in the airline industry. It focuses in on one simple human psychological need: the need for *safety and security*.

Anyone who took Psychology 101 in college, or perhaps even studied the basics of psychology in high school, should be familiar with Abraham Maslow. The twentieth-century psychologist worked on human motivation and self-actualization theories, and in doing so created a "hierarchy of needs" to illustrate his work. This hierarchy, modeled as a five-level pyramid, lists the basic human psychological needs required to reach fulfillment and self-actualization. They are (in order from the base to the top of the pyramid): physiological, safety, love/belonging, esteem, and self-actualization.[1]

Of interest to this discussion is the fact that in Maslow's model, *safety* is a primary basic need, and in fact it is second only to physiological needs (food, water, sleep, etc.) in importance. The simple point is that *people NEED to feel safe*. Once the basics of physiology and safety are met, humans feel fulfilled to seek the next higher levels of being human: belonging and interacting with others, seeking and attaining recognition, and finally developing knowledge and impacting the world around. But none of it happens unless they feel they are *safe*.

None of this should be surprising. As pilots, we are personally driven towards safety, not only through the demands of pilot vocation, but through our own psychological needs. A friend of mine related a story about a transatlantic flight he made recently that was progressing en route, at night, very smoothly. Many people had the window shades drawn and were sleeping. Suddenly, a small patch of turbulence bumped the drowsy cabin to wakefulness. People immediately opened their shades and peered out the windows. The interruption of the smooth flight triggered the psychological response that safety may indeed be in jeopardy. The reaction of looking out the window to find the cause would be, according to Maslow, quite natural! The next thing to happen, as you may have guessed, was the telltale chime of the "FASTEN SEATBELTS" sign illuminating, followed by an announcement from the flight deck reassuring the passengers that all was well and that the turbulence had subsided.

Here again we can see the link to customer service. People want their coffee, wine, cola, and ration of peanuts, of course. But more than anything, they want to feel safe. They want the crew to reassure them that they are safe. They want to confirm through sensory inputs, observations, and information provided to them that they are safe and will remain safe for the duration of their airborne excursion. Let's explore how we can help people fulfill their need for safety while aboard our airplane, and in doing so, master the essence of customer service.

NO MATTER THE FARE, THEY CARE

Our passengers board our airplanes with tickets of varying fare value. Some customers get cheap deals, and some pay through the nose. Still others are frequent fliers who routinely cash in their loyalty incentives for airfare. But no matter what ticket price they paid, they all care about their need to feel safe in the crew's hands. Whether you fly airplanes for a regional carrier, pulling connecting passengers from small towns into the big hubs, or you operate out of the large international big-city airports and take folks to foreign soil, the mission remains the same.

It is important to keep in mind that regardless of the type of flying we do, the type of aircraft we operate, or the types of passengers we carry, each and every one of our customers is human. They all care about the way we take care of their very basic needs, with safety being at the forefront. Therefore, we must construct a clear, consistent message that makes the passenger feel confident that the crew has made safety a priority.

COMMUNICATING TO CUSTOMERS: BEYOND THE PA

Without going into too much communications theory here, we should all be able to agree on several points. The first is the fact that communication can be verbal and non-verbal. In addition, communications should be planned and delivered in a clear and concise manner (again, regardless if it is verbal or non-verbal). And finally, it's easy to agree on the importance of regular communications, even including the delivery of messages containing information that was previously delivered. (In other words, a "no new news" update is more valuable than no update at all.) Given all of these points, we can begin to look at ways to appropriately communicate with our customers.

First, let's address verbal versus non-verbal communication. Verbal communication is the most direct method for delivering a message. It is the most natural, as well: humans are *talkers*. We use language, word choice, voice tone and inflection to convey a wide range of information, emotions, and intentions. But non-verbal communication can be just as effective. Unfortunately, so much non-verbal communication is unintentional. Whether it is our body posture, a frown, a scowl, a stomp, a sigh, a slam, a kick, or a shake of the head, all too often such non-verbal cues are negative. So a huge part of *intentional* communication is making the effort to be conscious of these negative cues, and making every effort to suppress them or to display positive ones.

Next, I want to talk about honesty in our messages. All too often I have heard announcements made—whether by pilots, flight attendants, or gate agents—that were blatantly dishonest or were not quite telling the whole story. I am certain that sometimes these messages were vague or misleading only because the person giving the announcement was in the dark themselves on the real honest truth of the situation. However, here are some of the problems with using even the smallest of fibs in your communications:

1. People see right through it. In fact, all too often when someone detects a lie, the truth is even easier to identify, making the lie all for naught.

2. Fibs, lies, and vagaries all can get out of hand quickly, especially if they are far-fetched or if the truth is easily at hand. The proverbial "hole" you dig with a misrepresentation of the facts can rapidly get deeper, and harder to emerge from.

3. When caught in a lie, you lose all respect from your audience and your integrity goes down the tubes. Any further communication, even if the communication is to rectify the lie, is sometimes useless because people disregard your message as lacking in the truth department.

Therefore, when you construct your messages to passengers, focus on the following goals for the message:

- The message is planned and reviewed before delivery.
- The message is factual, clear, and concise.
- The message is timely, relevant, and responds to feedback when necessary.

For each and every communication you make as a pilot, you should also endeavor to include a word on how it relates to safety, remembering that a primary concern of passengers is their own safety. Whether it is a pre-departure announcement, seat belt announcement, arrival announcement, delay at the gate, waiting in line for the runway, diversion, or an actual emergency, any message that includes the word "safety" or communicates that safety is not in jeopardy scores big points with your audience, every time.

VALUE-ADDED CUSTOMER INTERACTIONS

All too often, pilots end up being the men and women behind the curtain—oddly like the great and powerful Oz. Passengers know someone is in the flight deck flying the plane, and they understand the concept of flight deck security. All too often during pre- and post-flight, however, the flight deck crew clears out on the first chance to escape, remains behind the door, or simply occupies themselves with idle chatter with other crewmembers while the passengers move in and out. Passengers likely see this as the norm, viewing the pilots as ever-busy, too buried in dials, switches and charts to emerge. Granted, your duties may indeed prohibit your emergence, especially when the workload is high, but consider the impact you can have by making an effort to interact directly with passengers. Following are some ideas for ways to accomplish this.

Preflight Greetings

If you are able, stand near the entry door, perhaps even in the jet bridge, and welcome the passengers aboard. It's simple to do, and just by making yourself visible and available for any questions, concerns, or other needs lets your passengers know that they are *indeed* the priority for your flight. Alternatively, or additionally, if you are operating an aircraft that has first- or business-class seating, or know of a group of high-value customers, make a point to greet them separately. Walking back through first class, saying "welcome aboard" and asking customers if they have any questions reinforces the customer relationship. That small level of recognition may convince them to book again on your carrier, even in spite of a delay or other mitigating circumstance.

Inflight Interactions

On longer segments, it is common for pilots to emerge from the flight deck for physiological needs, including settling in for their rest period if operating with an augmented flight crew. This may be another opportunity to interact with passengers, greet them, and ask them if they have questions or need anything. On many of my flights, the "rest facility" for our breaks is a blocked seat in business/first class, and more often than not, it is located right next to a paying passenger.[2] I always make sure I have a business card on me when I head back for break. It is likely that I will converse with the passenger sitting next to me before I close my eyes, or after I wake, and a great way to "close" that interaction (akin to "closing the sale") is to write a thank you note on the business card and hand it to them. It is such a small thing, but it will go a long way to impress the customer that you care enough to share business credentials with them—a standard practice among professionals across all sorts of industries.

Post Flight

After you complete your post-flight duties and are all packed up (or even before you pack up), why not step out of the flight deck and thank the passengers while they deplane. It is more likely that they will say thanks before the words escape your own lips. This also makes you available as a resource for passengers needing a last-minute wheelchair, cart, help with a bag, etc.

Around the Airport

How often do you see passengers looking lost in the airport? My experience has been that I see them more often than not. And I also am frequently approached by passengers looking for assistance in finding a gate, flight information, baggage claim, or even a simple recommendation for a bite to eat. I encourage you to embrace these opportunities to interact with passengers. They may not be flying on your specific flight, or even on your specific airline. But taking just a few moments to answer a question with a smile on your face will be impactful. Don't forget to give a wink to the kids, too. Remember back to when you were a kid and a pilot gave you that wink or nod of confidence, and remember that your kindness today will encourage and inspire the next generation of professional aviators.

Chapter 15 Notes

1. Does the focus on human needs sound familiar? Review Chapter 4, where I describe the importance of briefing your crew to communicate that you want to know what their needs are.

2. It is preferable to have any seats adjacent to the rest seat blocked so as to avoid having to crawl over passengers and disrupt them.

16

Continuous Improvement, Continuing Qualification

Amazingly enough, the workforce of the world gets on about its business with very little in the way of required continuing education. There are plenty of jobs out there where you get hired, learn your role and tasks, and basically qualify through experience how to best do your job. Sure, there may be an initial training period, but once you are out from under the tutelage of a trainer or supervisor, you are pretty much on your own.

Airline pilots, however, are not just required to attend rigorous new-hire and initial equipment training, but also to participate in recurring training events. The airline industry term in the United States is *"Continuing Qualification" (CQ)*—aviation terminology for the more common *continuing education*. CQ is an important anchor point for the safety and integrity of our industry.

THE BASICS OF CQ

In Part I of this book, I went into great detail about Initial Qualification training under AQP. Again, with CQ, my main lens for explaining how you can be your best is one where AQP is the training method. If your carrier conducts recurrent training under Subparts N and O, my advice in this chapter will still apply.[1]

Continuing Qualification under AQP involves a regular exposure to training material and subject matter to bolster and refresh pilot knowledge, regular evaluations of flight proficiency during simulator events, and in some cases classroom seminar or instruction. Each carrier has a CQ footprint that applies to each pilot depending on the qualification and experience history of the pilot. Commonplace is the regularity of the CQ timeframe governing when a pilot visits classrooms, simulators, or has to complete online training modules.

Here is how my current CQ cycle looks over a 24-month period:

Continuing Qualification Component	Cycle Timeframe
Distance Learning (computer-based)	Every 4 months
Maneuvers Validation (CQMV)	9 months following previous CQLOE
Emergency Equipment/Doors Training	Every 18 Months
Line Oriented Evaluation (CQLOE)	9 months following previous CQMV
Line Check	At least once every 24 months

Keep in mind, under AQP, a carrier develops its own way of providing curriculum, training, evaluation, and qualification requirements that are required under Part 121, and the FAA approves the program on a carrier-by-carrier basis. This avoids the one-size-fits-all approach, as each carrier has cultural, operational, business, and fleet circumstances. For example, some carriers conduct classroom training (recurrent ground school) to cover general subjects. Others have different cycles and timeframes for Captains and First Officers so long as the data being collected and verified from the program shows the FAA that the program can "exceed minimum training standards in the greater interest of safety."[2]

AQP changed the paradigm for Part 121 carrier flight training. Under Part 121, Subparts N and O, the components for proficiency are basically curriculum and hours. AQP allows carriers to utilize a system that delivers curriculum, but instead of simply training or checking for a number of required hours to remain qualified, qualification is achieved through actual proficiency training and evaluation. Most importantly, as I described earlier in this book, AQP evaluations check the proficiency of a crew and how they safely operate together, not just of each individual pilot. The same holds true with continuing qualification events under AQP.

The Big Picture

Early on in my airline career I used to look forward to checking events with dread and despair. I attribute my bad attitude towards recurrent training to three main culprits:

- I felt that reviewing and being tested on the same material year after year was neither helping me become a better pilot, nor advancing my career.

- Proficiency checks were disparaged and bemoaned by co-workers as a punitive, unrealistic tests of our abilities as pilots. Due to the subjective discretion of the check airman, we could fail a checkride for even the simplest of errors, putting our careers on the line. I totally bought into this line of thinking.

- I believed that instructors, evaluators, and check airmen who spent 99 percent of their time in classrooms, briefing rooms, and simulators and 1 percent of their time flying actual trips couldn't possibly be tuned into the realities of the flight operation. I questioned their credibility.

These were limiting beliefs about recurrent training that were keeping me from performing at my best during proficiency checks and definitely while I was operating actual flights.

Eventually, I recognized that by lowering my expectations for CQ events, I was lowering the expectations I had for my own success. I decided that was completely counterproductive, and I turned my limiting beliefs into liberating truths when it came to my career and my own level of professionalism.

First, instead of believing that reviewing the same material year after year was a waste of time, I embraced the fact that without continual review and refreshment, I would lose the edge on my airmanship. I need the cycle of repetition to remain at the top of my game.

Second, I realized that proficiency checks, maneuvers validation, and other evaluations were actually crafted to qualify us in ways that lead to better proficiency. This was bolstered by the continued implementation of AQP across the industry.

Finally, I understood the truth about the instructors and check airmen who seem to live in the schoolhouse: *They really have seen it all.* This was something I gained clarity on when I became an instructor at my airline. One of my instructor mentors said, "We see it all here in the training environment. The good, the bad, and the ugly all get demonstrated during training events. The ways a pilot operates on the real-world flight line will all be revealed in the simulator."

So, to boil it down, here are the liberating truths I have come to embrace as I continue to work for continual improvement, ever sharpening my professional edge as a pilot:

1. Review and refreshment on a regular cycle keeps me sharp and at the top of my game.

2. CQ is designed to make me better, and if it doesn't, I am not the failure any more than the program is

3. Instructors and Evaluators are invaluable resources for me to use in my quest for superb airmanship.

PRACTICAL PERFORMANCE

A big part of having a successful recurrent training event is preparation. In my experience, that preparation begins in how you perform every day on the real flight line—executing normal everyday flight operations at a high level of airmanship and professionalism makes performance in a CQ event a cinch. Here are four practical ways you can take your performance during CQs, proficiency checks, LOFTs, or any recurrent event to the next level:

Line Performance Should Equal Evaluated Performance

As I said above, if you fly everyday trips per SOP, on profile, and with intentional efforts to fly professionally and with superb airmanship, your recurrent/CQ events will be a success. All too often, pilots get into the mindset that there is some higher level of performance required for CQ events. This is antithetical to the purpose of, and detracts value from, data-driven, crew-centered continuing qualification events. Flying at full performance in all operations is the professional pilot's goal. When we get to the simulator, that level of performance will naturally show up.

Armchair Flying Required for Non-Normals

Pilots cannot practice full-performance flying on engine failures, rejected takeoffs, emergency evacuations, and other non-normals as a part of routine flight operations. Therefore, we need to do some extra prep on non-normals prior to attending our CQ event. Ideally, we would all have some extra warm-up and practice time in the full-flight simulators or FTDs. Unfortunately, those opportunities are extremely rare for the average line pilot. The next best study method, in my experience, is good old armchair flying. Armchair flying becomes a lost art for many aviators as they get more experienced and confident. But even a couple short sessions of visualization of profiles, procedures, and repetition of memory items will sharpen you up and set you up for success.

Know the Obscure and Forgotten

Another way to advance our airmanship skills in a way that bolsters success in recurrent training and checking events is the ability to know and recall limitations, obscure supplementary procedures, and system operations that you last studied in initial aircraft qualification training. Take some time prior to your event to review memory action items and limitations you are required to know. Make sure you are solid on these knowledge areas. Then, go over the non-memory items, and non-memory non-normals that you think might be worth a read through (complex/compound hydraulic or electrical system faults are great candidates for this). Finally, go over any supplementary procedures you haven't visited for a while. Winter ops, alternative engine start procedures, and general operating policies are all fair game here. One key tip for studying this stuff: knowing where to look up a certain less-used procedure or piece of info is equally if not more important than knowing the details.

Embrace CRM and TEM

All your efforts to be compliant with SOP will be for naught if you are slack in CRM or TEM skills. One way to amplify your proficiency in CRM is to get just a bit more vocal. Gone are the days of the silent flight deck when the crew is focusing on crucial aircraft control and performance. Verbalize a bit more on what you are doing and what you are seeing your partner do. When aircraft configuration changes are called for, read back and confirm, even if it's not a standard call. Point out potential deviations from profile, speeds, attitudes, power settings, etc., before they become errors. Anticipate all threats verbally and be obvious about how you are identifying the threat.

Enjoyment Equals Improvement

Finally, in order to make your recurrent training or checking the best it can be, enjoy it! Relax, be encouraging to your training partner, and be confident. Take the opportunity to learn and expand your skill set. When the instructor or evaluator says at the end, "Ok! That's it. Is there anything else you want to see?" take the chance to work on something again you thought you could do better. Max crosswind landing? Engine failure, low altitude, on the missed approach? High altitude engine failure? Perhaps you want to see how well you'd perform a quick ditch maneuver, like Sully did? So long as your extra time in the sim is used targeting higher levels of proficiency and airmanship, your instructor/ evaluator and training partner should be game for it too.

Once you reach this level of enjoyment of your CQ events, your time spent will equal continuous improvement. Leaving the training center and heading back to the flight line should feel refreshing and, in a way, empowering. Completing a recurrent training cycle means you have not only demonstrated that you *continue* to show operational proficiency, but that you have added another notch of experience to your belt. Once you get back to the flight line, share the experience with your peers. Give them "the gouge" on how the training event and evaluation scenario played out. What did you do right? What could you have done better? Remember the debriefing from the event, be mindful of it, and use it to your benefit to strengthen your airmanship skills.

Chapter 16 Notes

1. Non-AQP recurrent training typically includes recurrent ground training (whether in-person, classroom training or remote, computer-based training), and proficiency checks on a 12 to 24 month cycle.
2. FAA AC 120-54 "Advanced Qualification Program"

17

The Superb Airmanship Model™

There I was, seat 21C, on a deadhead flight from one of our hub cities to another. I didn't know the pilots up front, but they seemed to be running a pretty tight ship. The cabin announcements were average, standardized, and quickly done between checklists and the closing of the main cabin door. We headed out to the runway ahead of schedule, but the taxi technique seemed stop-and-go, speed-up and slow-down. While airborne, you could *distinctly* tell when the autopilot was on and when it was off. Altitude changes were abrupt. The landing was firm, brakes applied swiftly to get the first high speed taxiway exit, and we seemed to race to the gate.

No margins of safety were threatened. It seemed like everything was on profile. We departed early and arrived on time. But as we were deplaning, one of the passengers who was sitting a few rows in front of me decided to complain to the pilots on his way out.

"That was the worst flying I have ever experienced," the passenger complained.

"Oh, I am sorry to hear that, did something happen?" the Captain responded with a confused but concerned tone.

"It just seemed like you guys were in a big rush. It just didn't feel smooth or calm like it should," the passenger said, now noticing that he was holding up the line of people behind him waiting to deplane.

"I am sorry you felt that way. Our job is to get you here safely, and as close to on-time as possible," replied the Captain. "Thanks for flying with us today."

"I guess I'll probably get a better ride in my cab this afternoon," the passenger fired his parting shot as he exited the airplane.

I was only a few passengers behind him as he said this. As I approached the main cabin door, the Captain recognized me in uniform and assumed I heard the exchange. He gave me the incredulous "what the heck" look with raised eyebrows and shook his head. I simply smiled and said, "Thanks for the ride."

Professional pilots can be so hooked up on following rigid SOP and ensuring they get the job done, they can forget that there is more to flying airplanes from A to B than just blocking in without bending metal. All too often we can get wrapped into the nuts and bolts of the vocation and lapse into a mechanical mode of operation. Simply meeting minimum standards, or just ensuring that basic rules are followed and proper procedures are adhered to, can miss an important aspect of flying. That aspect is commonly referred to as *airmanship*, and it lies at the core of what we do to fly the airplane safer while pursuing state-of-the art precision and performance.

While some would argue that airmanship is too elusive to define, several authors before me have taken on the task, and have done quite well. Dr. Tony Kern, who alone can be quoted time and time again without fear of misrepresentation wrote an entire book on the topic. In it he says, "Airmanship is the consistent use of good judgment and well-developed skills to accomplish flight objectives. This consistency is founded on a cornerstone of uncompromising flight discipline and developed through systematic skill acquisition and proficiency. A high state of situational awareness completes the airmanship picture and is obtained through knowledge of one's self, aircraft, team, environment, and risk."[1]

Notwithstanding my anecdote at the beginning of this chapter, airmanship isn't simply about smoothness, flying style, or greaser landings. Instead, as Kern pointed out, it encompasses all elements of our flying skills and faculties. A more concise definition of airmanship is provided in the FAA's *Airplane Flying Handbook:* "A sound acquaintance with the principles of flight, the ability to operate an airplane with competence and precision both on the ground and in the air, and the exercise of sound judgment that results in optimal operational safety and efficiency."

I could go on with several more definitions that authors previous to me have devised. Captain Dave English, who maintains a fantastic website and blog regarding his own journey of continual self-improvement in airmanship, and who has prolifically researched and written on the subject, writes, "Airmanship is a multi-dimensional concept that enables us to have skillful control of an aircraft, make good decisions about the flight, and is tightly linked to uncompromising flight discipline. *It is not something outside of the pilot, but rather is a personal state or mindset. Airmanship is an inner condition tied to continuous self-improvement and manifesting itself as optimal personal piloting performance* [emphasis mine]. This is the airmanship we will strive for."[2]

THE SUPERB AIRMANSHIP MODEL™

Achieving airmanship in the form of a "personal state or mindset" involves actual effort. I have found that there are ways to operate that I can commit to as a professional pilot. Over time, these have formed an operational model of airmanship that I continue to utilize every time I fly.

The Superb Airmanship Model™ uses some of the same components found in other definitions, models, and expressions of airmanship. However, this is my own formula, and one that I find works best within the context of everything else I have shared with you in this book.

Experience, judgement, proficiency, precision, efficiency, and performance are the synergistic components of airmanship in my model. When I fly, it involves pulling together everything I have experienced as a pilot, the use of sound judgement, and flying at my highest level of proficiency. Experience, judgement, and proficiency form the foundation for airmanship.

I use a combination of routines, debriefings, and study to enhance my mindfulness when I fly and to increase my knowledge about flying. I follow SOP while developing and using my own techniques and triggers to enhance my physical flying skills and faculties. By developing enhanced mindfulness, knowledge, skills, and faculties, I increase the levels of precision and efficiency I have when flying. High levels of precision and efficiency lead to the final outcome of the flight in terms of overall performance.

This model is driven by the practices I use to increase and enhance knowledge, mindfulness, flight skills and faculties. So, lets dig deeper into those practices.

Routines

High performing, professional athletes from all sports and disciplines are known for being masters of rituals and routines that give them the edge each and every time they play. If they aren't doing everything they possibly can to be at the top of their game, they won't be able to compete at the highest levels.

The same can be said for top professionals in all walks of life. This includes airline pilots: all pilots are called to be at the top of their game when they get on the flight deck. Our fellow crewmembers, passengers, employers, other flights, and the general public are counting on us to run a safe and sound flight operation each time we are at the controls.

Routines in the Superb Airmanship Model™ set me up for the mental and physical demands of flying professionally and serve to facilitate the increase of my knowledge and mindfulness as we work towards superb airmanship. These routines include actions I take before, during, and after my trips.

Pre-Trip Routine

Before every trip I have a set checklist of items I need to accomplish to feel completely prepared to operate. Along with the personal wellness routines I have, these set the stage for my best attempts to achieve superb airmanship. I follow this checklist 12-24 hours prior to the start of my trip:

- ☐ Schedule review and trip visualization
- ☐ Off-time planning
- ☐ Weather check
- ☐ Packing
- ☐ Commute planning

The pre-trip routine uses some of the same thought processes and skills I discussed in Part II, Chapter 6, Schedule Management. The framework in that chapter involved managing my schedule from the time it is originally awarded or assigned, up through and including the operation of each individual trip. Here, in the pre-trip routine I get more detailed while employing that framework.

Schedule review and trip visualization is straightforward in the pre-trip routine. I look over what is ahead of me for the trip—city pairs, flight times, layovers, and any other trip details of which to be mindful. I nail down my plans for the layovers and long breaks between flights as I check off *off-time planning.*

Next, I check the weather for my trip. A simple visit to a weather app, or even just to Google to do a quick *weather* check for the current conditions and forecast for the cities I will be operating in and out of on the trip. I make particular note of the forecast for my layovers so I can pack accordingly for my activities.

Packing for my trip is also done via a routine. I have found this to be extremely valuable to make this a standard routine that I repeat every time I pack. Simply stated, I pack the minimum I need for the trip.

Finally, the last task of my pre-trip routine is to plan my commute. If you live near your base of operations, this is a bit easier to accomplish— you simply plan out drive times or public transit schedules to get you to the airport safely in time for your trip. If you are like 60 percent of crewmembers, however, you don't live "in base," but rather take advantage of flight benefits (standby non-revenue, discounted fare, or jump-seat privileges) to enable a commute from your home city to your pilot base. For many carriers, there are commuter policies in place to allow for the possibility that your commuting plans may fall through (flight cancellations, sellouts, etc.).

Regardless of these policies, my *commute planning* always provides several backups. I allow myself two flights, both of which will get me from home to base at least two hours before I have to report. I start checking loads and seat availability to the extent possible to strategically eliminate flight options that have a higher risk of becoming unavailable to me.

Off-Duty Routine

After each duty period of my trip ends, I take time to do this relatively quick routine:

- ☐ Logbook/flight journal entries
- ☐ Required reports
- ☐ Weather check

The main focus of the tasks in my off-duty routine is to collect my thoughts and recollections from the duty period. To help facilitate that, I carry with me a combination daily planner and journal. Each day has a page for the my commitments and schedule, and a completely open page for notes, thoughts, etc. On the open page I jot down stand-out issues from any flights (for example, if I dealt with a customer issue, mechanical, or some non-normal that I may need to recollect in the future). I also note memorable flights, sights seen, websites or books I heard about during flight deck conversations, and so on.

As a matter of SOP, I debrief every flight with my flying partner. There may have been something from a debrief that I want to remember or focus on. Such entries really go to the heart of what I am trying to accomplish—an increase of knowledge and mindfulness.

Sometimes, especially if a safety issue or non-normal situation occurred during the duty period, there are reports I need to file. I also accomplish this in conjunction with my review and journaling of the duty period overall.

Finally, I ensure I have updated and recorded my flight details in my logbook. I use an electronic logbook on my smartphone that automatically uploads and updates schedule and flight time data from my airline, but I have to manually input landings, approaches, and other details. I then regularly transfer this to a spreadsheet-based logbook I keep on my personal computer.

Post–Trip Routine

Here is the checklist for my post-trip routine:

- ☐ Personal debrief/next times
- ☐ Required reports/expenses
- ☐ Rest and recovery

My routine after my trip is complete is to do a deeper evaluation of how the trip went and how I can be better. Considered by many to be the greatest NFL quarterback of all time, Tom Brady has several routines he uses to remain at peak performance. One that piqued my interest when I first heard of it is his post-game routine. In addition to athletic and physical recovery, Brady is known to debrief several times. Once with the quarterbacks coach and the offensive coordinator, another time with the team as a whole, and finally *on his own.*

My post-trip routine incorporates a similar approach. As I mentioned above, I already debrief after every flight. During my off-duty routine, I review those debriefs. After the trip is complete, I do one final debriefing where I purposefully write down my "next times" in my journal.

There are also some administrative items I often have to attend to, including once again ensuring any required reports are filed, and also submitting my expense report for the trip.

After my trip is complete, and I have arrived back home, rest and recovery are paramount. This can be a hard one to accomplish as there will undoubtedly be things to do around the house, activities, errands, and appointments to take care of when I get back home. Instead of getting overwhelmed by the things waiting to be done after my trip, I focus on—and plan—my times for rest, relaxation, and enjoyment. Aside from sleep, this includes planning meals, exercise, time with friends and family, hobbies and sports, reflection and worship, and even time to simply unplug without computers, phones, or TVs turned on.

Study

In the previous chapter, I wrote about the aspects of CQ, including knowing the obscure and forgotten when studying to prepare for a CQ event. Captain Chesley "Sully" Sullenberger who piloted the Miracle on the Hudson was known by friends and colleagues as someone who was always studying, reading, and increasing his knowledge.[3] Sully, having been named "Outstanding Cadet in Airmanship" upon graduation from the U.S. Air Force Academy, has lived his life with a drive towards continual improvement and superb airmanship—and many have attributed this as the X-factor for why he was able to achieve the nearly impossible feat of safely ditching into the Hudson River.

If there is one common thing I have learned from pilots who have come before me (Sully, Al Haynes, and my own pilot mentors), it is that the continued quest for airmanship requires study. This can include all methods of study, from reading to attending seminars.

Study is a key practice I employ in driving the Knowledge and Mindflness side of the Superb Airmanship Model™. Studying new techniques, best practices, new technology, research and development, industry journals, and even my own airline and fleet manuals keeps me sharp. Things I learn oftentimes will inspire me to research and discover new things that may help or enhance my craft.

Technique

A key practice I employ in the Superb Airmanship Model™ is the development and appropriate use of technique. My use of technique is the core driver of my increase in flight skills and faculties. Pilots know all too well that standard operating procedures are both clearly defined and required to be complied with. However, many pilots struggle with the intersection between SOP and technique.

What exactly is technique? A quick check of the dictionary tells us that it is "a way of carrying out a particular task, especially the execution or performance of an artistic work or a scientific procedure."[4] When we fly, can we effectively use technique when our manuals prescribe how to operate? How do we adhere to procedures when we think there is a better way to operate?

Technique is sometimes considered art, but more often recognized as talent. This is because technique should, by no means, involve bending the rules or breaking procedures. Rather, it involves an application of rules and procedures in a way that maximizes performance. For professional airline pilots, techniques are used in the operation to maximize comfort, efficiency, and safety.

Early on in a pilot's training and career, *technique* is used synonymously with *procedure* due to the lack of formal SOP. For example, we learn short-field and soft-field *techniques* for takeoffs and landings—such maneuvers can be accomplished by following a prescribed step-by-step *procedure* but the conditions (weather, runway, obstacles, etc.) are not available in one-size-fits-all. Adjusting the fuel/air ratio (mixture) on reciprocating powerplants is accomplished with several common *techniques.* But as technology on new engines has increased, the adjustment is now done via a manufacture mandated *procedure.*

When pilots move on to the SOP world of airline flying, technique no longer means the same thing as procedure. I can open up my airline's A320 flight manual and look up the LANDING PROCEDURE and find that it lists off the expanded version of the landing checklist, with additional steps in logical order that are required under the procedure to accomplish a safe landing. Some of these steps include FLARE... Initiate, THRUST... Idle. Both of these items seem intuitively obvious to a pilot, but the procedure also adds in some points of reference like degrees of pitch attitude to target in the flare and the approximate height above the runway to begin the flare.

What the airline procedure will not tell me is the triggers, cues, timing, feel, or other subjective information that may assist me in executing the maneuver. Incidentally, a few more pages after the LANDING

PROCEDURE is a subpart called LANDING CONSIDERATIONS which does grant pilots in our fleet additional information regarding establishing a visual aim point, the impact of threshold height, flare and touchdown, braking considerations, and crosswind landings. But still, this information is supplemental, and good to know, but it does not constitute technique.

Airline pilots need to understand that, just like the dictionary tells us, technique is a way of performing a procedure. In the context of the Superb Airmanship Model™, *technique is the professional execution of a procedure with a high level of skill and proficiency which maximizes the characteristics of comfort, efficiency, or safety of flight.*

Technique that Maximizes Comfort

One thing that most flight manuals don't write into detailed SOPs is comfort. We rely on our stick-and-rudder skills to maximize comfort for our passengers. This is where pilot technique finds a very prominent home. The smoothness of transitions between climb, cruise, and descent; the soft roll into heading changes; a keenness to pressurization changes, cabin comfort, and noise. These are all learned techniques, and pilots aspiring to superb airmanship are constantly working on such techniques.

Sully described an instance where he employed technique in this way in his book *Highest Duty:*

> It was up to me how I wanted to travel the final 110 miles, and how I would get from thirty-eight thousand feet down to the runway in San Francisco. It was an incredibly clear and gorgeous night, the air was smooth, and I could see the airport from sixty miles out. I started my descent at just the right distance so that the engines would be near idle thrust almost all the way in, until just prior to landing. If I started down at just the right place, I could avoid using the speed brakes, which cause a rumbling in the cabin when extended. To get it right, I'd need to perfectly manage the energy of the jet.[5]

Professional pilots pull together a host of resources including knowledge of the airplane, finesse in operating the flight controls, proficiency with automation, and input from crewmembers to make their flights comfortable. As procedures are carried out on every flight, the application of proficient flight skills combined with technique maximizes comfort. From preflight, to engine start, taxi out, takeoff, cruise, descent, approach, landing, and postflight—every procedure can be executed as prescribed, but with a learned and practiced technique that maximizes comfort.

Technique that Maximizes Efficiency

Similar to comfort, efficiency is another area where SOPs have limited detail, and again airmanship rules the day. Some carriers employ flight planning techniques and teach maneuvers and procedures designed to maximize efficiency. Pilots understand how to do, and have done, constant rate/power-off descents, reduced thrust takeoffs, limited APU burns, single-engine taxi, and the like. It is, however, the actual use of these procedures consistently that constitutes a technique that maximizes efficiency. A pilot's coordination with crewmembers and dispatchers is key. The level of skill and proficiency in this technique coincides with the level of leadership and professionalism a pilot operates at.

Technique that Maximizes Safety

Standard operating procedures are developed with safety as the primary directive. The evolution of airline SOP resulted from research that procedures needed standardization in order to maximize safety. Checklists, flight deck flows, callouts, and profiles were written to be common among the crews and fleets. Through the implementation of SOP, technique has taken a sideline, but safety has not. In fact, it was the sidelining of technique that enhanced safety. Instead of several different ways of operating the airplane existing, a standardized system of procedures was defined.

So, wait... do we have SOP and technique at odds with one another? By no means! As a matter of fact, the technique that maximizes safety is the proper execution of SOPs itself. Not complying with SOP, even for the sake of your own technique, erodes the margins of safety. For pilots, exerting leadership in SOP compliance is paramount in this technique. Without adherence to SOP, CRM breaks down, standards are deviated from, and threats become unmitigated errors.

SOP COMPLIANCE AND TRIGGERS

Here is a rule that all aviators should remember when it comes to SOP compliance: Nobody is perfect. While we strive for it, perfection is unlikely to be a result we attain. Even the most strict rule followers will tell you that they can have momentary lapses in judgement, instances where they become distracted, or times where they simply forget a callout, a checklist item, or a step in a profile.

In order to mitigate the risk of not being perfect when it comes to SOP compliance, we need to be honest about *intentional* non-compliance. There really isn't any room for it in our business. If there are any rules, procedures, or standards that you ignore, dodge, or are lazy about, ask yourself why. If you have a legitimate safety or operational concern about a certain checklist, flow, profile, or other procedure, talk to your chief pilot, fleet manager, or someone in your carrier's training department. They will either help allay your concern, help you understand the reason for the procedure, or work on a change or correction that you have helped them come to realize was necessary.

Even after taking intentional compliance out of the risk factors, we still are faced with our imperfection. In order to mitigate those risks further, I have developed sets of SOP triggers that help me remain compliant. They come in three varieties: verbal, physical, and visual. These triggers can occur singularly, or in combination, but they always cause me to take a procedural action.

Verbal SOP Triggers

When we operate a checklist that is read aloud, we should be focusing on the meaning of the responses. The same applies for when we perform standard callouts. For example, at my carrier it is a standard callout on takeoff for either pilot to say "POSITIVE RATE" after confirming via change in altimeter and VSI that the airplane has broken ground and is in a positive climb. This callout is a verbal SOP trigger for the PF to command "GEAR UP."

Physical SOP triggers

Physical SOP triggers function based on a tactile or mechanical cue. Continuing on the example of our SOP for the takeoff profile, once the "GEAR UP" command is called out by the PF, the PM selects the landing gear lever to UP. On the A320 fleet, selecting the landing gear is a physical SOP trigger to also select the speed brake lever either to ARM or DISARM the ground spoilers. (When the gear is selected UP, the ground spoilers are DISARMED; conversely when the gear is selected DOWN the ground spoilers are ARMED.)

Visual SOP Triggers

Visual cues are the most common ones we use when we fly. Hence why we use the idiom "flying blind" to describe doing something without guidance or experience. Airline SOP is riddled with visual cues from instruments, warning systems, indicators, gages, and even things we see out the windshield. As airliners have become more advanced with automation, verification of autoflight modes is crucial to safe operation and SOP compliance. Many carriers don't require it, but a visual SOP trigger that I have seen many pilots use is the change of a Flight Mode Annunciator (FMA). For example, when an ILS localizer signal is captured, most modern primary flight displays will annunciate "LOC" with a display of the abbreviation, a change in color, a flash, or an outline, and sometimes a combination of several visual cues are displayed. The common response, if not written in SOP, is for a pilot to say "LOC captured" or something similar. It is a visual trigger that elicits a verbal response. That response then can be a verbal SOP trigger, which can then cue other responses. See where this is going?

Batching SOP Triggers

My favorite explanation of SOP triggers overall is the missed approach or go-around procedure we use at my carrier. The SOP for a missed approach is a standardized set of callouts and actions performed by both the PF and PM. When done in proper sequence there is a distinct cadence to the procedure that highlights the natural grouping or batching of triggers that occur.

There are multiple cues pilots receive that can lead immediately to the execution of a go-around. For this example, let us consider a flight that has to execute a published missed approach procedure upon reaching minimums on an instrument approach. Assume the missed approach procedure has been briefed prior to the approach commencing, and that the PF has turned the autopilot off (hand flown approach). Upon reaching the decision altitude the PM calls out "MINIMUMS," a verbal SOP trigger for the PF to determine whether or not to continue the approach (a visual SOP trigger).

The PF responds with: "GOING AROUND, FLAPS THREE, CHECK THRUST"—a batch of verbal SOP triggers that coincide with the PF pitching the aircraft up, and selecting TO/GA on the thrust levers.

A second or two passes, and after receiving the visual SOP trigger of altimeter and VSI change, the PF calls out: "POSITIVE RATE, GEAR UP, SET MISSED APPROACH ALTITUDE, NAV" —another batch of verbal SOP triggers that command the PM to retract the landing gear, set/verify the missed approach altitude in the altitude pre-selector, and then select NAV on the mode control panel of the autoflight system.

Breaking down any checklist, flow, or profile in your SOP to understand the triggers used in each step helps you increase airmanship by deepening your flight skills and faculties. The triggers aid you in conducting the procedures, but being cognizant of the triggers actually reinforce your compliance with SOP. Taking a non-negotiable stance on SOP compliance requires that you have a method to mitigate the risk of *unintentional* non-compliance.

AUTOMATION

In the twenty-first century, aircraft have become technologically advanced to the extent that, especially with the proliferation of drones, some are betting that automation that is commanded by artificial intelligence will enable us to *remove* the pilot from the flight deck altogether. Perhaps someday that will come to pass, but in the meantime pilots who are striving for superb airmanship need to remember that they are still in the flight deck and remain in command of their aircraft. Automation management involves the use of aircraft automation to reduce workload, increase efficiency, and enhance safety.

Proper use of automation includes knowing when to turn off automation and requires pilots to maintain proficiency in hand flying. However, many operators worldwide have opted to lean into automation and require pilots to utilize the autopilot or autoflight systems more often than not. This can cause a conundrum of sorts. How do pilots maintain their proficiency at flying sans-automation, while complying with company SOP which requires them to use automation?

I like to think of the solution has having three distinct parts. First, pilots need to embrace automation by maximizing their understanding of it. Second, use of automation requires discipline. Third, pilots need to hand fly as much as possible, whenever possible.

Getting Geeky with Automation

Embracing aircraft automation requires a pilot to become intimately aware of how their aircraft automation works. In their book *Automation Airmanship,* Christopher Lutat and S. Ryan Swah outline nine principles through which pilots can gain better understanding, control, and results from automation.[6] Many of the principles, such as planning, briefing and debriefing, situational awareness, and workload management are predicated on well known and utilized CRM skills. But they take them to a level that applies the CRM soft skill aspect into a flight skill context in using automation.

I will boil it down even further for my application in the Superb Airmanship Model™. You simply need to get geeky with automation. Pilots need to become experts in their aircraft's autoflight systems— from the FMS/FMGC, to the autopilot servos themselves. We drill down on understanding our powerplant, fuel, and hydraulic systems in extreme detail. Why not do the same when it comes to autoflight?

As part of my airmanship, I enjoy being that pilot that can show a function or technique in the FMGC to my flying partner and hear, "Nobody ever showed that to me before." I like talking about how the VNAV path is determined and what logic is being used by the automation. When someone asks me a question about how the autoflight system works, and I don't readily know, I revel in poring over the manuals to find the answer. This is what getting geeky with automation is all about, and it is what drives better skills using and mastering the automation.

Autoflight—The Three A's

I used to chuckle when someone turned on the autopilot and said, "Ok, George has got it." Or, "Awesome Pilot on." (Many autopilot switches are marked "AP.") Now I wonder if people really think they are handing off the airplane to an artificial or imaginary actor? Most are saying these things tongue-in-cheek, but it does raise a question over the pilot mindset of discipline when the autopilot is engaged.

Airbus pilots are especially familiar with the level of discipline required for their airplane, as it is completely fly by wire. Whenever an unexpected turn, climb, descent, or thrust setting occurs, it is sometimes uttered, "What's it doing now?" It again raises the question—who is flying? George? Awesome Pilot 1? Obviously, the unexpected aircraft state is corrected, but as we know from our study of TEM, some threat or error led to it.

So, what can we do to mitigate the threats and errors that happen with use of automation? I have a simple alliterative for you to remember:

- Anticipate
- Act
- Adhere

Anticipate

When using automation, pilots need to constantly be anticipating what the aircraft will do. This involves paying attention to triggers, understanding what cues and indications the autoflight system has for your benefit, and constantly processing that information. Anticipate: What will the autopilot do when you get to the TOD? Anticipate: What will happen when we cross that green tennis-ball-looking dot on the nav display? Anticipate: What will change flight-path wise when I make the numbers big on the FMGC? Verbalizing what you anticipate the automation will do with certain inputs lets your flying partner in on the mental model you have for the flight path and what role automation is playing in making it happen.

Act

Be prepared to take action to intervene when necessary to ensure the autoflight system isn't doing what you anticipated (or what you didn't anticipate). Monitoring the modes and states of the autoflight system is crucial here. Did you dial in a heading on the flight control panel but the airplane isn't turning? Act. Did your partner preselect an altitude but the airplane isn't descending? Act. Did you select TOGA thrust on the takeoff roll and the message "TO THRUST NOT SET" posts? Act!

Adhere

On a flight inbound from Manchester, United Kingdom, to Newark, New Jersey, I was serving as the relief pilot and sitting in the flight deck jumpseat as we started the descent for Liberty International. The Captain was one of our Quality Control Line Check Airmen, and well known for being a stickler for accuracy (hey, it was his job to be that way). The First Officer was PF for the leg, and was nervous about how the Captain would judge his performance. The autopilot was engaged and ATC had held us higher than usual, requiring a steeper descent rate to achieve an altitude crossing restriction on the arrival. As the airplane approached 10,000 feet MSL in the VNAV-controlled descent, it began its programed deceleration to 250 KIAS. Except, it needed more drag which the First Officer didn't aggressively apply with speed brakes. On its quest to make the crossing restriction at 7,000 feet MS,L the aircraft continued below 10,000 feet MSL at 270 KIAS.

"Two hundred fifty below ten isn't a recommendation; it's a rule," the captain dryly said.

The First Officer quickly applied full speed brakes and changed the vertical mode from VNAV to FLCH and re-selected 250 knots on the mode control panel.

My point in retelling this anecdote is to underscore the necessity to adhere to all restrictions, rules, minimums, and limitations when using automation. Autopilot engagement doesn't relive you of your responsibility to control the airplane. If the autopilot can't adhere, you need to intervene (act). And, if in order to adhere, you need to deviate, it is incumbent upon you to do so safely and in accordance with operating rules and practices.

Hand Flying—The Antidote to Automation Saturation

In recent years, a large amount of discussion has occurred in aviation safety circles regarding the overuse of automation. Several investigations have found overreliance on automation as a contributing factor to the fate of many accidents and incidents. As a result, the FAA started making recommendations to operators, beginning with a SAFO issued in 2013 encouraging "operators to promote manual flight operations when appropriate."[7] Airlines wanted more clarity and guidance, and the FAA wanted to stress the importance of hand flying, so another SAFO was issued in 2017 detailing suggestions for carrier's training and line operations policies to encourage more hand flying.

Simply stated, manual operations of the aircraft should be conducted as much as is safely practical. I brief my flying partner when they can expect me to hand fly, and I base it off of the present conditions. Manual operation isn't prudent when the flight has several threats already present—weather, traffic, complexity, experience, and other operational threats need to be considered.

I do take every opportunity to click off the automation, however. As a part of my overall quest to become a more proficient, efficient, and high performing pilot, I need to continue to keep my manual flying skills sharp. Developing those skills makes a better pilot overall and helps me achieve superb airmanship.

Chapter 17 Notes

1. Tony Kern, *Redefining Airmanship* (New York: McGraw-Hill, 1997), 22-23.

2. Dave English, "Inner? Art? Airmanship?" The Inner Art of Airmanship, accessed 2020, innerairmanship.com/asstd/index.html

3. US Airways Flight 1549, which ditched in the Hudson River after a dual-engine failure due to bird strike shortly after departing KLGA on January 15, 2009.

4. "Technique." *New Oxford American Dictionary*, 2020. Apple iOS Dictionary App.

5. Chesley Sullenberger, *Highest Duty* (New York: HarperCollins, 2009), 149

6. Christopher Lutat and S. Ryan Swah, *Automation Airmanship* (New York: McGraw-Hill, 2013).

7. SAFO publications are made by the FAA to promote safety information and guidance to Part 121 and Part 135 operators.

18

Tips, Tricks, and Tools of the Trade

One of the best things pilots learn from one another is technique. Everything from flight maneuvers, customized flight deck flows, and FMC shortcuts, to the way they set up the flight deck, record flights in a logbook, or stay organized—everyone has their own methods. The purpose of this chapter is to introduce you to some common-sense practices that will aid you in being a safe, effective pilot-in-command.

FLIGHT DECK ORGANIZATION

Being organized in the flight deck is fundamental to safe and efficient flying. Preflight routines of most professional pilots start with "building the nest"—the simple steps pilots take to settle into the flight deck and get organized for the flight. It is so fundamental that most line check airmen and instructors tell pilots who are training in new aircraft that before anything else gets done, a pilot needs to build their nest or "set up" their side of the flight deck.

This set up does *not necessarily* include preflight flows or checks of the actual aircraft. Rather, this activity focuses on personal equipment. Let's look at it in terms of hardware and software.

Hardware	
✓ Bag stowage	✓ Electronics
✓ Seat adjustment/positioning	✓ Writing utensils/scratch paper
✓ Lighting	✓ Personal "comfort" items
✓ Headset setup	✓ General area cleaning and organization

Software
✓ Charts
✓ Checklists
✓ Flight deck cards, TOLD cards, etc.
✓ Manuals

Although these are short lists, to be sure, they include the most common things that pilots unpack and prepare before any other preflight action takes place. Let me give you a brief description of how I get my nest built every time I step into the flight deck. (This routine has been the same for me for years in the airline business, and varied only slightly in each different aircraft type. (I currently fly the B757/B767 and this narrative follows the lists of hardware and software.)

Once I get access to the flight deck, I stow and secure my suitcase, flight case, and my carry bag in their appropriate locations in the flight deck. I then move my seat into a position that I can get into it, and before sitting down in it, I check the condition of the seat:

- Seat cushion condition
- Seat belt/shoulder harness/buckle condition
- Headrest condition and position (if installed)
- Ability to move and adjust seat

Then I sit down. I immediately adjust the seat for height and distance from the controls, as well as for comfort. If anything on the seat doesn't work or is soiled, worn, etc., I immediately notify aircraft maintenance to get it fixed. This might seem trivial, but believe it or not, the seat and all of its components are designed for appropriate performance and safety. If a component is not serviceable, you have no business operating the aircraft from that control position until the component is repaired or replaced.

Lighting comes next. I check every map light, spot, or dome light I have access to for operation, aim, brightness, etc. This can be difficult if it's a bright sunny day out, but catching a light that is inoperative at high noon will avoid a problem at sunset and thereafter! I also check flashlights if they are installed, and I get mine at the ready from my flight case.

Headset installation and setup is another non-negotiable item for me. First of all, it's required to use a boom mic below 18,000 feet MSL per 14 CFR §125.227, the regulation governing flight deck voice recorders. Second, I want to ensure my headset works. I get out my rig, plug it in, and make sure it works, and confirm that the airplane's audio control panel is set up to work with the headset.

Electronics are a recent addition to my preflight nest-building routine, as my company has issued an iPad electronic flight bag (EFB) to every pilot. The iPad itself requires preflight action: I have to ensure that it has at least 66 percent battery power, that all available and authorized updates are installed to the apps and manual revisions on the EFB, and that the EFB can be powered up and is available and within my reach on the flight deck. (We have yet to utilize the iPad EFB in a mounted and shore-powered way, but that day is coming and will require additional preflight actions.) My other electronic item is my iPhone 5, which has on it several aviation apps I use during my flights: my logbook and schedule management program, my go-to weather and airport information app, and one or two airline apps and flight tracker apps.

Next, I make sure I have pens and highlighters within reach or on my person (and that they work, too). I also grab some scratch paper and put it in an easy-to-reach spot or on one of my chart clips.

I grab some personal comfort items, such as tissues, galley wipes, and a bottle of drinking water. These get put in the stow bin next to my flight kit.

Finally, I get out some cleaning materials: I carry my own large-size Wet Ones® Antibacterial Wipes, and the company supplies me with Sani-Com and Aerospace Lens wipes by Celeste Industries. I wipe down all surfaces I will be touching, including toggle switches, knobs, switch lights, PTTs, etc. If the CRT screens or indicator lenses need touch-up, I wipe them as well. Then I make sure cup holders, bins, and other areas are cleared of debris and clean.

All of the above "hardware" setups take me no more than three to five minutes. The software setup is even easier:

Charts: I typically pull the Jeppesen charts I need for the trip the day prior to the trip and place them into my "1" binder. In the flight deck, all I need to do is get the binder out of my flight case and put it at the ready, typically sitting on top of my case.

Checklists: While checklists are provided for me by the airline, I want to make sure that (a) I have one, (b) it's a current revision, and (c) it's in good condition.

Flight Deck Cards/TOLD Cards/ATIS Cards, etc.: Sometimes I use them, sometimes I don't. At my carrier, we print everything off of the ACARS printer, so ATIS cards aren't that useful. But sometimes I want an organized template on which to jot stuff down or to help remember certain things. This is where my flight deck cards come into use. I developed my first flight deck card when I upgraded to captain in the Saab SF340, and continued to improve the card as well as revise it for use in other aircraft types. Many pilots have developed their own versions of it; if you have a particular way you write down certain pieces of information (flight number, SELCAL code, fuel, times, SOBs, gate info, route info, frequencies, etc.), you are basically writing a flight deck card. Preflight, I just get one out or write up the template for one on scratch paper.

Manuals: I make sure that they are accessible. In my case, I have most of the manuals on my iPad, so I make sure that the reader app is loaded with tabs preset to the manuals I use most often.

The software part of building the nest is so quick, and really is more of a check than anything. But it rounds out the setup of the flight deck for the pilot. As soon as my nest is set up, I move on to aircraft preflight duties, and global flight deck setup, the routines for which are prescribed in my flight manual.

FLIGHT DECK CARDS

I mentioned these in the previous section. When it comes right down to it, these are so common in the industry that I think most pilots don't even realize they are making their own versions. I have developed some template versions that I can readily print and have on hand, rather than having to draw up each leg on a piece of scratch paper.

Each pilot will indeed have their own versions and information that they want to have in front of them. Some pilots want a few items of go-to info; others want an extensive list. I have seen flight deck cards made up of small Post-It® Notes, and others that take up an entire steno-pad-size piece of paper. To each their own.

So, what are flight deck cards? They are basically simple reference or note cards that pilots use to keep track of common useful information on each flight: flight number, flight times, reference speeds ("V" speeds), weights, fuel, navigation information, memory-joggers, frequencies, clearances, weather, deicing info, micro checklists...the list is not exhaustive. For demonstration purposes, below are three examples of flight deck cards I have used over the years.

CRJ900 Flight Deck Card:

757/767 First Officer's Training Flight Deck Card:

In the CRJ900 flight deck card example, you will note that I have listed some briefing mnemonics (SEAICE, IMSAFE). On the second card (757/767 FO's training flight deck card), I have briefing columns ("DEP" and "TO") containing items I want to cover in briefings. For the third (757/767 ETOPS flight deck card), I still follow the SEAICE technique in my briefs, but rather than printing out all the pertinent items my carrier likes to hear in a brief, I reference a handy lanyard card that is clipped to my badge. This is partly because my ETOPS-based flight deck card for the 757/767 needed more areas to jot down quick-reference items.

Again, there is no special format, rhyme, or reason to constructing a flight deck card of your own. But make sure that it is functional and useful for your particular operation.

757/767 ETOPS Flight Deck Card:

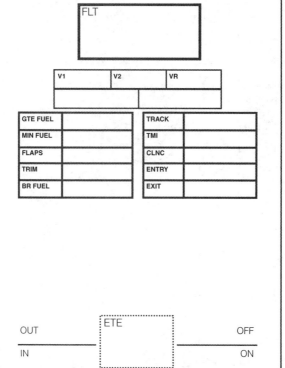

MONTHLY UPKEEP

Pilots are all too familiar with the array of regular maintenance checks required for aircraft. From line checks to heavy checks, the planes get looked over on a routine basis to make sure that they can safely continue in service.

Taking a cue from these aircraft maintenance routines, one day I thought it might be a good idea to have a regular check of all the things I myself need in order to remain in service as a pilot. It all started when I was cleaning out my flight case. Removing expired memos, replacing antibacterial wipes, restocking pens, and reviewing some new manual revisions made it clear that it might not be a bad idea to make a monthly checklist of things to keep up on. The checklist I developed covers three main areas: personal currency, procedural currency, and pilot parapher-nalia. My checklist is as follows.

Personal Currency

1. Pilot certificate

2. Medical certificate

3. Passport

4. Currencies

   a. 90 Day (landings)

   b. Cat II/III/Autoland

   c. Line check

   d. PC/RFT/CQ

5. Logbook updated

Procedural Currency

1. Pilot Operating Manual/Aircraft Flight Manual revision

   a. Aircraft bulletins

   b. Aircraft memos

   c. Airport Directory

      i. Airport Directory bulletins

2. Flight Operations Manual

   a. FOM bulletins

   b. FOM memos

3. Electronic Flight Bag (EFB)

   a. Operating system updated

   b. Applications updated

   c. Navigational databases/chart updates completed

Pilot Paraphernalia

1. Flight Bag
   a. Remove garbage
   b. Check pockets
   c. Supplies
      i. Pens, pencils, ear protection
      ii. Alternate glasses/sunglasses
      iii. Wipes/Sani-Com
      iv. Perf cards
      v. Flight deck cards/note cards
      vi. Screen/lens cleaners
2. Flashlight
   a. Batteries
   b. Ops check
3. Headset
   a. Check connections/plug
   b. Clean earpieces

This checklist simply helps me keep things in order, so I am more effective in the flight deck. I encourage you to develop a similar routine for yourself.

SHARPENING THE SAW

One of the biggest challenges for a pilot is remaining proficient. Pilots are all normally checked in continuing qualification cycles, line checks, and proficiency checks. However, in-between the checks, they can lose the edge a bit. This can be attributed to two main factors: complacency and absence from the flight deck. Here is a primer on how to combat complacency by maintaining expertise in the airplane, and what to do after an extended absence to get back in the saddle.

Becoming an Expert

I once heard the following from one of my mentors and colleagues in the airline schoolhouse:

"You have no business training or flying the company's $100 million airplane unless you are an expert."

Truer words were never spoken, right? But what does it mean to be an expert? Does it mean you have to be able to recite the most obscure manufacturer specifications for the tensile strength of the wing spar? Does it mean you can have a greaser landing no matter the conditions? Must you have a Joe Friday-esque ability to rattle off FARs and Ops Specs with machine-gun rapidity and accuracy? If expertise is knowledge based, then those with the most knowledge are experts...right?

Knowledge is part of it, for sure. Skill also plays an important role. But perhaps the most often overlooked aspect of being an expert is knowing the right way versus the wrong way—discernment and judgment is the hallmark of expertise.

As a matter of fact, the Wikipedia entry for "expert" states that "an expert is someone widely recognized as a reliable source of technique or skill whose faculty for judging or deciding rightly, justly, or wisely is accorded authority and status by their peers or the public in a specific well-distinguished domain." One needs to have the skill and knowledge, and the ability to discern, which sets them apart in the eyes of one's peers.

Pilots-in-command are required to be experts. You cannot be directly responsible for, and be the final authority as to, the operation of an aircraft without the knowledge, skill, judgment, and discernment required to garner the recognition of your peers (fellow crewmembers, operations personnel, etc.) as pilot-in-command. If you are not feeling very much like an expert as a pilot, there are some easy and straightforward steps you can take to become one:

1. Stop Worrying About Being Chuck Yeager

When Yeager broke the sound barrier (and then did it repeatedly thereafter), his talent at the stick made him legendary. Many people believe there isn't an aeronautical challenge he couldn't have conquered. It is a reasonable claim, for Yeager made his mark of expertise at being a test pilot (and before that in air combat). But we are not all test pilots. Our callings and vocations as aviators may be oriented in many different ways. We can become experts in our own unique way we do our jobs. The focus on the skills required to do our jobs is then what becomes our expertise.

This was true for Yeager. He focused on improving certain things related to being a test pilot, practicing and expanding his skill. Yeager certainly did many things well, but where he excelled as an expert he made deliberate efforts to focus on what he could improve upon. Had he been an airline pilot, a charter pilot, or even a bartender (like the one he played in his cameo role for *The Right Stuff*) he would have endeavored to be an expert in each vocation, separately.

That same focus should be incumbent on all pilots who want to be experts. Find out what you can improve upon and focus intensely on it. Do you need to improve your systems knowledge? Focus on it. Do you need to improve on crew briefings? Focus on it. Does your technique on landings need an edge? Focus on it. Soon your skill set becomes not just "things you do" but "things you do with expertise."

2. Be Intentional About Your Goals for Expertise

Dovetailing with the idea of intentionality discussed in the previous section is the concept of specificity. We have all heard the phrase, "Jack of all trades, master of none." When you try to spread focus around to too many different things, you lose the focus. Being deliberate and specific about your goals for expertise is crucial.

First and foremost, set your goals. For example, if you need to work on flight deck management, make a goal specific to that. Write it down: "Goal: Become an expert at flight deck management." Then break that goal down into small, but achievable steps you can take to improve.

Secondly, become deliberate about practicing to become beyond proficient in the skill targeted in your goal. Work on improving that skill to perform it at a slightly higher level every time, with each practice improving on the last. Speaking of practice...

3. Practice in Environments and Situations that Allow You to Improve

This is an extremely poignant step in an aviation context. It is the reason we utilize flight simulators and flight training devices for practice as well as evaluation. The nature of flying airplanes, especially in the airline context, doesn't allow us to practice all skills on the job. You can't do V_1 cuts, emergency descents, high-altitude stalls, or total electrical failures on the flight line for practice. So we head to the simulator for recurrent training and evaluation. Experts relish the opportunity to practice, train, and improve. Nobody who wishes to be an expert should have fear of the simulator. If you have such fears because of the training environment itself (horrible instructors and check airmen who choose to use intimidation as a "teaching tool") you need to address those fears directly with management. But if you have a great training and evaluating environment, you need to embrace it.

All too often we hear the groans about having to go in for that CQ simulator event. Experts don't do that—period. They look forward to going in, focusing on what they need to improve, and taking steps to do so. When the instructor or check airman says, "Any questions?" or "Do you want to see anything else?", experts say "Yes!" and are eager to take hold of that opportunity to improve.

4. Seek Immediate and Accurate Feedback

If you are going to be an expert, you will need to be vulnerable. It can be hard for many Type A, Joe Ace Pilot personalities to understand, but face it: when you are seeking to become an expert, you have to admit first and foremost that you are a work in progress. In order to get feedback, you have to ask someone who you can trust to evaluate whether or not you have improved, or whether or not what you are doing is working. Alternatively, you need to seek results that show improvement. But prior to all of this you need to admit that "you're working on it."

Experts seek feedback all of the time. This is not to be confused with being a recognition seeker—one who is always looking for a pat on the back. Instead, experts look for actual feedback, asking questions such as, "How is this going?", "Did that work out properly?", "What can I do to improve this?" and "If I could do that all over again, what should I do differently?" Experts want to hear tips and tricks for improvement, not "attaboys."

5. Guide Yourself with Known Standards, and Exceed Them

Every checkride or recurrent training utilizes known standards for evaluation. From Private Pilot certification on up to ATP, pilots have to meet the FAA's Practical Test Standards (PTS) under Part 61. As you get into Part 121 ops, more standards are prescribed. Many pilots retain copies of evaluation forms from their CQ events that list out those standards and the results of the ride. Why not use them as a guide for your expertise?

Part 121 Appendix F prescribes the maneuvers and elements required for a proficiency check (14 CFR §121.441). Wordy as it is, it is a good guide. So is any PTS book. Use these or any stage check, evaluation, or check-out form as a guide to target the areas you would like to improve. Then set the goals (step 2), practice (step 3), and get feedback (step 4). Repeat the process. Work to exceed the standards for the skill, and to be able to repeat the skill with minimal effort needed to excel.

Stretch yourself to be an expert. You don't have to be a know-it-all. You don't need to be Chuck Yeager. You simply need to know what you are doing well, discern what you need to do better, and push yourself to exceed standards to improve on specific skills.

Getting Back in the Saddle

It happens to virtually every pilot at least once, and sometimes several times, during their career. Extended absences happen for a myriad of reasons: illness or injury, family leave, dequalification, extended vacations, or even long spells on reserve duty without assignment. At some point you will walk away from the airplane and not return for several weeks, or sometimes months.

When pilots get back to work, they typically have a self-awareness that they are returning to a vocation that involves the application of complex skills. Pilots tend to communicate to their co-workers that they are back from a long absence, not so much to talk about why they were away, but to either directly or indirectly put people on alert for their behavior.

I am sure you have (or soon will have) experienced a flying partner who, during the preflight brief, says something akin to, "Hey, just keep an eye on me. I have been out on leave for the last three months, and I know there will be some cobwebs to knock out." Don't get me wrong, this is a perfectly fine thing to say in a briefing. Pilots should communicate the concern that personal performance may not be 100%, for any reason.

However, comments like this are indicative of self-awareness. If not handled directly, and even when you do put your coworkers on notice, that self-awareness sometimes manifests itself in several different re-sponses that can negatively affect performance:

- Anxiety
- Insecurity
- Unassertiveness
- Complacency and/or resignation
- Indecisiveness

The underlying cause of these responses is the feeling of unprepared-ness experienced when returning to work. There are ways to combat these responses, however. Even when you are away from the airplane, you can still "sharpen the saw," remain prepared, and keep the dramatic pronouncements of your cobwebs to a minimum. Here is how:

1. Remain Tuned-in to Company News, Fleet News, etc.

This can seem really antithetical, especially if your extended absence is purposeful, like a planned long vacation. We often go on vacation to forget about work, right? Well, that is why this is the first suggestion as well as the easiest one to comply with. Remaining tuned in doesn't mean you have to engross yourself. In fact, this task should only take about five to ten minutes of your time each week.

Most operators post regular updates on their business. Log in to and skim your company's website. If you see any operational updates from chief pilots or fleet managers, skim them. If there are other memos or postings that you would normally read and digest on a regular basis while at work, find them and skim them, too.

You probably noticed my suggestion to skim these pieces of informa-tion as you read them. There are two reasons for this: First, to save time (try to limit this to five to ten minutes a week), and second, to glean the highlights so you can go back and easily find them when you return to work. A great example is an operations memo that was recently posted at my carrier about some ACARS functions that have changed. Rather than reading the line-by-line nitty-gritty on the procedural steps, key-strokes, and indications the new functions utilize just to forget about it all before returning to work, it would be wiser to skim the memo, make note that there are new ACARs functions, get a general sense of what is affected by the changes, lock that "headline" information in your memory bank, and get back to enjoying your vacation. (When it is approaching time to get back to work, you will recall this memo, and therefore remember to get more familiar with it near the end of your absence; this step will be covered in more detail later in this section.)

2. Do Some Armchair Flying

Have you ever done armchair flying before? 99.9% of pilots have. Every pilot is encouraged by his instructor to "armchair fly" maneuvers prior to lessons or checkrides. If you are a Part 121 pilot, you likely have at least done it to prep for a checkride by sitting down and envisioning and/ or acting out flows, techniques, and procedures. If you haven't done armchair flying for some time, it is time to revisit this extremely useful technique—especially if you are going to be out of the flight deck for a long period of time.

For the chair flying exercises, don't visualize a checkride. Visualize your typical day and typical flight. Visualize everything you do from arriving at the gate to postflight (skipping ahead with a virtual "fast forward" when you come to periods of waiting). Go through the motions of the flows and checklists for preflight, engine start, push, taxi-out, normal takeoff, departure, climb, cruise, descent, arrival, approach, landing, taxi-in, shutdown, and postflight. Perform this once halfway through your absence, and once near your return date.

3. Keep Your Charts and Manuals Updated

Granted, there may be some logistics involved in keeping charts and manuals updated. Some pilots can get them electronically, while others still have to go to their mailbox on base and retrieve them. Others may have a mix of both. If possible, check that your books are current when you are halfway through your absence, and again near your return date. If you are out for more than 120 days, there are two paths you can take: (1) revise your manuals every month, or (2) if possible, wait until a few weeks before you return to work and get new, fully revised issuances of the manuals from your company. The upshot here is that you should take care of this task with some scheduled regularity so that you don't have a pile of documents to revise just prior to your return date.

4. Make a Point to Contact a Fellow Pilot to Talk Shop

Again, this may seem weird to those of you heading out on extended vacations. But here's the deal: when we as pilots are in work mode, on a typical cycle of fly days and off days, we are talking shop with fellow pilots all of the time. We have casual conversation both in and out of the flight deck about layovers, hotels, new procedures, airports, airplanes, and all kinds of experiences that occur on the flight line. It is through these conversations that we learn from each other and keep each other sharp. When we are away from work, we lose that completely. So find someone you know, like, and trust to give you the latest scoop on what's been happening at work. Do it as often as you like, but at the very least, make this contact halfway through your absence and again just before you return to work. For longer absences, try to catch up with coworkers no less than once per month.

5. Do a Final Ops Review Prior to Your Return

Just before you come back to work (e.g., within the last week of your absence), conduct a "Final Ops Review." This is an opportunity to complete three main tasks to prepare for your first trip back.

Task 1: Run a Monthly Upkeep Checklist

Earlier in the chapter, I provided a monthly upkeep checklist to help ensure that every month includes a regular check of all the things needed to remain in service as a pilot. The checklist covers three main areas: personal currency, procedural currency, and pilot paraphernalia. Run this checklist and take stock of anything you need to get, to update, or to do before you report for the trip, and then make sure you get those things settled. Do this no later than 72 hours prior to reporting.

Task 2: Review All New Company Information and Procedures

In step one of this section, I recommended you remain tuned-in to all the company news, fleet news, and updates on procedures by skimming the memos, bulletins, and postings. Now it is time to tap into your memory bank and recall the major headlines, remember the new procedures to review, and review them. Set aside some time to clearly read and study this information. Keep in mind that as you return to the flight line, the people you fly with will likely be already accustomed to any new changes in operations or procedures. Be prepared and up-to-speed before you report. Do this no later than 24 hours prior to reporting.

Task 3: Do a Procedures Refresher

This is similar to chair flying but is a little more structured, and is designed to go back over your procedures in a way that will aggressively spark your memory back into action. Here is how to do it: Pick the most complex non-normal procedure or maneuver and the most complex normal procedure or maneuver. Find them in your manual. Read them in that order (most complex non-normal, then most complex normal). Then chair fly them in the same order. Finally, review all checklists you normally use on your airplane. That's it! There's no need to spend hours on end reviewing every single procedure and maneuver. By focusing on the two most complex ones and then doing a simple review of the checklists, you will have "primed the pump" for your mind to reengage the activity of line flying. Do this sometime 12–24 hours prior to report.

By implementing all of these recommendations, you hopefully can keep the cobwebs at bay during your extended absence from flying.

CONCLUSION

There is a reason this book is subtitled "*Your Best Trip, Every Trip.*" Anyone who truly loves flying and understands that the act of flight is an amazing technological wonder that man was not designed for has a deep respect for it. As professional pilots, we "cheat death" with every operation. We run complex, sophisticated machines that expend an enormous amount of energy, travel at speeds that approach the sound barrier, and are subjected to mechanical stresses that are tempered and withstood by amazing feats of engineering. And we carry precious cargo: people just living their lives, wanting to get somewhere faster than land-borne travel will allow. People like you and me heading to weddings, funerals, vacations, graduations, business meetings, new lands, new homes, and perhaps new lives.

Being a professional pilot means you cannot forget about your job—your duty, and your debt, to your crew and passengers as mentioned in this book. Your job includes your duty to coworkers and citizens on the ground, your employers, and fellow aviators you share the skies with—all who count on your professionalism.

No matter what your background is, how many hours you have under your belt, or how many type ratings you have, you can start improving today by making a difference in how you operate. If you are a new pilot just entering the industry, this book may set a firm foundation in how you operate in your new career. As a pilot in upgrade training, this book may have given you a new perspective, new methods, or new interest in how to be the best captain you can be. Perhaps you are a seasoned pilot leader, and everything in the preceding pages simply resonates with how you already conduct yourself as a pilot. Whatever the case may be, it is my sincere hope that this book has connected you with information that strengthens your leadership, professionalism, and airmanship.

I encourage you, from the moment you set out for the airport to start a trip, to think about this duty. Think about how you carry yourself as you make your way to the gate. Plan ahead how to brief your crews, how to work with the flight attendants, and how to make CRM work for your flights. Consider the impact of your resources, from the dispatchers to the mechanics, the ramp personnel to the gate agents. Be prepared for how to handle non-normal situations. Do your best to engage with your customers. Take a responsible approach to rest and fitness for duty, and take pride in professionalism.

This is how you make *every trip your best trip*.